THE COMPLETE IDIOT'S GUIDE® TO

Remodeling Your Kitchen

Illustrated

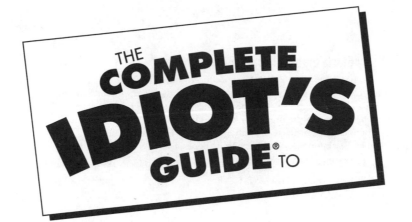

THE COMPLETE IDIOT'S GUIDE® TO

Remodeling Your Kitchen

Illustrated

*by Gloria Graham Brunk and Sue Kovach
with Michael Jones*

ALPHA

A member of Penguin Group (USA) Inc.

Publisher: *Marie Butler-Knight*
Product Manager: *Phil Kitchel*
Senior Managing Editor: *Jennifer Chisholm*
Senior Acquisitions Editor: *Mike Sanders*
Senior Development Editor: *Michael Thomas*
Production Editor: *Billy Fields*
Copy Editor: *Cari Luna*
Illustrator: *Chris Eliopoulos*
Cover/Book Designer: *Trina Wurst*
Indexer: *Heather McNeill*
Layout/Proofreading: *Rebecca Harmon, Mary Hunt*

Contents at a Glance

Contents

Foreword

Several days ago I heard a radio commercial for a large grocery store chain. They calculated how many meals the average person might eat in their lifetime. The number is just under 100,000. Of course, a certain number of these meals are eaten away from home, and many are eaten while we are younger (and don't care about the surroundings we eat in). But my guess is that you might be like me, and tens of thousands of those meals will undoubtedly be prepared and eaten within the walls of your own home.

In my opinion, the primary purpose of a kitchen has not changed much in the past 50–100 years. Kitchens can and should be a warm and inviting space where family members get together and obtain physical and emotional satisfaction. Granite countertops, lavish stainless appliances, and custom cabinets are not needed to achieve this goal. If you have been lucky enough to camp in the great outdoors and sit on a stool or log around a glowing campfire after a meal, you know a kitchen has that same magical allure.

I distinctly remember spending lots of time with my mom and dad at the table in our 10 foot long by 9 foot wide kitchen. Yes, we had a sink, oven, refrigerator, some counter space, and a table four people could squeeze in around, all within this small space. Nearly forty years ago I used to watch the popular television series *Lassie*. Every episode seemed to have one or more scenes in the kitchen, where little Timmy talked with his mom. Lassie, the wonder dog, usually interrupted the conversation or meal so she and Timmy could save a life or solve a problem.

Numbers do not lie. Since you're going to spend so much time in your kitchen, it only makes sense that the room be efficient, practical, spacious, and inviting. These qualities don't happen by accident. If you are about to embark on a kitchen remodeling job to create that oasis within your home, it takes thoughtful planning and a knowledge base to make sure you get what you need. The information in this book helps you achieve this goal.

The kitchen remodeling process is by no means easy. It is a journey fraught with obstacles that can cause you to go over budget and miss your completion deadline by weeks. I have remodeled more than my fair share of kitchens for my wife Kathy and for countless customers and can tell you that kitchen remodeling is perhaps the most stressful project a remodeler and homeowner can undertake.

This remodeling experience should be a happy one, where you see progress each week and headaches are few. Put to use the checklists and accumulated knowledge and tips in this wonderful guide and nothing but happy memories will flood your mind as your children and grandchildren marvel at the wonderful room where you and they meet and eat. When they ask you how your wonderful kitchen came to be, simply tell them you were no idiot—you got advice from the best in the business!

Tim Carter
AsktheBuilder.com

Introduction

You look at your kitchen and sadly shake your head. Brash Harvest Gold countertops and appliances, avocado-green cabinets, droopy drop ceilings, and loopy linoleum—sound familiar? Face it, your kitchen could be a set for the TV sitcom *That '70s Show*! No wonder you want to tear it all out. You're a victim of '70s Style!

Don't worry, you can recover from '70s Style and a host of other kitchen ills, including the old country kitchen "pigs and cows décor," lack of space, dark, cramped quarters, worn-out countertops, old rundown appliances, and peeling paint. Your vision of an efficient, up-to-date kitchen can become reality, and it can happen within your budget. Best of all, you can do it all yourself, and you've already taken the first step with this book.

The Complete Idiot's Guide to Remodeling Your Kitchen, Illustrated will show you the way to new kitchen Nirvana. With clear step-by-step instructions, it will help you turn your tired old galley into the sparkling new kitchen of your dreams. You'll find loads of information on kitchen products, accessories, appliances, and finishes to help you discover your own style and design a room that will do you and your home proud. Hundreds of photographs and drawings guide you through the process from start to finish.

I'll be your teacher, and don't worry, I know what I'm talking about—I've been a kitchen designer for more than a decade. I also write a newspaper column on kitchen design tips to help people create their own beautiful, functional kitchens. Helping me teach you is Michael Jones, licensed building contractor extraordinaire, who specializes in kitchen and bath remodeling and general interior construction work. From installing cabinets, moving walls and raising ceilings to plumbing and electrical work, Mike has done it all, and he knows how to teach others to work on their own kitchens. Mike and I worked together to create a new kitchen for a 1920s house on the popular TV show, *This Old House*.

How to Use This Book

This book is divided into three parts that lead you through the logical steps of remodeling your kitchen. Let's take a look.

Part 1, "Before You Begin," provides you with all the tools you need to make important design decisions for your new kitchen. You'll look closely at the reasons why you're dissatisfied with your current kitchen, answer numerous questions about your lifestyle and preferences, and explore your options for a complete top-to-bottom redo or a partial remodeling job. Surveys and quizzes help you organize your thoughts regarding what you want in your new kitchen and, most important, what you need. Valuable information about budgeting is included, as well as reference material and discussions about finding help for your project if you need or want it. Photos of finished kitchens stimulate your imagination and creativity.

Part 2, "Designing Your New Kitchen," puts you right to work getting your design on paper. Instructions for the critical job of measuring your kitchen space are detailed in photos and drawings. Different types of kitchen layouts are discussed, along with loads of tips to create a functional design you'll love. Detailed information and photos are provided for all the elements you'll want to consider in your kitchen, including appliances, plumbing, electrical considerations, lighting, floor and wall finishes, cabinets, hardware, countertops—everything up to and including the kitchen sink. You can feast your eyes on plenty of photos in this part.

Part 3, "Getting It Done," is where you roll up your sleeves, pick up your tools and jump right in. Don't worry—by this point, you'll not only be ready for it, but quite able. First you'll learn how to schedule your work and obtain the proper construction permits. Then you tear out the old kitchen, make preparations for the new, and finally do the installation according to your plans. Photos and drawings show you exactly what you need to know and simplify even the tasks you feel might be a bit tough. And it's all done in a logical order, so you won't miss a step or forget anything.

At the end of the book are a glossary of terms, resources, and graph paper to help you draw your designs.

Extras

Throughout the book, sidebars provide you with extra information about safety issues, tips from the world of professional kitchen design, the lingo of professional designers, and cost-saving measures. Sometimes a sidebar will explain a particular procedure in detail, or just give you some insight into the design process. Put it all together, and you have *The Complete Idiot's Guide to Remodeling Your Kitchen, Illustrated.* Let's get remodeling—and have a good time, too!

CAUTION | **Don't Get Burned!**

It's easy to get burned in the kitchen if you're not careful, and I'm not talking about a hot stove. Here you'll find warnings and cautions about issues that can affect your budget, your design, and most important, your health and well-being. So take heed.

Mike's Installer Notebook

Here's where to look for the how-to know-how from professional kitchen installer Mike Jones. He'll share his hard-earned knowledge about installing kitchens, and can help you avoid costly mistakes, injuries, and other set-backs with his sound, seasoned advice.

 Bang for the Buck

Everyone wants to save as much money as they can, and this is where you'll learn little tricks of the trade for pinching a few pennies here and there. This info is definitely valuable!

 Designer's Notebook

Look here to find all the secrets of professional kitchen designers. I use information like this in my work on a daily basis. And I promise I won't send you a bill for my consultation.

 Pro Lingo

Have you ever wondered what a mullion is? A reveal? A framastat? (Okay, I made that one up.) Here's where you'll learn the language of kitchen design and remodeling. It's important, because it will help you communicate when you're shopping for your kitchen elements and discussing your issues with designers.

Acknowledgments

Writing a book while working full time is no small feat. I would like to thank Sue Kovach for bringing the opportunity to my attention, and for her photography, writing skill, and guidance. This book would not have been possible without her hard work and efforts. Thanks also to Mike Jones, my installer and my "other half" in the business. He translates my vision into reality on a daily basis, and always with a smile!

Anything I accomplish is to the credit of my family. Thanks to my parents Carl and Yvonne Graham for giving me a happy home, and a love and respect for books and writing. Also, my sister Pam for rooting her big sister on and always being there. Heartfelt appreciation to my husband, Greg, and my precious children, Graham and Sabrina, for enduring the months of the writing process. And to my wonderful, close-knit and always supportive extended family: Jackie, Lu, Mags, Bill, Malcolm, Dorothy, and Angie.

I wish to thank editors Mike Sanders and Mike Thomas, and Alpha Books for publishing this timely and much-needed source of information, and to agents Marilyn Allen and Bob Diforio for involving me in this project.

We all wish to thank Jim and Vilma Medler for letting us transform their "before" kitchen into a beautiful new kitchen they'll enjoy for years to come. Their patience and good humor during the remodeling process, made longer by photography requirements, is much appreciated.

I'm grateful to my boss and "work dad," Ron Kimball, of Masters Kitchen Gallery, for his support. Thanks to Dean Fleming for giving me my first chance in the business, Malcolm Thomas, my patient kitchen design mentor, and my colleague, Barbara, for her support at work during the writing process. Special thanks to everyone at Ferguson Design Gallery in West Palm Beach for their contributions.

Thanks also to Christine, Brenda, Sue, Garrett and Mike of my creativity group for their weekly dose of encouragement, and to Katie Deits and Bill Huttunen of the *Palm Beach Post* for promoting the project with my Kitchen Karma column. A very special thanks to Shawn, Karen, Vicki, and the Rising Phoenix Dancers, who are my dear friends that keep me going.

Last but not least, thanks to my many clients who have allowed me to help them create kitchens to live in and enjoy, and who have given me the experience to write this book.

—Gloria Graham Brunk

Many thanks to Gloria and Mike for allowing me to enter their world of professional kitchen design and remodeling. What a fun and fascinating place it is, and made more so by top-notch pros like them. A special nod to Gloria for the long hours she put into this book, in addition to her regular work and the never-ending work of being a mom. And to Mike, for his unwavering dedication and patience during the long hours of photography, and I promise I'll never ask him to hold a heavy cabinet up in the air for ten minutes again! Thanks to my agents, Marilyn Allen and Bob Diforio—always there with support and encouragement, through thick and thin. I'm grateful to all my friends and family who help keep me grounded, and especially Neal Rawls, who sees me through all that life brings.

—Sue Kovach

Special thanks to Gloria for giving me the opportunity to be involved in this project, and to Sue for her excellent writing skills and ability to convey the ins and outs of kitchen remodeling to you, our readers. I'm forever thankful for my wife Loren, and our four boys, Eric, Christopher, Michael, and Andrew. To all my past and future clients, thanks for giving me the chance to work with you and your projects. And I thank God for giving me talent to excel in the trade industry, for the joy and accomplishment I get from my work, and for the doors He opens to new and exciting things for my family and me.

—Michael Jones

Trademarks

In This Part

Part 1

Before You Begin

Kitchens, kitchens, kitchens—so many layouts, designs, and options to choose from, so many questions you're eager to have answered. Galley or eat-in? A "U" shape or an "L"? Cooktop or stove? Breakfast nook or not? This part takes you through the process of deciding everything about your new kitchen. You'll explore what you *want* in a kitchen and what you *need* in a kitchen, peruse plenty of photos to get your creative juices flowing, and learn budget management so you can pay for it all.

You'll also learn where to go for help if you want or need someone to assist you with your remodeling project. Let's get started!

In This Chapter

- ◆ Kitchen remodeling—a good investment

- ◆ Why do you want to remodel?

- ◆ The good, the bad, and the ugly—analyzing your kitchen

- ◆ Where to find helpful resources

Chapter 1

The Heart of Your Home

My house has a small kitchen, but somehow it's always full of people. You've probably noticed that happening in your home, too, especially when you have guests over or throw a party. No doubt about it, everyone usually ends up gathering in your kitchen. That's because the kitchen has always been the heart of the home, and with today's open floor plans, it's more true than ever.

Not only that, but the kitchen has evolved into a room that supports even more functions than just cooking, eating, and entertaining. Integrated laundry centers are fast becoming kitchen elements, and a computer desk/homework center will soon be a ubiquitous part of most kitchens. Even a bar with a winecooler can be part of the kitchen. Whatever works for your lifestyle, just do it.

No matter how small or large, at a minimum, the kitchen is a place to cook and a place to gather, almost as much as the TV room. It's one of the most important rooms in your home, and for many households, it's *the* most important room. No wonder you're willing to go through the time and expense to remodel it!

The fact that you're tired of your kitchen and want something fresh is reason enough to consider remodeling. But how about another reason: Kitchen renovations are the top return on investment in your home. You can realize up to 95 percent of the cost of your project when you resell your home! That's money in the bank, and an obvious motivating factor for many homeowners.

It's easier than ever to create an incredible kitchen, even on a budget. New products and materials have made it possible for even the most budget-minded remodeler to have a kitchen that looks high-end. Even those once-costly luxury features of custom cabinets such as roll-out drawers, cutlery trays, and spice racks are now available in all price ranges. If you do your homework and shop around, you can truly have it all at your price.

Today's kitchens are more integrated into the rest of the home than kitchens of the past, which were separate rooms for the sole purpose of cooking. *(Wellborn)*

From laundry centers to winecoolers—today's kitchens do it all for your household.

Once utilitarian rooms, the kitchen today is often a showplace in the home, but still highly functional. *(Dupont)*

Choose a traditional style, or go modern—even futuristic—in the kitchen. Your options are many.

Traditional kitchens are a big favorite of many people. This one has plenty of warm woods and a comfy, homey feel. *(Craft-Art)*

There's a lot to love about this kitchen, including ample storage space, lots of light, and a terrific décor. *(Wellborn)*

Looking for a Reason

Your first step to creating a new kitchen is to find out what's wrong with your old one. Do you hate the layout? Are you bored to tears with your cabinets, the outdated appliances, the dull floor? Do you complain about your lack of counter space, about insufficient lighting? In other words, why do you want to remodel your kitchen?

A simple way to begin to organize your thoughts is to take a sheet of paper and divide it into two columns. On one side, list what you like about your kitchen right now. On the other side, write down what you don't like. You can use the handy organizing sheet provided here. This information helps you to determine what changes you want to make, and what features of your kitchen don't need to change.

Don't like the kitchen sink? Replace it! Your choice of sinks is huge, and you're sure to find something you'll love. *(Kohler)*

Glass cabinet doors, cookbooks at hand, and a shiny new sink with a view—maybe these are some of the elements of your dream kitchen.   *(Kohler)*

It's tempting to want to rip everything out and start all over again. But it might not be necessary to do that. And if you're on a tight budget, you may have to leave some things unchanged, or plan on doing your remodeling job in phases. So it's crucial to discover what you can live with in your current kitchen, and what must go.

Analyze Your Kitchen

Take a sheet of paper and divide it into two columns. You're going to use this sheet to organize your thoughts about your current kitchen. This will help you make decisions for the design of your new kitchen. Your sheet should look something like this:

What I Like About My Kitchen

_____

_____

_____

What I Don't Like About It

_____

_____

_____

_____

Open up your critical eye and take some time to fill out this sheet. Stand in your kitchen while you do it, and study everything. Open doors and drawers, turn on the lights, dig around in those hard-to-reach cabinets to remind yourself how really hard to reach those pots in the back are, especially if you're in a hurry to get one. Examine your appliances, turn on the garbage disposal—in short, give your old kitchen the once-over, and write down what you like and don't like about it.

First, let's take a closer look at what you don't like about your current kitchen. Does your list of dislikes look like this?

Old ugly cabinets

Hate the wallpaper

The '60s linoleum bugs me

Can't stand the low cove ceiling

Countertops—yuck!

Dislikes such as these indicate that your primary reason for wanting to remodel is aesthetics. If most of your answers fall into this category, it means you're fairly comfortable with your current layout, and you may not need to extensively rework it. Thus, your planning will be strongly focused on color choices, floor and cabinet materials, wall treatments, and other such style considerations.

Now, suppose your dislikes look something like this:

Not enough counter space

Lack of storage for pots and pans

Fridge is too far away from the work area

Kids and dogs are underfoot when I'm cooking

I bump into the peninsula every time I walk to the sink

These dislikes show that a big focus of your remodeling plans will be layout-oriented, dealing with function, storage, and traffic patterns through the kitchen. Your planning focus might involve rethinking your work centers and moving some of your kitchen elements to new locations.

Pro Lingo

You don't just encounter traffic patterns on the city streets. Your kitchen has traffic patterns, that is, the way people move in, out, and through it. This is important to consider when deciding whether or not to change your layout. You just might find that you can make changes that will restrict the kids and dogs from getting underfoot while you're working, and make your kitchen more efficient. It can make it safer, too.

Roll-out drawers are just one accessory that can make your kitchen more functional, and your kitchen life easier.   *(Merillat)*

A kitchen design like this can solve a lot of common "kitchen complaints," like lack of counter space. This one has plenty.   *(Dupont)*

You'll flip over the fantastic faucets available for your new kitchen, especially if your drippy old leaky faucet has got you down.   *(Kohler)*

Look now at the things you like about your kitchen. This is important, too, because you can save your budget by not reworking things that you're actually happy with. For example, if you love your lighting, don't change it. Moving lighting fixture boxes can be costly and possibly involve hiring an electrician. Maybe you like the location of the lights, but the fixtures are a bit tired-looking. Replacing the fixtures but not moving the lights is the answer, and the economical answer to boot.

Bang for the Buck

Wait! Don't rip out everything yet, unless you need to and/or don't like it. You can save money by keeping the things you like about your kitchen. There must be something you like about it, right? Maybe not. But it's worth considering.

Who wouldn't want to cook, eat, and gather in this fabulous kitchen? It's probably everyone's favorite room in this house.   *(Merillat)*

Going through this process will lead you to the answers you seek. Then you can plan to change what you don't like, and keep what you do.

As you get ready to make decisions about your new kitchen, make use of Appendix B. I've put together some great places to find help with design, layout, buying kitchen elements, even kitchen installation issues.

Mike's Installer Notebook

Sure, you're just getting started. But while you analyze your kitchen, consider what remodeling work you're likely to be doing, and think about your tool collection. Will you have what you need when the time comes to start tearing out the old and installing the new? Make a list of what tools—major and minor—you may need to acquire by purchasing or renting. You'll need this list when you make your budget.

Even small spaces have lots of potential to be your dream kitchen. This one is small, but efficient— and beautiful. *(Kohler)*

Lights, camera, kitchen! This kitchen is picture perfect, and one that any homeowner would be proud to have.   *(Wellborn)*

Let's move on to Chapter 2, where we'll go into more detail by looking at what you *want*, and what you *need* in your new kitchen.

The Least You Need to Know

◆ Examine your reasons for wanting to remodel the kitchen.

◆ Analyze your kitchen for what you like and want to keep.

◆ Determine what you don't like about your kitchen and would like to change.

◆ Get ready to remodel!

In This Chapter

- ◆ Determining what you need in your new kitchen
- ◆ The User Profile for evaluating your lifestyle
- ◆ Defining work centers for a functional kitchen
- ◆ Developing a wish list of your wants for your new kitchen
- ◆ Taking a preliminary look at your new kitchen design

Chapter 2

I Need, I Want

Remodeling the kitchen is no small undertaking. So before you start designing and tearing things out, it's important to gain a firm understanding of what you *need* in your new kitchen, and also what you *want*, so that you can incorporate both into your new design.

This chapter takes you through the process of determining your needs and wants, and explores how to resolve those issues in your new kitchen.

I Need

You know that you need more storage space, or a new refrigerator. But you may have some real needs that you can't quite express, those nagging peeves that you can't seem to locate the cause of in order to devise a solution. This is where the following User Profile can help you. Use it to take stock of how you and those in your household use your kitchen, and organize your thoughts regarding its functionality and usefulness. From the results of the profile, you can come up with solutions to your problems.

User Profile

It's time to play "20 Questions." Okay, it's actually 25 Questions. But these are 25 important questions regarding your lifestyle and how you use your kitchen. The answers will help you design a new kitchen that's functional and adequately addresses your individual needs. After you answer the questions, we'll discuss your answers and how you can transform the information from the profile into your new kitchen design.

A. Length of Time in Your Home

1. How long do you intend to stay in your home?

B. Your Current Kitchen

2. What do you like about your current kitchen? (Refer to your list from Chapter 1.)
3. What do you dislike about your current kitchen? (Refer to your Chapter 1 list.)

C. People Issues

4. How many people are in your household?
5. Are there children in the household? Ages?
6. Who will be doing the most cooking?

   Is this person left-handed or right-handed?

   How tall is this person?

   Any special considerations for physical disabilities?

D. Household Lifestyle

7. What other activities besides cooking take place in your kitchen (e.g., eating, laundry, paying bills)?
8. Where do you prefer to eat most meals?
9. Do you entertain frequently?

   Formally or informally?

E. Cooking Preferences

10. List the types of cooking done in your household (for example, cooking from scratch, bulk cooking and storing, etc.).
11. Does the primary cook *like* to cook?
12. Does the cook specialize in a type of cooking?

    Explain.
13. Will there be multiple people cooking or preparing food at the same time?
14. Do others who cook specialize in a type of cooking?

    Explain.
15. Do any of the cooks like to bake?
16. Are there special cooking needs, such as Kosher or vegetarian, gourmet, ethnic?

F. Storage Needs

17. Do you cook in quantity and freeze food?
18. How often do you shop?
19. Do you buy pantry items in bulk?

    What types of items do you buy (e.g., cans, bottles, jars, boxes, bagged foods)?
20. Are you partial to fresh fruits and vegetables, buying smaller quantities at a time?
21. How many sets of dishes, silverware, pots and pans do you have?
22. Do you buy and store paper products in bulk?
23. How many cleaning products do you typically store and use?
24. What types of small appliances do you have?

    Which do you use most often?

    Least often?
25. Where is your trash receptacle currently located?

Analyze Your User Profile

You've answered all the questions—now what do your answers mean, and how do you translate them into your kitchen design? Let's cover the topics addressed.

Length of Time in Your Home

This first question is important when planning to remodel. Your answer will determine how much money and effort you put into the remodeling project.

If you're planning to stay in your home for any length of time, you'll have to live with whatever you do, so it must appeal to your needs and wants. However, if you have an eye toward selling the home in the near future, and getting the best possible price for it, your kitchen remodeling job can be entirely different.

In the latter case, focus your efforts on aesthetics so that the kitchen will "show" well and look reasonably updated. Thus, an all-out gutted-to-the-slab remodeling job may not be necessary. This could be the perfect situation for quick fixes like giving old wood cabinets a fresh look with paint and decorative doorknobs, replacing old linoleum with new luxury vinyl, or simply replacing the tired old countertop and the appliances. (See Chapter 5 for more quick fixes.) Since you wouldn't be in the home for much longer, you could limit your monetary investment, but protect your home's value by making some improvements.

In this case, it wouldn't hurt to run your kitchen upgrading options past a real estate professional. A fresh pair of eyes will have a different view of the things you look at every day and take for granted.

This old kitchen is a mess, but the owners plan to sell the house soon. Rather than spend a lot on replacing the cabinets, they decided to paint them, install a new sink and faucet, and freshen up the walls.

Bang for the Buck

If your cabinets are sound, but look old and tired, an economical solution could be cabinet *refacing*. Laminate is applied to wood or laminate boxes and new doors are hung. It's like having new cabinets for much less money.

If you're in your home for the long haul, your efforts should be focused on your wants and needs. Take your time, and don't be afraid to spend the extra money for features you love, like granite countertops, pull-out drawers, wine racks, lazy Susans, door-mounted spice racks, and pull-out trash cabinets.

Your Current Kitchen

You know the things about your current kitchen that you love and the things that drive you crazy. Remember that likes and dislikes list you made in Chapter 1 and transferred to the User Profile? Look at it again to make sure you don't sacrifice any of the precious features you love in your present kitchen when planning your new one.

People Issues

The next group of questions involves how people in your household use the kitchen. Unless you live alone, you'll want your design to address the needs of others in your household as well, from functionality, sturdiness, and ease of maintenance to safety.

If there are lots of people in your household and you want an eat-in kitchen, you'll have to provide a space large enough to accommodate the size of eating surface and number of chairs you'll need. An eating surface can be a table, peninsula bar, even seating at an island.

In general, your kitchen should cater to the person who cooks the most. This leads to consideration of some ergonomic issues. Counter height, for example, can be an issue for taller- and shorter-than-average persons, for obvious reasons. Standard kitchen counters finish at 36" high, and all under-the-counter appliances are made with this dimension in mind. To customize the whole kitchen for a taller person, the cabinets would need to be custom-made, and therefore, more costly. However, you could raise the height of the counter only where the tall person works the most, such as the food prep work center, to cut costs. You can also lower the counter height for a shorter person.

Eat-in kitchens require a lot of space, especially if you have a large household. A smaller household could get away with a small table in a corner or cozy nook.

This kitchen has a work area for a shorter person.

The dishwasher lends itself to some adjustment, too, and can be raised to minimize bending as a taller person loads and unloads it. One way to raise it is to place it on a platform with a working drawer or panel below it. Keep in mind, however, that you'll have to make sure this height will be compatible with your plumbing. Generally, this only works at the end of a run of cabinets, where the raised countertop won't occur in the middle of your work space.

Perhaps you need to consider a shorter person. You can reduce the standard space between the upper cabinets and the countertop, called the backsplash, which normally is 18" high, to a more user-friendly 15". This allows you to bring the upper cabinets down to a more reachable height. Don't go any less, however, or you won't have a comfortable height to accommodate countertop appliances. Even at this height, a little person still might not be able to reach those top shelves. Here's a neat fix: Plan a 9" wide base cabinet to store a stepladder. Stepladders are also available that will fit under your cabinets in the toekick space. Talk about efficiency! (It's not a bad idea for average-sized persons in a standard kitchen, either.)

Whether the primary cook is right- or left-handed can bring some ergonomic issues into play. The dishwasher location, for example, can make cleanup tasks easier or more difficult based on where it is, and on where you store your everyday dishes and eating utensils. If you're left-handed, placing cooking utensils in the drawer to the left of your range goes with your natural tendency to use your left hand to grab things. It's the other way around for a right-handed person. Give thought to these issues as you're working. There aren't any "rules" regarding placement, however. Whatever you choose to do should work for you.

Designer's Notebook

A special note regarding disabilities. If anyone in your household uses a wheelchair, you need to provide extra access space beyond the recommended 36" width of walkway in order for the person to be able to turn around. A minimum of 42" is suggested to accomplish this. You may also wish to provide a work area or seating area with enough room for a wheelchair to fit under a tabletop surface. For information on *adaptive* design standards, see the Resources appendix of this book.

Don't forget kid-related issues when contemplating your new kitchen. If you have small children, you should think about ease of maintenance and cleaning, and above all, safety. Here are some tips:

◆ Select finishes that are easy to clean. Stainless steel is *not* kid-friendly, as it easily shows the little ones' fingerprints and smudges.

◆ Don't place glass doors below the counter, where small ones can break the glass.

◆ Avoid open display shelves at this height—it's an invitation to curious toddlers, making them more trouble than they're worth (the shelves, that is).

◆ Vinyl or wood flooring are kinder on the chef's legs and feet—and on falling children.

◆ Beware of sharp points, known in the kitchen design biz as *hip clippers*. Soften sharp corners, especially on countertops. Remember, if it's at your hip level, it's at a child's head level.

Household Lifestyle

Does your kitchen serve purposes other than cooking, such as laundry, eating, or a homework station for the kids? If so, you'll consider special kitchen elements for these purposes.

You can create a laundry center for a stacked washer/dryer combo using cabinet panels with doors. You can't order a standard cabinet for this purpose, but you can put one together using panel and door components. You can discuss this option with your cabinet supplier. Be sure to provide the specs of the washer/dryer combo, and know where the dryer vent is located.

You can buy nonstacked front-loading models sized especially to fit under kitchen counters. If your kitchen is large enough to give you what you need and support a laundry center, this is a good way to go. The countertop is a ready-made folding area, an essential component of a laundry center.

This front-loading washer and dryer fit perfectly under the kitchen counter. If you've got a kitchen large enough, you can do this.

Today, a lot of people like including a desk work area in their kitchens. It's a convenient station for bill-paying, menu-planning and organization. Some families like having the kids do their homework in this area, so it's also a good place for a family computer. Consider putting a drawer or cabinet in this area for children to store their school supplies.

Bang for the Buck

Unlike the stacked washer/dryer combos of yesterday, today's models are full capacity and can serve even a large household as well as individual units can. So don't ignore them if you're planning a laundry center, as they can save both money and precious space.

For those who entertain, plan for storage for extra dishes, glassware, and other items you use when having guests in your home. If you entertain frequently and for large groups, it's not unheard of to install two ovens, even two dishwashers, to accommodate this aspect of your lifestyle. Don't forget to plan for space for guests to congregate. Remember, everyone always ends up in your kitchen, or at least nearby. In Chapter 9 I'll discuss how you can use peninsulas as barriers to keep guests from interrupting the work flow in the kitchen. These can also be serving spaces for informal buffet entertaining.

A peninsula/bar can serve two purposes: A casual place for a few people to dine, and a barrier that separates cooks from those who might get in their way. *(Wellborn)*

Cooking Preferences

Here's where the real function of a kitchen comes into play. Though your kitchen may serve several purposes in your household, cooking is obviously the primary one.

What type of cooking you do and how often plays a big part in what kitchen elements you choose. If you're known as The Microwave Maven, you'll want to give that appliance a place of honor in your kitchen design, and would have little need for the design elements a gourmet chef couldn't live without. For those who cook often and from scratch, a food prep center with plenty of counter space that's close to a sink,

preferably with a garbage disposal, is a great idea. So are important tools of the trade such as knives at the ready and a collection of spices.

Someone who specializes in Asian cuisine may even want to add a wok station to the cooking center. (More on *work centers* later in this chapter.) Vegetarian households will likely require additional cold storage for fresh fruits and vegetables. You can see that different types of cooking and lifestyles lead to different kitchen priorities, so tailor your kitchen to your household's custom needs.

The Kosher Kitchen

Families who follow kosher dietary rules will have special design needs. Kosher cooks must have separate storage areas for dishes, cookware, and utensils, and the ability to wash these items separately. This can call for two dishwashers, two sinks, and enough storage for at least two sets of dishes, cookware, and utensils.

What about more than one cook or other helper in the kitchen at the same time? And the noncooks, those persons who hang out in the kitchen while you're at work? If you do a good job planning the work centers, your kitchen will be able to accommodate multiple people cooking, cleaning up, or preparing food at the same time.

Even the best planning won't always allow a small kitchen to handle multiple cooks and well-separated work centers, however. But small kitchens can still be efficient for one cook, and actually have an advantage of being able to save steps for the cook. In this case, focus your efforts on finding the most efficient usage of the space you do have.

Small kitchens aren't so bad after all! This one is a dream for the cook, who can easily work from the fridge to the stove, sink, and dishwasher. *(Whirlpool)*

Storage Needs

Inefficient storage, or lack of storage space, is the number one complaint people have about their kitchens. The problem often arises from builders cutting corners and trying to use the least amount of cabinetry. You can probably find a few lost storage opportunities in your kitchen, such as dead corners, which are corners made unusable due to design constraints, or blank walls where some type of storage could be used.

Your User Profile outlines what type of storage you need. If you buy in bulk and cook in bulk, you probably could use a tall pantry, and perhaps a larger freezer compartment in your fridge. Someone who buys lots of fresh produce may want to consider separate refrigerated vegetable drawers, a real convenience that costs more, but could be worth the price if this is a big part of your lifestyle.

Refrigerated vegetable drawers can be located in a cabinet in a food prep center.

Your collection of cookware and dishes also drives your storage requirements. If you have good china, everyday dishes, and some specialized cookware, you need more space than someone who has service for four, one set of pots, or uses paper plates a lot (don't laugh, lots of people do this). Most kitchens have a drawer below the range where pans can be stored. But did you know that cabinets are available with big, deep drawers for holding cookware? They're called pot and pan drawers, and are more efficient than standard base cabinets with doors for storing cookware. Don't forget to check these out in Chapter 3.

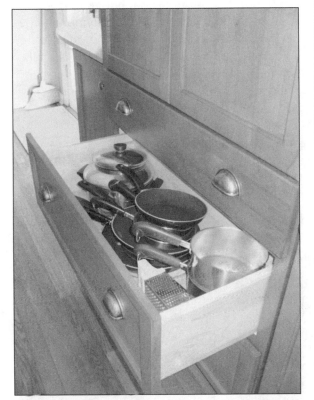

Pot drawers—an idea whose time has come. They're more efficient for storing cookware than standard base cabinets.

Small appliances can burn up countertop space and cause storage problems. The ones you use most often can be kept on the countertop, which is the most functional place for them. But if you lack space, you should store them in a readily accessible area, while the least used can go "down under" in a less-accessible place. You may consider getting rid of those small appliances you don't use at all. Why have

them if you don't use them? Remember, small appliances can be trendy—bread makers are a good example. You may have a few white elephants on your hands.

Nice juicer, but how often is it used? It sure takes up a lot of countertop space. Better to store it in a cabinet somewhere and have more room to work on the counter.

Work Centers

If you're researching ideas for remodeling your kitchen, you've probably come across the term *work triangle*. It's that ideal geometry that allows you to work easily from stove to sink to refrigerator. Much is made of this concept, which was developed by the University of Illinois Small Home Council over half a century ago. By setting "standards" for distances a cook would move from one work station to the next, efficiency was supposed to be insured.

The concept states that each leg of the triangle should be between four and seven feet in length, and the total of all three should equal between 12 and 26 feet. This can be a convenient and familiar guideline, but it should be only one of many considerations in planning your new kitchen space.

Today's kitchens have evolved from being closed-in separate rooms to larger, multifunctional open spaces. The average kitchen has more appliances and more cooks than those of yesterday. With this in mind, the concept of work centers has become more practical than the old triangle idea. A work center groups like appliances and functions in one area. This concept is the most helpful consideration of a functional kitchen design, especially in a larger kitchen.

Let's look at typical kitchen work centers.

Cleaning Up

The cleanup center is composed of the main sink with garbage disposal, dishwasher, trash and recycling receptacles, or possibly a trash compactor. Not every kitchen has all these amenities—after all, the cook and the dishwasher are often one and the same! But every kitchen will at least have a sink and a trash receptacle, which should be located near one another. When possible, locate trash, sink and dishwasher in a row so that you can scrape dishes, rinse them, and load the dishwasher conveniently. The order can be reversed according to necessity or preference (left- or right-handed), but the sink should remain in the center.

Food Prep

Since the primary purpose of the kitchen is preparing food, the food prep center will be one of the most important work areas. Your habits and personal preferences as noted in the User Profile will dictate how much space you need. The avid cook who enjoys preparing meals from scratch will generally require more space than the "microwave maven." The food prep area should be located near the refrigerator, should have adequate countertop space for

your needs, and be near a sink and trash receptacle. Note that in smaller kitchens, the trash and sink will be the cleanup center just described, but you would use the counter on one side of the sink for food prep, with the opposite one being used in cleaning up.

If space and plumbing considerations allow it, consider having a secondary sink for food preparations. Its location should be convenient to the refrigerator and trash, but away from the main sink. This allows for both functions to be performed simultaneously, but without causing a kitchen traffic jam. Note that "near" is a relative term, and should mean what *you* consider to be near with regard to the number of steps you take while working.

Cleaning up is a breeze if you've designed your cleanup center efficiently. *(Master's Kitchen Gallery)*

This food prep center has everything handy, including utensils, spices, even a cutting block on a cart that can be moved to anywhere in the kitchen.

The heart of the heart of the home: The Cooking Center. *(Master's Kitchen Gallery)*

Now You're Cookin'

The cooking center is also important, and is composed of range or cooktop, oven, and ventilation. Interestingly, the oven is the *least* used of the major appliances, so if you choose to go with a separate cooktop and oven, the oven's location may be more remote from the cooking center. In any case, the cooktop and ventilation should be located close to the food prep center.

 **Don't Get Burned!**

Be careful of traffic patterns intersecting work areas. In addition to being distracting and inconvenient to the cook, it could be dangerous when it comes to children and hot pots.

For Microwave Mavens

The microwave is the second most used appliance in today's kitchens, running second to the refrigerator. The micro can be part of the cooking center when it's a microwave-hood located over the cooking surface. Or, consider locating a freestanding or built-in micro near the refrigerator for convenience. This works well technically, too. Installing the micro in an upper cabinet requires at least an extra six inches of depth, and that works great next to the depth of a refrigerator.

Microwaves can also be installed under the counter, an option that's becoming more popular. The benefit is that you're not taking upper cabinet or counter space, and it's more accessible to shorter family members, like kids. For convenience, include a handy drawer below the micro for storing micro bowls, dishes and storage containers.

The microwave has become a mainstay in many households. Give it a place of honor in your kitchen.

Specialty Centers

You may wish to add some specialty work centers when customizing your kitchen, depending on your needs and lifestyle. For example:

1. Coffee Center. You don't need a big budget or lots of space. A coffee center can be as simple as a nice little corner where you locate your coffee pot with a cabinet for coffee, filters, teas, sugar, mugs, and other related items. Maybe your special spot is by the window, where you can sip your first cup as you watch the sun come up.

2. Baking Center. You might select an area near the oven where you can have special storage space for baking items, and perhaps a slab of marble for rolling out dough.

3. Beverage Center or Bar. A peninsula is perfect for a beverage center or bar. Cabinets in the peninsula can store glasses, bottles, even a water cooler if you're really clever with your design.

This coffee center has a built-in espresso machine, and all the necessities handy for making great coffee.

When designing work centers, don't hold back! Give yourself permission to think outside the box. It's your kitchen, so if it's safe and it functions for you, it's right!

I Want

You may have many needs in a new kitchen, but you surely have plenty of wants, too. In fact, it's probably your wants that led you to decide to remodel in the first place. Make a list now of the things you want in your new kitchen. You may not even need these things, but if you're going to remodel, you want the final result to make you happy. You shouldn't remodel without making provisions to include what you want.

Based on these wants and the needs you've outlined, you can now determine your remodeling objectives, in order of priority. Your list might look like this:

1. Improving inadequate storage and poor planning of existing layout (Need)
2. Updating the outdated look (Want)
3. Trading up on quality if possible (Want)

These priorities will drive your decisions and keep you focused. They'll lead you to give special consideration to layout and accessories that will allow you to use your space more efficiently. Blind corner cabinets, which go all the way into the corner but are partially concealed by the adjoining perpendicular cabinet, can be made more accessible with half lazy susans. Second, you could choose a newer door style and moldings which will blend with your décor, yet remain timeless and not too trendy. Last, you'll investigate the price difference of going to a wood door instead of laminate over particle board.

A Quick Look

At this point, you've defined your needs and wants. You probably have at least *some* idea of what it is you'd like to do with your own kitchen. It's a good time to do a "quick look" at the direction you're heading.

Use this simple checklist to narrow down the areas you should focus on, and help you determine the scope of your project.

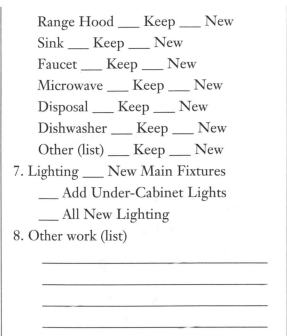

Kitchen Remodeling Project Quick Look

Check all items that apply:
1. Floor ___ Refinish ___ Replace
2. Walls ___ Paint ___ Wallpaper ___ Other
3. Ceiling ___ Paint ___ Replace ___ Other
4. Cabinets ___ New ___ Reface ___ Paint
5. Counters ___ New ___ Refinish
6. Appliances:
   Refrigerator ___ Keep ___ New
   Stove ___ Keep ___ New
   Range Hood ___ Keep ___ New
   Sink ___ Keep ___ New
   Faucet ___ Keep ___ New
   Microwave ___ Keep ___ New
   Disposal ___ Keep ___ New
   Dishwasher ___ Keep ___ New
   Other (list) ___ Keep ___ New
7. Lighting ___ New Main Fixtures
   ___ Add Under-Cabinet Lights
   ___ All New Lighting
8. Other work (list)

   _____
   _____
   _____
   _____

You have now narrowed your focus and can go on to the next chapter to study the kitchen elements you're most interested in.

The Least You Need to Know

◆ When planning to remodel your kitchen, it's important to distinguish between your wants and your needs.

◆ Fill out the User Profile to determine what your needs are with regard to your new kitchen.

◆ Think about work centers and how you perform the various functions within your kitchen so you can design the most efficient layout for your needs.

◆ Prioritize your wants and needs in case budget or time constraints require you to break your project into phases, or eliminate aspects entirely.

◆ Use the Project Quick Look to define the scope of your job and make sure you're on the right track.

In This Chapter

- Appliances
- Cabinets
- Countertops
- Sinks and plumbing
- Lighting
- Wall, floor, and ceiling options

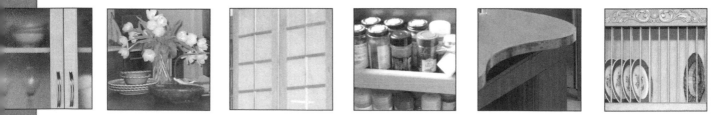

Chapter 3

Kitchen Elements

Now comes the fun part—learning all about the different elements of kitchens and what options are available to you. This chapter takes you step-by-step through each kitchen element, providing descriptions and specification information that will help you make the best choices possible for your new kitchen. It's like shopping without going to the store, though you'll have to do that soon, too. But believe me, you don't want to leave home until you've read this chapter!

Appliance Applications

If the kitchen is the heart of the home, then appliances are the heart of the kitchen. Unless you don't cook and your kitchen is merely a showplace, you rely on your appliances for preparing meals. Therefore, your primary concerns are function and aesthetics. Whether you're keeping the appliances you currently have or are planning to buy new ones, this section tells you what's available so you can find appliances to serve your wants and needs.

Beautiful and functional kitchens are made up of different elements, from appliances and counter-tops to sinks, lighting, and floor materials. Coordinating and buying these elements is a fun and satisfying part of remodeling.

You're Finished!

Actually, you're just getting started. And you should know that standard finishes for most appliances include white (the most economical), black, bisque, or almond, and stainless steel.

What's Cooking?

Your cooking choices come down to traditional ranges (formerly called "stoves"), cooktops, microwaves, and ovens with broilers. Ovens can be separate wall-mounted appliances, or those incorporated into a range. Here's the rundown on all of these options.

Ranges

The technical definition of a range is a single appliance that has an oven and a cooktop surface. This is the most typical and economical cooking option. You'll find a variety of ranges when you go shopping, from gas and electric models to those with conventional radiant or convection ovens (we'll cover that when we discuss ovens). Ranges can be freestanding, the most common type, or slide-in models, which have unfinished sides and are designed specifically to fit between two cabinets. The controls on these models are located on the front of the appliance, allowing your countertop to continue across behind it. The sides also overlap the countertop, eliminating the gap. It's a clean look that simulates that of a separate cooktop, but for much less money.

Range Standards

Ranges are 30" wide and 36" high to work with adjoining countertops. This standard applies to both freestanding and slide-in models.

Freestanding ranges have finished sides, so you could place one all by itself, without cabinets around it. But then you wouldn't have any work space close at hand.

Cooktops

If you're not feeling at home on your range these days, you can change that. Cooktops are more popular than ever. It's a surface cooking unit with no oven, and is built into a counter-top. Cooktops are great on islands, even penin-sulas. They're available in gas or electric, and generally have four burners, though two, five, and six-burner models are available. Some models also come with indoor grills.

Cooktop Standards

Cooktops are typically 30" wide for four-burner models. Sizes of larger and smaller cooktops vary, from 20" to 48".

They're usually made to fit in a 24" deep cabinet.

Most sit between 2½" to 6" high, with most of that depth below the countertop.

A reason to want a cooktop is for the extra burner, which requires a 36" width that you can't get with a range.

A slide-in range has a nice, built-in look.

This gas cooktop is on an island, and is both functional and beautiful.

For both cooktops and ranges, the cooking elements for electric models can be conventional coils, or glass-top surfaces. The coils, though cheaper, are quickly becoming obsolete. Smooth tops lend a clean, updated look and are easy to maintain. They tend to work best with flat-bottomed metal cookware.

For gas ranges and cooktops, you can choose sealed burners or traditional open-style. Sealed burners offer the advantage of preventing grease and cooking debris from getting caught in difficult-to-clean areas.

A cooktop on an island can easily and efficiently accommodate more than one cook.
(Whirlpool Corporation)

Cooktops come in many styles with varying numbers of burners. You can see the different cooking element choices here.

Designer's Notebook

Not all electric cooktops are created equal. Gas cooking used to offer the most control, but new technology in electric cooktops is giving it some competition. These technologies include:

1. Induction cooking. The food gets hot, but the cooking surface doesn't.

2. Radiant cooking. Old technology, but elements heat up faster, use less energy, and clean up better.

3. Halogen cooking. Heats up and cools down quickly, and offers fine temperature control.

Technology usually means higher cost, so these cooking surfaces are generally more expensive.

Ovens

When choosing an oven, either in a range or separate built-in model, you'll have to decide between a conventional radiant or a convection type. Radiant ovens cook food via the broiling element on top of the oven and the baking element on the bottom. Convection ovens incorporate a fan in the back of the oven that helps

cook food more quickly, more efficiently, and more evenly by moving the heated air around the food. This is especially handy if you like to bake. Convection ovens are about 25 percent more expensive than radiant ovens, but can save you money in the long run, since the increased efficiency reduces cooking times.

Oven Standards

Built-in ovens range from 22" to 50" wide. But be careful to check the manufacturer's size specifications before ordering your cabinet, since sizes vary according to manufacturer and model.

An advantage of built-in ovens: You don't have to bend to work with them, or to clean them.
(Jenn-Air)

Speaking of oven cleaning, gas or electric can have the standard cleaning option, which means you do the cleaning. If you don't want to get to know your oven on such an intimate basis, you can spend a little more and get a self-cleaning model. Cleaning is accomplished by actually burning off grease and debris using extreme heat. Heat shields are required for these ovens to protect adjacent cabinets from the heat, or you can remember to open neighboring doors and drawers when cleaning.

CAUTION Don't Get Burned!

All new appliances come with a manufacturer's warranty, usually one year. Know what's covered by the warranty before buying an additional service warranty, which may extend the manufacturer's warranty into the future. Be sure you aren't duplicating coverage.

Microwaves

Microwaves have become a mainstay in most households. You can choose from stand-alone models, built-ins (which are simply stand-alones built into a cabinet), or over-the-range microwave/ventilation hood combinations. The stand-alone models are available in varying sizes, from those that will accommodate large items such as turkeys, roasts, or hams, to more compact units that are great for everyday duty, such as warming, defrosting, and cooking smaller items.

Built-ins require a trim kit that fits onto the face of your cabinet opening surrounding the microwave to achieve an integrated look. A built-in located under a countertop can be a good idea in some households, since it frees up countertop space, and makes the microwave accessible to little ones. But it would require bending on the part of adults.

Microwaves are now available with the same convection features found in regular ovens.

Microwave Standards

Full-size microwaves vary by manufacturer, but typically are 16" deep, 15 to 18" high, and 24" wide.

Compact micros also vary, but typically are 12" deep, 12" high, and 22" wide. Always measure before finalizing layout plans.

Microwave/hood combinations are generally 30" wide to fit over a standard 30" range or cooktop, and 15" high. The depth is compatible with adjacent 12" deep wall cabinets—not perfectly flush, but usually not greater than 16" deep.

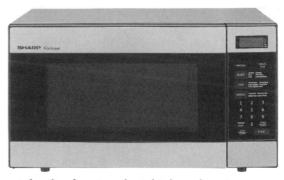

A familiar face in today's kitchen, the microwave has become a mainstay. *(Sharp)*

For small kitchens, the microwave/hood combination mounted over the range or cooktop is a good choice. It's convenient in the cooking center, and the hood can be vented to the outside or recirculated.

The over-the-range mounted microwave/hood combination is preferred by many people because it saves countertop space.   *(Sharp)*

A microwave cabinet with a drawer. The microwave opening must be cut out to specification of microwave and trim kit. These models require extra cabinet depth, anywhere from 18" to a full 24", so be sure to account for this in your planning.

Ventilation

Cooktops and ranges should have ventilation hoods to eliminate smoke and cooking odors. The most common type fits underneath the over-the-range cabinets. The next most common is the microwave/hood combination. There are two freestanding types of hoods as well: An island hood, which works with a cooktop on an island, and a wall hood, which mounts on the wall.

Ventilation hoods can also be concealed behind special hood cabinets. Whatever type you choose, cooking surface appliances are required to have ventilation of at least 150 cubic feet per minute (cfm), either venting to the outside, or recirculating.

This wall hood is a stand-alone over a cooktop.

The Big Chill

If refrigerator shopping leaves you cold, consider this: Besides being the most essential item in your kitchen, it's also the only one you depend on for reliable service 24 hours a day. The choices are extensive, and the price tag can be expensive, but thorough research helps you make the best choice for your needs.

Full-sized refrigerators come in a wide variety of widths and depths based on capacity, measured in cubic feet. How much the fridge holds is generally the driving factor in your purchase. Eighteen cubic feet is the minimum suggested capacity for a family of four, but you could easily use up to 25, depending on your lifestyle, cooking habits, and storage needs.

How that capacity is configured is another choice. You can choose a two-door with freezer on top or bottom, or a side-by-side model. The freezer on top type is the most affordable. Top over bottom compartments offer full width, and can hold large items from holiday turkeys to children's birthday sheet cakes easily. Side-by-sides limit this ability, so choose carefully according to your lifestyle. The freezer on the bottom style is gaining popularity. It's a new look, and the refrigerator portion is at eye level, a good idea since it gets opened about 20 times more than the freezer compartment.

Options include adjustable shelves, glass or wire shelves, egg trays, deli meat drawers, even fruit and vegetable crispers that are climate controlled.

Refrigerator Standards

Refrigerators run from 30" to 48" wide for standard models.

Refrigerators with regular freezers over or under the refrigerator compartment are typically 33" or 36" wide.

Side-by-side models are 36", 42" or 48" wide.

Depth for all models can be as much as 33", not counting handles. This will stick out beyond all cabinet depths. Height is typically 72".

Built-in refrigerators fit better with cabinets, and are 24" deep. However, they're generally 84" high, and widths vary. You can also have a happy medium with counter depth or semi-built-in models, which are gaining popularity. These are also about 72" high, but the refrigerator depth is only 24", excluding the doors. So the part that sticks out will only be the door, about another 3".

Cabinet panels can be added to the front with a trim kit.

Not quite a built-in, but a high-end, finished look, with functionality.

The freezer on the bottom model is becoming popular for its updated look, and for its functionality. *(Amana)*

Designer's Notebook

Use refrigerator side panels for a custom built-in look at a reasonable price. This allows you to bring the over-the-fridge cabinets forward, so you can actually use them with ease.

Dishwasher Duty

A dishwasher has got to be the greatest convenience in the kitchen. Just load it up, and go relax. This appliance has also undergone some major high-tech revolutions.

Standard dishwashers offer a few wash and rinse selections. But newer features include pot and pan, crystal, or china settings; digital controls; hidden controls; stainless steel interiors; even two drawers that can be used to wash dishes separately or at the same time. Features such as those add to the price. Even the most common models today, however, offer more energy efficiency and water savings than older models, and operate more quietly than ever.

Dishwasher Standards

Dishwashers are almost all 24" wide, but some 18" "slimline" models are also available.

They're made to fit under a 36"-high countertop.

Panels to match your cabinets may be applied to the door with a trim kit.

If you're unsure about what model dishwasher you'll eventually use, consider finishing the exposed sides of the adjacent base cabinets, just in case you choose a model that exposes them. Then you're safe no matter what you get.

A two-drawer dishwasher is practical—use one drawer for smaller loads, both for big loads, or use it to separate dishes for washing in a kosher kitchen.

Cabinet Members

Cabinets make the kitchen, and the basis of your kitchen plan essentially consists of filling the space with cabinets in the appropriate sizes for maximum functionality. But more than that, cabinets define the look and feel of your room, so aesthetic appeal is a big factor in choosing the boxes you'll use.

A general rule of thumb: The more cabinet boxes you have, the more money you'll spend. That includes contractor help for installation if you choose to go that route. So if your cabinet budget is a bit tight, plan to use the largest sizes you can without compromising function and good sense.

Let's run through the most common cabinets you'll use.

Basics of Base Cabinets

Stock cabinets (standard sized boxes) come in 3"-width increments, starting at 9" wide and going up to 48". All are 24" deep and are 34½" high. Anything wider than 48" would need a door that would be too heavy to be supported by a standard cabinet hinge.

Cabinet widths from 9" to 24" have one door, or can have a door and a drawer, or up to four drawers, if it's strictly a drawer base cabinet. Boxes over 24" wide will have two doors. There may be one or two drawers on top of this. Drawer base cabinets can be drawer-only, typically three or four, and the wider ones (30" or 36") can be used for pot and pan storage.

The toe space on base cabinets can be from 3½" to 4½" high. This is part of the cabinet height of 34½".

Here are several types of base cabinets, including a sink base and door with drawer bases.

You can have all drawers in a base cabinet.

Sink base cabinets are simply base cabinets without a shelf, since the plumbing needs to go into it. Also, the drawer front is false, if you have one. Otherwise, it could have a full-height door. Standard sizes are 33" to 36" wide.

This interesting sink base cabinet is curved, requiring curved doors. But this is a custom item, and more expensive than standard sink bases. Note the full-height doors.

Peninsula and island cabinets aren't any different from regular base cabinets, with one exception. A true peninsula cabinet has doors on front and back for access from either side of the peninsula. These can be upper or base cabinets.

This irregularly shaped island has cabinets all around it, offering a large amount of storage space.

Wall of Cabinets

Wall, or upper cabinets, come in three main heights. They are either 30'', 36'' or 42'' high. Shorter cabinets that are used above the refrigerator, range, or microwave hood are available in 3''-inch increments starting at 12'' high. Widths are the same as base cabinets, ranging from 9'' wide to 36'', with some cabinet manufacturers offering up to 48''.

Cabinet boxes come in two types:

1. Frame. Frame boxes have a frame applied to the face of the box, as if a picture frame was glued to the opening. Normally, only wood cabinets have frames. The door can either cover the whole frame (full overlay) or just the opening, leaving some space around the door (standard overlay). The same for drawer fronts. The door hinges are visible with a standard overlay. The look is more traditional.

2. Frameless. There's no frame on the box, so doors and drawers always cover the opening completely, with no visible space. Frameless cabinets are also called Euro-style. The look is sleek and modern.

A kitchen with frameless cabinets. Very sleek and high-tech looking.

Mike's Installer Notebook

If you plan to mount your cabinets flush with the ceiling and aren't planning to use crown molding, you must include a starter strip. This element is installed between the cabinets and the ceiling to give the cabinets some breathing room, so to speak. Without the added clearance, your doors will rub on the ceiling when you open and close them. Even worse, if you have high hat lighting fixtures, which are mostly recessed but the housing extends a bit beyond the ceiling, the doors could hit them if you don't use starter strips! Starter strips are available in 96'' lengths.

The more traditional look of framed doors and drawers.

Glass doors can be ordered for wall cabinets. You can choose frame-only doors for a full door of glass, or you can opt for a more traditional window look, where mullions or *muntins* divide the glass. Use glass doors as a visual element on cabinets that can be seen from other rooms. Since you'll be able to see the cabinet interior, it should be finished to match the exterior. Otherwise, cabinet interiors are typically white or natural maple-colored, no matter what the exterior finish.

These doors are a traditional window look using mullions to divide the glass.

Pro Lingo

Are you mulling over mullions? You should be if you're considering glass-front cabinet doors. You can choose the look and profile of these wood dividers.

Cornered

Builders often cut corners in the kitchen by not utilizing corner space with corner cabinets. Why? Because they cost more than simply using standard cabinets and ignoring all that extra space. Fortunately, you can make up for that when you remodel by considering some terrific corner cabinet options.

Both base and upper cabinets offer corner solutions such as easy reach, which is aptly named. You can easily reach everything in the cabinet and use all the corner space. The door is actually in two parts (see the accompanying figure). To use an easy reach base cabinet, you must have 36″ of space from the corner in both directions.

Once you have an easy reach corner cabinet in your kitchen, you'll wonder how you ever did without one before!

Blind corner cabinets are more common, and you may see them in standard kitchens. They're available in widths from 36" to 48". They're not as easy to use, but do give you the extra storage space. You can make blind cabinets more user-friendly with half-lazy Susans (see the accessories section later in this chapter). Blind upper cabinets are too narrow to use lazy susans, so they're harder to get into.

You might also choose a diagonal corner cabinet. For something a little different, use a diagonal base for a sink cabinet. Diagonal wall cabinets aren't as easy to get into as an easy reach because the opening is smaller and there's only one door. Also, they're deeper to reach into and it's harder to get into the back.

This blind base cabinet has a half-lazy Susan to make it more user-friendly.

Diagonal upper cabinets are stylish, and highly functional.

Using a diagonal base cabinet for your sink is out-of-the-box thinking—and a unique design.

Designer's Notebook

Would you like wood, or MDF (medium-density fiber board) construction for your cabinets? Here's the scoop. MDF is often looked down upon as "cheap," and that can be a misconception. Good MDF cabinets are dense and stable, meaning they're strong, steady, can support heavy countertops, and won't move. Wood, on the other hand, is always expanding and contracting, which can cause problems, particularly with doors. In terms of water damage from a flood, wood or MDF will suffer about the same damage.

So which one is better? It's a matter of budget and personal preference. Some people like the naturalness of having all wood. When you find cabinets you really like, the material won't matter as long as it's good quality, and the box has 5/8" to ¾" thick sides. Anything less is considered to be less than adequate.

Install Tall Cabinets

Tall cabinets can serve several functions, including pantry storage, broom closet, and built-in oven housing. Widths range from 12" to at least 36", while heights are 84", 90" or 96," corresponding to wall cabinet heights of 30", 36" and 42". Tall cabinets have the same toe space as other base cabinets.

With roll-out drawers, tall pantries are another "How did I ever do without it?" cabinet. A broom closet is simply this type of cabinet without shelves, and generally more narrow.

Built-in ovens are housed in a tall cabinet, with storage space at hand for bakeware—or whatever you want.

Specialty Cabinets

We've covered the basics of kitchen cabinetry. Now let's look at some specialty cabinets that can make your kitchen highly functional, while offering some luxuries you may have been missing in your old kitchen.

Different cabinet manufacturers offer different specialty cabinets. When you choose a brand, study the offerings carefully. As a rule, the more expensive the cabinet line, the more types of cabinets it will offer, and the more modifications to their stock line will be available.

Here are photos of some of the more common specialty cabinets available from many manufacturers.

Trash cans don't always have to go under the sink or sit out in the open. If you have the space, consider a pull-out trash cabinet. They will hold one to four containers, more commonly one or two: One for trash, and one for recycling.

This is a terrific cabinet for those who buy lots of canned goods, but it can only be used for canned goods.

These open shelves act like "cubby holes" to store and/or display whatever you want.

Frequent entertainers might want a tray cabinet for all their party trays. They're also good for storing baking sheets and cutting boards.

A bookshelf goes nicely above the range, an area often difficult to reach for regular kitchen use. But it works well for cookbooks or to display items.

This type of cabinet can end an open-ended run of wall cabinets in any situation where you would prefer a more finished look, rather than looking at the blank side of a cabinet.

Accessorize Your Kitchen

Accessories are the little luxuries of the kitchen. Imagine a built-in spice rack, wine rack, or open plate rack storage for your favorite family china. If digging in the back of blind cabinets bugs you, half-lazy Susans and roll-out drawers are accessories to the rescue. Again, the availability of accessories varies from one cabinet manufacturer to another. If you do your research, you'll find cabinet lines that offer the luxuries you desire.

Here are some common accessories.

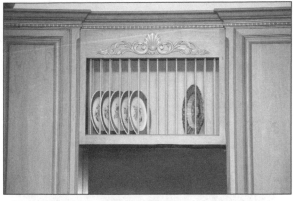

Plate racks function as storage and display for your special dishware.

No more disorganized spices—an on-the-door spice rack keeps your spices in order, and thus keeps your kitchen in order.

You may find room for a stylish built-in wine rack in your new kitchen.

Customize your drawers and organize your eating utensils with cutlery drawers.

That useless space in front of the sink doesn't have to be useless. A tilt tray gives you a place to store sponges, scouring pads, and other cleaning items that clutter up your sink.

Appliance panels match your cabinets and are mounted, using special kits, to the front of dishwashers, refrigerators, or trash compactors to blend them with the rest of the kitchen. These are especially good to use with white appliances, which can stand out harshly against dark or wood cabinets, and even some lighter-colored cabinets.

You can have a breadbox in a cabinet to help keep bread fresh.

Moldings and Fillers

There are some miscellaneous cabinet elements you need to know about. Let's start with moldings, which are the coordinating trim pieces you use to finish the tops and bottoms of your cabinets.

From ornate to simple, molding makes the difference in a kitchen, providing a high-style polished look to even the simplest cabinets. There are three types:

1. Crown molding tops off your upper cabinets and can go directly against the ceiling, or not. Typically, crown molding is 2" to 3" high.

2. Undercabinet light rail is smaller molding that finishes off the underside of wall cabinets. It can be used to conceal undercabinet light fixtures if you're using them.

3. Toekick, or toe board, is molding that finishes the bottoms of cabinets at the floor.

There are many molding profiles to choose from, and they vary by manufacturer and style of cabinet. You'll specify moldings when ordering your cabinets. Molding strips are 96" in

length—be sure to order enough to cover for potential cutting mistakes. It's generally recommended to order an additional 12" for every cut you'll make.

You don't have to use molding if you don't want to—it's strictly an option. However, you should at least order matching toe kick, or the cabinets could look a bit rough.

You're sure to find a molding profile to suit your tastes, and the style of your cabinets.

Fillers are trim pieces that literally fill the gaps in a kitchen. It's a rare kitchen with dimensions that work out exactly when you install cabinets. For all those little spaces an inch to a couple inches between walls and cabinets, a filler makes it fit. Take a look at your kitchen cabinets and look for fillers. Look under the wall cabinets, and you'll definitely see them, because they'll have nothing behind them.

Wall fillers, base filler, and tall fillers are the three types, and are available in lengths that correspond to the standard cabinet heights. You cut them to fit your needs at installation time.

Fillers aren't bad things—they're a necessary part of kitchen design and installation. So use 'em if you need 'em!

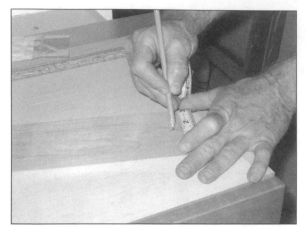

Fillers are cut to your specific needs. They fill the gaps between cabinets and walls, and where cabinets meet at corners.

Designer's Notebook

Moldings, especially crown molding, can be a headache if you don't have enough on hand. Always order an extra eight-foot length to allow for mistakes. Hey, even really good installers can make a mistake every now and then! Also, allow at least a foot of molding for each mitered joint in the project.

Knobby Needs and More

Cabinet hardware includes drawer slides, shelf clips, and door hinges, but these items come with the cabinets. The only hardware you need to be concerned with buying separately are door and drawer knobs and handles.

There are literally thousands of handles, pulls, and knobs available in a myriad of materials, from glass and ceramic to metal, plastic, rubber—whatever you can imagine. Honestly, selecting door and drawer knobs can be one of the most difficult tasks when remodeling, simply because you have so many to choose from.

Remember from Chapter 2 how to minimize confusion: Decide between two choices at a time. And check for quality materials and manufacture.

Designer's Notebook

Check the quality of hardware that comes with your cabinets. You may love the cabinets, but if you're not satisfied with the hardware, consider upgrading it.

Knobs are easier to install than handles, since there's only one hole to drill.

Counter Toppers

Countertops are an important functional and aesthetic element in the kitchen. When you look at a kitchen, you see the cabinets and countertops almost as one entity. You should take your time and do a lot of research before purchasing countertops to make sure you get what you need, as well as what you want. For example, avid cooks make heavier use of countertops, and may want to allot a larger percentage of the budget to this aspect of the job.

Before we discuss all the countertop options, let's look at backsplashes, which go hand-in-hand with counters.

Make a Splash

Countertops usually come with a 4" high backsplash. However, the whole 18" area between the countertop and the bottom of the wall cabinets is also called the backsplash. People often choose to paint or wallpaper this backsplash area above the 4" countertop extension. However, you can use countertop material on this entire area, or select a different material that matches and works with your countertop material. You can even view this area as a blank canvas to make art—many people do artistic designs with tile, faux painting, stenciling, punched tin, whatever works. Most important, do what you like.

Be creative with your backsplash area to put your personality into your kitchen.

The backsplash can be any material you wish. Or, you can extend your countertop material up to the cabinets.

Decorative tile makes a great backsplash.

Laminates Unlimited

Laminate is a thin sheet of the finish you select that is applied either to plywood or particle board countertops. They're sold under the brand names of Formica, Wilsonart, and many others. They're the least expensive, and are what you'll typically find in an economically built kitchen. Advantages of laminates include the availability of a wide range of colors and textures, and the fact that a do-it-yourselfer can install them, especially the self-rimmed variety. (See Chapter 12 for installation instructions.)

Disadvantages of laminates include sensitivity to heat, and the fact that you can't cut directly on the surface and must use cutting boards. Home improvement centers or laminate countertop fabricators make the top to your dimensions and specifications. You'll have to indicate finished edges, backsplashes, and sink cutouts unless you plan to do them yourself. It's best if you can take your dimensions directly from your base cabinets once they're installed, as this final dimension can vary slightly from your plans.

There are more choices in laminate countertops than ever. This one has a unique crackle finish—and looks fantastic.

Tile Style

Tile countertops are a popular option, with a wide range of choices. Ceramic tile is the least costly way to go. Natural stone such as tumbled marble is more expensive, and has to be sealed and maintained. Prices are more expensive than laminates.

Tile countertops are functional and attractive, but can be a maintenance headache because of the grout.

Advantages of tile countertops include greater heat tolerance and custom appearance. But if you're a down-and-dirty cook, you're not going to enjoy keeping grout joints clean. Grout sealers help, but you'll still have to put some work into keeping grout clean. Generally, it's not advisable to cut directly on most tile surfaces.

Would You Like Wood?

Wood or butcher block countertops are growing in popularity thanks to new sealing technologies that protect against water. They're an excellent mid-range option priced in between laminate and solid surface. They're available in varying thicknesses, which you need to keep in mind as you plan your kitchen design. This option is also installer-friendly, and the tops can be refinished by sanding when the surface becomes nicked or scratched. Price is determined by the type of wood. An option: Use wood tops in just one section of your kitchen such as the food prep work area to cut costs and add efficiency.

Wood is functional, and the look is unique and warm. *(Craft-Art Countertops)*

Solid Choices

Solid surface countertops are just that—the color goes all the way through the man-made polyester or acrylic resin material. Corian by Dupont, the most well-known brand, is also the original, and it comes with a ten-year warranty that's transferable if you sell your home! The advantages of solid surfaces are that you can get integral or molded sinks that are seamless, and since the material is man-made, you can have just about any shape or edge you can think of.

While the surface is hard and nonporous, it's not impossible to scratch or stain. However, it can be buffed out and refinished. Solid surfaces are a higher priced option. Also, they require expert installers with special equipment, so plan for this in your budget if you choose these countertops.

Another up-and-coming choice in solid surface counters is quartz agglomerate. It simulates the look of granite without the natural variations and is made of 93 percent quartz. You can cut on it, put hot pots on it, and, in the unlikely event that you scratch it, you can buff it out. The well-known brand is Silestone, but Dupont also makes this material under the brand name Zodiaq. These tops are made and installed by authorized fabricators only, and the price ranks right up there with granite.

 Bang for the Buck

You can save money on solid surface countertops by opting for a thinner edge. Typically countertops are 1½", but a ¾" looks just as nice, and can save money.

Corian brand from Dupont is the original solid-surface countertop material. *(Dupont)*

Take It for Granite

Natural stone countertops are absolutely the most luxurious. No two can ever be exactly the same, as they are natural products. The most popular stone used in kitchens is granite. It's harder and less porous than marble, and if scratches do appear, they can also be buffed out. Durability, luxury, and beauty are the benefits, plus it can handle your hot pots without a problem. The natural coolness of this surface makes it an excellent choice for bakers who spend time rolling out dough.

On the downside, fabrication and installation must be done by pros. Also, natural stone is quite costly.

Designer's Notebook

If you have a bar or peninsula and plan to use a granite or solid surface top, note that the overhanging portion of the top may need additional support. Angle irons or brackets can be used to support this cantilevered weight. Standard overhang is 12" for an eating area to allow leg room, but if your countertop fabricator doesn't think you can get away with 12" without support, you may be able to do with 10".

This unusual granite countertop has beautiful variations found only in natural stone.

Steel Yourself

Stainless steel can also be used as a countertop and can work well in a contemporary design. Born in commercial kitchens, it definitely yields a commercial look that is sleek, while being an excellent work surface in terms of heat as well as cutting. Its use in homes is uncommon; one reason might be that it's quite expensive.

Unique, sleek, shiny—and expensive. Stainless steel has a lot of pluses, but you'll pay for those advantages.

Concrete Ideas

Poured concrete is quickly becoming more accepted as a countertop for the kitchen. It can be made in any shape or color you want. This is an expensive and labor-intensive choice that you certainly wouldn't want to tackle yourself.

A final word about countertops: They can make or break a kitchen in both aesthetics and function. Don't be afraid to mix materials, such as tile backsplash with laminate counter. Consider your needs. If you bake and you really want the granite work surface, you can do your own tile backsplash in a complementing color for a great look that saves money by cutting down on the square footage of granite you'll need.

Concrete comes to the kitchen, and can be molded and shaped any way you want. This kidney-shaped countertop is a bold design element of this ultra-modern kitchen. *(Buddy Rhodes Studio, San Francisco)*

That Sinking Feeling

The type of sink you choose for your new kitchen will be determined by the size of your sink base cabinet, and your personal preference in terms of bowl size, number of bowls, and configuration. Standard kitchen sinks are single or double bowl. There are two types:

1. Drop-in. The most common sink, these extend over the countertop cutout to rest on the counter.

2. Under-mount. These sinks mount underneath a solid surface countertop, and the sides are flush with the sides of the cutout. Under-mounts have varying support requirements, and require the most space as the entire sink must fit under the counter.

Solid surface countertops use an under-mount sink.

Kitchen faucets are many, and are best chosen to coordinate with the sink. Also, the styling should blend with the décor of your kitchen. A highly stylized Jetsons model won't look right in an English Victorian kitchen.

Faucets can be single lever with a pull-out spray feature, or three-holed with a separate lever for hot and cold water, which can also have a separate sprayer. Make sure your sink choice has enough holes to accommodate your faucet choice.

Standard sinks drop in the cutout and rest on the countertop.

Sink materials range from stainless steel in various grades, or gages, to cast iron and solid surface countertop material, these being manufactured as an integral part of the solid surface countertop.

Kitchen faucets come in all sizes, shapes, styles, finishes—and prices, from inexpensive to whopper-sized price tags. Choose carefully for quality and function, as well as aesthetic appeal. *(Price Pfister)*

Don't forget garbage disposals, part of the sink and plumbing system. In-sink garbage disposals will grind any type of biodegradable waste so that it flushes into your septic tank or sewer system. The price range is wide, depending on motor horsepower, component material, insulation, and warranty.

Consider how much you use a disposal. If you use it a lot, you should consider a higher horsepower model. Power ranges from ⅓ HP to 1 HP, with ⅝ to ¾ HP adequate for most households. Warranties run from one year to seven years. Stainless steel components add to the quality, efficiency, and durability of the unit. Adequate insulation will keep noise to a minimum as you grind away.

Putting a bit more money into a disposal means more power and efficiency, and less noise. It can be well worth it. *(In-Sink-Erator)*

Watts Up!

Adequate lighting is important in the kitchen so you can see what you're doing. But light for working isn't the only reason you'll want to spend time thinking about lighting.

There are four different sources of lighting to consider for the kitchen: general, ambient, task, and accent.

1. General, as the name implies, is the source of overall illumination, and is provided by your main overhead fixture(s). These can be anything from recessed fixtures such as high hats to hanging fixtures. However, this general lighting isn't enough for all the detailed functions that are carried out in the kitchen. In fact, general lighting is usually located on the ceiling in the center of the kitchen, so if you're working at the perimeter countertops, your body will cast a shadow on what you're doing. This is where task lighting comes in (#3).

2. Ambient lighting can also be referred to as "mood lighting." An example is to install lights above your upper cabinets to create a soft glow in the room.

3. Task lighting is the light that enables you to see what you're doing as you perform the tasks of the work centers. Under-cabinet lights are an example of task lighting, as is a track light pointing directly at a cutting board, or over the sink and cleanup area.

4. Accent, or decorative lighting, is used to create an effect. A track light to illuminate a focal point in your kitchen is an example of this, as is lighting inside a cabinet with glass doors.

Some lighting can perform more than one task. Undercabinet lighting can be both task lighting, and can provide ambient lighting that can be seen from an adjacent living area, especially if you install dimmers on them.

The minimum lighting required in all kitchens would be a source of general lighting and adequate task lighting.

Designer's Notebook

Bulbs for today's kitchen lighting run the gamut from the traditional incandescent bulb to fluorescent, halogen, and xenon.

Halogen and xenon are more expensive initially, but can save you money in the long run due to fuel efficiency and longer lasting bulbs. If you prefer the price of fluorescent, you can find bulbs that cast a natural no-flicker light, unlike those of the past.

Lighting the way in the kitchen takes thought to make sure you have all your work areas covered, and have a pleasing lighting environment overall. *(Armstrong)*

All Around the Room

Like any other room in the house, you'll address design issues for redoing your kitchen walls, floor, and ceiling—if you choose to do so. Most likely, you will at least paint the walls. In this section, I'll list several options for each, with pros and cons.

The most important thing about making choices for these kitchen elements is that you choose items that blend with the décor of your kitchen, and offer functionality and durability.

Wall Wants

At the least, you'll paint your walls. We recommend semi-gloss paint for ease of cleaning, particularly if you plan to paint the backsplash area. It's the most economical option, and it's easy to enhance with faux finishing techniques. Plus, it's the ultimate do-it-yourself wall finish.

The kitchen walls are an opportunity for expression. Use colorful paint, unique wallpaper, even wood to obtain the look and feel you want.

Wallpaper is also popular for kitchens. You want to make sure that the color and the pattern style work with the mood of the kitchen. The wallpaper you choose should be easy to clean and wipe up. Some wallpapers have a waterproof finish, which is a good idea.

Another fashionable option is wood paneling. Wainscot paneling is sometimes used in country and traditional kitchens, and is a good way to finish the backside of a peninsula.

Flawless Floors

What you walk on in the kitchen is important. Kitchen flooring must be durable and attractive, and be able to blend in with the rest of your home, especially adjoining rooms. If you plan to replace your current floor, take time to research all the floor options available to you.

Here are the most popular kitchen flooring choices:

1. Tile. There are so many types of tile to consider, including mosaic, ceramic, Mexican, quarry, marble, granite, and porcelain in all shapes, sizes, and colors. Tile is practical for the kitchen, durable, and lasting. It can fit any décor, from traditional to ultra-contemporary. One downside: It's hard on the feet. If you spend a lot of time in the kitchen, you could place cushiony throw rugs at the work areas where you stand.

2. Vinyl. Today's vinyl flooring is a long way from the old linoleum of the past. Materials are tougher, and the selection of patterns and colors is greater. Luxury vinyls are easy on the feet and high-quality. You can choose patterns that look like tile, stone, even wood. Vinyl is generally the most economical choice, though the best grade vinyls can be comparable to tile in price.

3. Wood and Wood Laminates. Wood brings a feeling of warmth, which is perfect for the kitchen. Types of wood flooring include strips, which range from 1½" to 3½" in width and are nailed or glued to the subfloor; planks, which are at least 3" wide and install the same way; or parquet, wood patterns in 6" × 6" squares, though specialty squares of any size can be made. Parquet is usually glued to the floor. Wood laminates, a plywood base with veneers applied, are thinner than hardwood flooring, often by about half. They are typically glued in place. Many wood or laminate floors connect with a tongue and groove system.

Choosing tile flooring can be difficult, because there are so many choices.

Wood and wood laminate floors bring warmth to a kitchen.

Over Your Head

Ceilings are just like walls, for the most part. You can paint your ceilings, but you probably wouldn't wallpaper them. Don't despair, though. You don't have to live with a vast expanse of drywall ceiling. You have other options, such as:

◆ Beadboard wood paneling for a casual, island look.

◆ Punched tin panels can augment a wide range of styles, from industrial to Victorian.

◆ Ceiling tiles aren't what they used to be— tiles mimic other more expensive ceiling options, such as tin, but can be applied quickly and are much less expensive.

This tin-look ceiling is actually made from less costly ceiling panels from Armstrong.   *(Armstrong)*

What about popcorn? At this point in time, most people would want to get rid of that white, rough-textured ceiling. Popcorn is an outdated look. If you've got it, and your whole house has it, you'll probably need to live with it, unless you choose to remove it from the entire house. But most people wouldn't choose to apply popcorn.

Your Specifications List

As you select all the elements of your future kitchen, be sure to keep detailed notes about your choices. This way you won't forget anything important that you'll need to know as you shop for the various elements in your design. Call this list your Spec List.

For example, in your cabinet details, you'll want to note your choice of framed or frameless design, wood or particle board construction, painted or stained finish. Do this as you research and educate yourself in each kitchen element category.

In the next chapter, I'll show you how to organize and catalog these choices for quick reference and easy shopping.

The Least You Need to Know

◆ Research your options for kitchen elements.

◆ Think about the elements you like and need for your new kitchen.

◆ Consider costs as you peruse your kitchen element options.

◆ Research product information when selecting your elements, including potential sources.

◆ List details of these items so when you make your choices, you'll have a detailed specifications list.

In This Chapter

◆ How to minimize confusion and make sound decisions

◆ Put your personal style and preferences into your kitchen design

◆ Where to find ideas for your new kitchen

◆ Create a kitchen design scrapbook to collect your thoughts and ideas

◆ A rundown of design considerations for kitchen remodeling

Decisions, Decisions

Now that you've explored in detail the various elements that will make up your new kitchen, you have some choices to make. But there are so many products available for your kitchen in so many varieties and options, it's enough to make your head spin! Faced with literally dozens of choices in cabinets, flooring materials, appliances, accessories, and more, how can you eliminate confusion and make sure you're choosing what's really right for you?

This chapter helps you to process all that information as it pertains to you, so that you can arrive at decisions that you'll be happy to live with for years to come.

This, or That?

Shopping for kitchen elements can make you feel like a kid in a candy shop. It's easy to like *all* the cabinets you see, and *all* the countertops. But you do have to choose. To get to the right choice for your needs and wants, I like to take a two-point approach.

When I was first starting out in the kitchen design business, my boss taught me a nifty little trick to help clients clear the clutter in their heads when trying to make those design decisions. Here's what you do: You take just two—only two—options, and decide between them to arrive at your choice with a minimum of confusion.

For example, let's say you're selecting your cabinet door style.

1. Ask yourself: "Do I want wood or thermofoil?" Let's say you want wood.
2. Now ask yourself, "Do I like oak or maple?" Maple it is.
3. Next, "Do I want traditional or contemporary?" You're a traditionalist at heart.

4. Now ask, "Do I want just a raised panel door, or a simple flat panel door?" You want flat panels.

And so on. You get the picture. It's just a process of elimination using only two choices at a time to whittle down the options and eventually arrive at the final decision, without unnecessarily confusing yourself.

This, or that? There are many cabinet door choices, like these different types of wood. Using a two-point approach can help you decide which one is best for your kitchen.

You can use the same process to eliminate several choices. Let's talk flooring. You like tile, wood, wood laminate, luxury vinyl, and cork. The process might go like this:

1. Do I want wood, or tile? I like tile better.

2. Do I want tile, or cork? Cork's easier on my feet, but I like the look of tile better.

3. Do I want tile, or wood laminate? I still like tile. Wood laminate is still wood.

4. Do I want tile, or luxury vinyl? I can have a tile look at a vinyl price, and go a bit easier on my feet. So I think I'll take the luxury vinyl.

In this example, the choice was tile all the way, until luxury vinyl was examined. After having eliminated all the other choices, it really came down to the two that were the most similar, but the vinyl had more advantages over the tile. It was discovered that even though tile was the primary choice, the advantages of vinyl outweighed the tile. Notice that price and practicality were also considered in the decision. Using the two-point approach can help you make good, educated decisions that weigh all aspects of your choices.

Once you arrive at your first choices, you can examine the options within those choices. In the example above, luxury vinyl was chosen for flooring, so now comes the decision of exactly which vinyl flooring selection to go with. Sheet vinyl or squares? Pick one. Does the one that looks like wood flooring work better with the other design choices, or the product that looks like mosaic tile? Once again, keep applying the two-point selection method until you arrive at your final decision.

Keeping *You* in Your Kitchen

There are two important words to remember as you go through the process of designing and remodeling your kitchen: *Your* kitchen. As you collect ideas from different places—magazines, TV shows, someone else's home—you can fall into the trap of designing a kitchen that, well, essentially belongs to someone else. It's important to put your own personality and ideas into the plan. You want to make sure you're creating a room that reflects who you are, and is a joy for you and your family to be in.

Your research on the Internet and in books and magazines is simply to inform you of what design elements and products are available. The finished project should be your own interpretation. It should be *your* kitchen.

Here's what I mean: Let's say you love to travel, and you treasure all the souvenirs and mementos you collect. You can incorporate them into your kitchen design. A photo of a colorful green market in San Francisco, showing close-ups of rows of bins filled with bright red tomatoes, brilliant green peppers, and eye-popping orange carrots not only fits in as a piece of kitchen artwork, but you took the photo and can tell the story behind it. A decorative plate from Australia, salt and pepper shakers from Colonial Williamsburg, a palm-tree painted pitcher from Florida—all of these things can find a home in your kitchen, and make it much more personal and meaningful to you.

The more of yourself you put into your kitchen, the more *right* it will feel to you. You're probably entertaining some thoughts and ideas right now as you read this. *That's it*—pay attention to those thoughts, and adapt them to your design. Okay, so maybe nothing came to mind, and you really have *no* idea. That's all right, too. Here's where you hit the books and magazines.

Ideas abound in newspapers, and many books and magazines on kitchen design and remodeling. Browse to your heart's content, and clip away when you see things you like.

Start simple, and look for anything that strikes you. The sky's the limit here, because you're just looking for *ideas* right now. Once you've collected five or more images, you may begin to see a pattern emerging. It can be as simple as a color scheme, or maybe it's a full-blown design theme such as Island style or Cape Cod. This is *you* coming alive, and begging to be incorporated into your kitchen design.

Don't worry if it seems as though you like too many things or have collected a lot of ideas. This is what you should do to discover the real you. It's from this collection of ideas that you'll make your decisions by applying the two-point approach.

Your Kitchen Scrapbook

The best way to collect your thoughts is to create a kitchen design scrapbook. Making such a book helps you focus your efforts, and thus make better decisions. There is nothing worse than walking into a cabinet dealer's showroom or a home improvement center without a game plan. You'll be confronted with a hundred different door styles, finishes, countertops, and other products, and will probably walk out frustrated and confused, accomplishing nothing.

Fortunately, it doesn't have to be that way. You can make choices and decisions at home, over time and without pressure, before going shopping, and record them all in your design scrapbook. A simple three-ring binder will do the trick, along with tabs and dividers for the different categories you need to consider in your kitchen design. The idea is to collect clippings, photos, color samples—anything you like that can help you arrive at your final design. Sheet protectors are handy for storing magazine clippings. You might include pocket dividers to slip paint swatches into, even laminate samples.

The result is a kitchen scrapbook you can take shopping with you to eliminate confusion and keep you focused. You can include photos, clippings, and information about appliances, cabinets, countertops, and hardware. Don't forget any sketches you make of your proposed floor plan. Be sure to include notepaper for jotting down your thoughts as they occur, and for taking notes as you shop to record what you've seen and where you saw it. For larger projects, an expanding file can be more functional. But keep it manageable, or you might not want to haul it around with you.

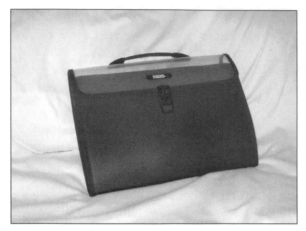

This is a handy carry-along case for your folders. When you open it up …

This book uses a three-ring binder with dividers, tabs, and some pockets to hold loose items such as paint swatches.

Your kitchen design scrapbook allows you to mull over the possibilities before you have to make a final choice. Again, anything goes here. After a few days—and price quotes—you'll be able to whittle it down using the "this, or that" method.

Not only that, but your scrapbook can save you time, and often enable you to obtain ballpark prices for kitchen elements right on the spot.

Design Considerations

As you make decisions about the elements of your kitchen, you should think about how your kitchen will blend in with the rest of your home. This means taking the architecture of your home and room into consideration, as well as the decor.

Let's look at these two important design aspects.

… it looks like this. It holds a lot, is convenient to work with, and closes up for carrying to the stores and showrooms with you.

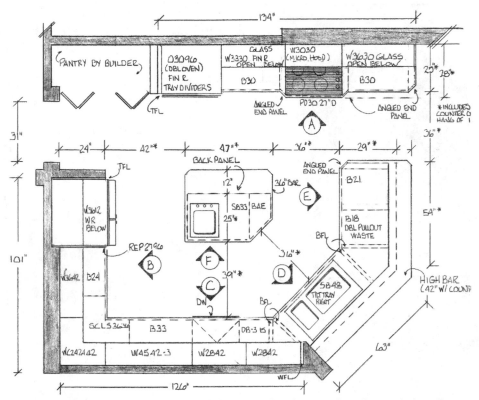

Notice how the angled corners and shapes in this design reflect the angled walls.

Architecture

Your kitchen should fit in with the architecture of your house. For example, if your home has arched doorways, the radius of the arch can be reflected in the door style you select for your cabinets. You can also round off the edges of your countertops rather than keep them square. Some floor plans have angles, octagons—all types of shapes throughout—and all present opportunities for integration into your kitchen design.

High ceilings are another example of architectural considerations. Older homes built before air-conditioning often had high ceilings. Newer homes are touting high ceilings as a selling point. One way to take advantage of this design element is to stagger the height of your cabinets. It's visually interesting, and it draws the eye upward, opening up the room. If all the cabinets seem low, in one line with lots of space above them, it shortens the room.

This kitchen has high ceilings. The staggered cabinet heights look much more interesting than would rows of cabinets the same height with lots of space above them. *(Wellborn)*

Designer's Notebook

Is your kitchen closed? No, this doesn't mean you can't eat after 11:00 P.M. In older homes, the kitchen is usually a separate room, closed off from the rest of the house. There were no open floor plans back then. The kitchen was strictly a utilitarian room with one purpose: Cooking. Today, a kitchen can be a multipurpose room, and as visually important as any other room in the house. If your kitchen is closed, and you're not particularly fond of that, you may want to consider the idea of opening the kitchen up by eliminating a wall, or by cutting one down. Keep in mind that if you choose to open it up, it will be especially important for the style of your kitchen to match, or at least blend, with the décor in the adjoining room or rooms.

Here's another architectural element to work with: Built-in furniture. Older homes often have shelves, even cupboards, that are built in to the room. Even if you're updating a kitchen, elements such as these might work well and could be kept.

This built-in corner cabinet is a wonderful architectural element that can work well in a new kitchen.

Décor-um

Finishes, moldings, door styles, color and texture are all décor considerations. So what exactly is décor? It's the decorating style of your home, such as traditional, contemporary, country, southwestern, Victorian, and cottage. Oh, you think you don't have a décor? Actually, you do, even if it's not evident to you at first.

Perhaps your style is *eclectic*, which is the most popular décor for a reason: Essentially, anything goes. It's what comprises your own style and taste, and is the unique arrangement of elements that are *you*. Whatever you like, use it. The important thing is that a common element ties everything together into a visually appealing result. Color, material, and shape can work as a common thread that brings together normally disparate elements.

For example, if you like contemporary, which has clean simple lines, you can mix something that is Shaker country. It also has clean, simple lines, though it's a different design style. Even a traditional cabinet selection and modern stainless steel appliances can coexist in style with the addition of stainless steel plumbing fixtures and cabinet hardware. These accessories can still be traditional styles. It's the stainless steel finish that ties them to the appliances, and the traditional design that unites the appliances and cabinets.

Designer's Notebook

Does your kitchen have a *focal point?* In interior design, every room has a focal point. In a living room, it can be a view, a fireplace, a baby grand piano. The kitchen is no different. Common focal points include a pot rack, a shiny stainless-steel refrigerator or hood, prominently placed glass cabinet doors, even an open shelf for showing off a Fiesta Ware collection. Whatever it is, the focal point should be located in the center of the kitchen, where it can be easily seen.

The elements in this kitchen reflect eclectic design. It has the clean lines of contemporary style, but uses some traditional elements such as cup drawer and door pulls, hardwood floor, and simplified molding.
(Masters Kitchen Gallery)

Choosing the elements of your kitchen takes time and thought. Remember, you're making decisions that you'll likely be living with for a long time. It's important to make them from an enlightened perspective. This will leave you feeling confident, give you peace of mind, and lead to a final result you'll be proud of.

The pot rack is the focal point of this French country kitchen. *(Masters Kitchen Gallery)*

This kitchen design has lots of interesting shapes and visuals. Notice how the floor tile laid on the diagonal matches the angle of the peninsula in the foreground. *(Masters Kitchen Gallery)*

This clean, simple kitchen has a bay window on the left. The kitchen design takes advantage of this feature, letting in plenty of light and providing a view.   *(Masters Kitchen Gallery)*

The Least You Need to Know

◆ Educate yourself on your choices of kitchen elements.

◆ Make decisions using a two-point approach: This, or that?

◆ Find your unique style. Make a scrapbook of ideas to stimulate your imagination.

◆ Give thought to design considerations such as architecture and décor.

In This Chapter

- ◆ How to determine your kitchen remodeling budget
- ◆ Allocating the budget for your wants and needs
- ◆ Where to find funds for your project
- ◆ Controlling remodeling costs
- ◆ Quick, economical fixes for smaller budgets

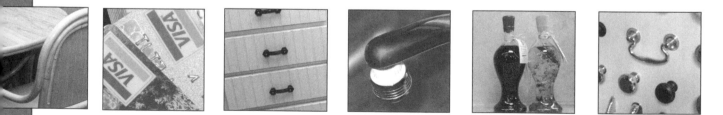

Chapter **5**

Show Me the Money

You already know that remodeling your kitchen will bring you the biggest return on your investment of any room in your home. For that reason, it's typically the most expensive room to remodel. If you fear kitchen remodeling sticker shock, don't worry—we can help you find ways to get the right kitchen for you, and do it within your budget.

This chapter helps you understand the costs involved in remodeling your kitchen, guides you through the process of determining your budget, and presents options for obtaining the funds you need. You'll also learn how to juggle the numbers to get what you most need and want out of your remodeling project. Money-saving solutions for those with smaller budgets are also presented.

Calculating Your Budget

It's true that the kitchen costs more to remodel, and this makes sense when you think about it: Of all the rooms in the home, the kitchen contains more items that are costly, such as cabinets and appliances.

In fact, cabinets are probably going to be your greatest expense. If you don't plan to do all or most of the labor yourself, the cost of contractors will be right up there, too. Appliances, countertops, and flooring are the next most costly items. Hardware, wall coverings, accessories and lighting consume the rest of the budget.

First, the Bottom Line

To determine your remodeling budget, you need to sort of work backward. That is, you first determine how much money you want to spend, or are able to spend, then allocate the funds to the different kitchen elements you plan to purchase.

At the same time, you want to be sure that you're making a sound investment. So you must choose a budget figure that's reasonable as it relates to the value of your home. For example, if your home is worth $85,000, you wouldn't want to spend $50,000 on a new kitchen, because it's unlikely that you would ever see a good return on that money, unless the real estate market in your area doubled in the next few years. While that's not out of the question in some areas of the country these days, it's still a big gamble that most people can't afford to take.

Here's how to determine a sensible remodeling budget:

1. Determine the current value of your home. You can hire an appraiser to obtain a true figure. The fees for an appraisal vary, but generally start at $250. You can also research the recent sales prices of homes in your neighborhood that are comparable to yours. You can then work with an educated "guesstimate" of your own home's value.

How much does the new kitchen of your dreams cost? With careful budgeting, you can have what you want and need.

2. Decide what percentage of your home value you wish to spend on your kitchen remodeling. Typically, 15 percent is a good number for a complete remodeling job. However, you may decide you don't want or need to go all out, and thus choose a lower figure. A good rule of thumb: Stick to 10 to 15 percent of your home's value, or you'll be spending too much relative to what your home is worth.

3. Study the resulting figure and decide if it's realistic for you.

Play with the figures. Even the "rule of thumb" may not work for you, depending on your financial situation. You have to make decisions based on how much available cash you have to spend, whether or not you want to take out a loan, and how much debt you're willing and able to take on. If using 15 percent in your calculations yields a figure larger than you think you can handle, try a lower percentage.

That's the first phase of determining your budget. Spend time thinking about it and discussing your options to arrive at a realistic and doable figure for you. Once you arrive at a figure you can work with, you can move on to the next phase of budgeting.

Budget Breakdown

No, that's not what you suffer when you work on your remodeling budget. Once you've determined how much money you can spend, you create a basic breakdown of costs according to the various kitchen elements you plan to purchase.

In practice, I have found that the following budget breakdown is typical and workable, and tends to reflect the vast majority of homeowners' wants and needs:

◆ Cabinets: 45 percent
◆ Countertops and backsplashes: 15 percent
◆ Appliances: 10 percent
◆ Flooring: 10 percent
◆ Labor: 10 percent (required contractors and optional help)
◆ Wall coverings: 5 percent
◆ Lighting/electrical: 5 percent

This is your first-level breakdown, and it isn't carved in granite. Depending on your personal wants and needs, you can adjust these figures to reflect your own remodeling considerations.

For example, if you plan to keep your appliances, you can redistribute the 10 percent allotted for them throughout the rest of the budget, adding 2 percent to each remaining budget item. Or, you could put the entire 10 percent toward an item that you wish to spend more money on. Suppose your greatest desire is for solid surface countertops—you love to bake, and baker-friendly countertops would really make you happy. Then add the 10 percent from the appliance allocation to the countertops budget, and you can have the countertops you really desire.

Using that example, here's what your reworked budget breakdown might look like:

◆ Cabinets: 45 percent
◆ Countertops and backsplashes: 25 percent
◆ Appliances: 0 percent
◆ Flooring: 10 percent
◆ Labor: 10 percent (optional, except for required contractors)
◆ Wall coverings: 5 percent
◆ Lighting/electrical: 5 percent

Even if you spread the amount among other categories and increase some budget items by only one percent, it can make a difference in a remodeling budget. One percent of a total budget of $10,000 is $100. In the labor category, that could buy you some plumber time if you wanted it, or allow you to choose a different wallpaper.

The preceding list covers your basic budget items. You'll build your detailed budget from this list, breaking each category down into components. For example, let's look at flooring:

Flooring

Tile	$ _____
Cork soundproofing layer	_____
Tools	
Tools for old tile removal	_____
Tile cutter rental	_____
Tile laying tool kit	_____
Materials	
Adhesive	_____
Grout	_____
Sealant	_____
Delivery of tile	_____
TOTAL FLOORING COSTS	_____

Do this for each budget item, remembering to take into account "hidden" costs, i.e., those easy-to-forget items that can really add up. These include:

- Tools. For a remodeling job this size, you may need to acquire some specialty tools you'll either buy or rent.
- Disposal costs. Often overlooked in planning and budgeting, disposal may not be cost-free, depending on how your community handles larger trash items. You may need to dispose of debris yourself if your usual hauler can't take items, or you may need to pay extra for them to do so.

- Safety equipment. Construction jobs require safety equipment such as eye and ear protection, dust masks, lumbar support belts, perhaps even safety shoes.
- Miscellaneous items. The small-ticket things that can really add up, such as: Joint compound, putty knives, dry wall tape, caulking, plumber's putty, sanding paper, and so on. Account for them in the main budget category where they'll be used.
- Delivery charges for materials and appliances.
- Cost of eating out. A major expense if you can't find ways to improvise cooking at home while work is being done.

Murphy's Cushion

Don't forget to add "Murphy's Cushion" to your budget. No, I'm not talking about your Irish neighbor's recliner. It's a contingency added to your budget, a financial fudge factor, if you will, to take care of those annoying little unforeseen costs that can catch you off guard and really wear down the budget.

For example, you may tear out your old cabinets and discover that the wall behind the sink is rotted and needs to be replaced. If you've padded your budget with a contingency, you'll have extra funds for materials and labor to do the repairs so you can continue installing your new cabinets.

What's a good contingency? Figure at least 10 percent more than you anticipate spending for each category. So if you're planning $2,000 for flooring, $200 is the contingency. Or, simply figure it on the total budget: A $10,000 budget would have a $1,000 contingency. Be sure to keep a careful eye on your expenditures as you progress in the project to minimize surprises.

Bang for the Buck

Once you get the costs of hauling junk away, check with the suppliers of your new appliances and cabinets. For a fee, they'll often take away your junk, and it might be cheaper than taking it to the dump. Or, you might be able to make some money on your discards. If your appliances are in working order, you might consign them for resale if they're clean enough, or donate them to a charity and take a tax deduction.

Paying for It All

Now you've got the sticker price on your new kitchen, and hopefully you don't have a case of sticker shock. So how are you going to pay for it? There are several options, including asking Uncle Harry for a loan. But if he's not inclined to help you out, check out these sources of financing:

1. Savings. Weigh the pros and cons of using personal savings for your project. If you plan to sell your home within a few years and the new kitchen adds good value to the house, you just may see a better return on those funds. Do some math on your interest rates and decide. Just be sure you're comfortable with how much savings you use, and don't drain your account completely.

2. Loans. Personal, home equity, or home improvement loans are the best choices.

   ◆ Home equity loans can have terms similar to a mortgage, which means a long term in which to pay it off. That also means racking up a lot of interest charges too, however, even if the interest rate is low. Be sure to ask for a detailed amortization of the loan, so you can see exactly how much you'll pay out over the life of the loan.

   ◆ It might be better for you to try a home improvement loan. These are often like a line of credit—you are given a lump sum figure that you can borrow, and a checkbook. You write checks as you need the money. If you don't spend it all (you can hope!), then you're paying interest only on what you did spend. The interest on both home equity and home improvement loans may be tax deductible, so check with your accountant or tax adviser.

   ◆ Personal loans typically have higher interest rates and bigger payments. You should probably check out the first two loan options first.

3. Credit cards. Depending on how much money you need, using your credit card could be an option. Don't take cash advances, however, as the rates are much higher than for purchases. Use your lowest rate cards, or look for cards with special offers, such as low or no interest for a year. This could be a real budget saver.

4. Refinancing your home. When interest rates are low, you can take advantage of the equity in your home by refinancing for a higher amount and using the additional cash for your remodeling project. Remember, remodeling the kitchen brings a high return on the money, so going through the process of refinancing can be well worth it. The increase in your monthly mortgage payment can be small. Or, you just might lower your payment if your current interest rate is much higher than the going rate, even if you take additional funds for remodeling.

Bang for the Buck _____

Here's how refinancing your home to get remodeling funds can really work for you. A homeowner bought a condo eight years ago for $68,500 with an 8 percent mortgage. With taxes and insurance, the monthly payment is $568. In her area, real estate has appreciated nicely, so her condo is now worth $130,000, and her mortgage balance is $57,000. She decides to spend $20,000 to remodel the kitchen, which is about 15 percent of her home's value. She can obtain a new 30-year mortgage at 5 percent, so she refinances for $80,000—$20,000 for her kitchen remodeling project, and some extra cash to cover any expenses involved in acquiring the mortgage, and maybe to take a vacation to the islands to boot. Her new payment: $496! She actually saves $72 a month, _and_ gets her new kitchen! So in this example, the homeowner is actually getting paid $72 a month to get a new kitchen. This is a true example. Amazing, isn't it?

You may not need a loan for remodeling. Credit cards are a viable option for funding.

Keep It Under Control

Remodeling your kitchen is an exciting undertaking. It's something you've dreamed of, and now you're making it a reality. But please, come back down to earth for a moment. It's easy for homeowners to get carried away, suddenly deciding to remodel both bathrooms, add a master suite and install an in-ground pool, "while we're at it."

It's also tempting to make changes and upgrades while the work is going on in the kitchen. This is why it's so important to carefully plan your design, go through the process in Chapter 4 for making quality/price comparisons and tradeoffs, and _stick to your guns!_ Otherwise, you can go over budget and run out of money, or be forced to go deeper into debt than you had planned. Neither option is good for your mental and financial health, so work to keep it under control.

The next section can help you keep costs under control with money-saving ideas.

Budget-Friendly Ideas

You want wood cabinets and granite countertops—but as you do your budget, you find that _it_ prefers laminate all the way. The bottom line is this: The bottom line. Unless you have unlimited financial resources, the decisions you make when choosing kitchen elements are pretty much going to be budget-based. That pesky money always gets in the way of great ideas, right? Wrong!

Doing research and putting your imagination to work for you can still give you a stylish kitchen that you'll love and that, most important, is functional. This means taking time to explore all the options for different kitchen elements to come up with a workable plan that fits your budget and your style tastes.

While you're keeping your budget in mind when choosing products, it's also important to consider quality and value. Don't base your product choices *solely* on cost. Value and quality of products does equal money, because going with a poor-quality product could end up costing you more in the long run.

Consider the following money-saving ideas to help you keep your budget in line. Always keep quality and value in mind.

Accept Your Appliances

If you're still tossing logs into your wood-burning cook stove, you may want to consider a nice modern cooktop. Sure, the wood stove works fine, but get real. It's time to enter the twenty-first century! Seriously, though, your old appliances may still be able to work for you, and thus save you a lot of money in your budget—literally thousands of dollars, in fact. Especially if your appliances are only a few years old, there may be no real need to discard them. As long as they're in good working order, look okay, and will fit into your design, living with them for a while longer can allow you more money to spend on kitchen elements that really need a makeover.

However, do consider the age of the appliances. Even if the refrigerator works fine and looks good, if it was purchased before the year 1990, it's not nearly as energy-efficient as what you can buy now—actually, it's about half as efficient! If it's *really* old, then it's consuming more power than you can imagine. Plus, the older the appliance, the more likely it is to develop problems, even if it's working fine right now. And that goes for your wood-burning stove, too.

If you've got the budget for new appliances, use it. If not, careful planning and consideration can save you some bucks, and still give you a lot of new kitchen for the money you do have.

Designer's Notebook

What do you think is the single biggest energy consumer in most households? (That's electrical energy, not *your* energy.) You might be surprised to learn that refrigerators have earned that title. In the year 1992, the U.S. Environmental Protection Agency (EPA) founded the Energy Star program to promote energy-efficient products in order to reduce greenhouse gas emissions. The program has expanded from its humble beginnings and now encompasses all manner of products purchased by business and consumers. From computer monitors and AC/heating units to kitchen appliances and even ceiling fans, the Energy Star label on products has become familiar to most consumers. If you're planning to replace any appliances, give consideration to those with Energy Star labels. They not only save energy, but can save you money almost immediately, and certainly in the long run.

Cabinet Meeting

Custom cabinets are expensive, there's no way around that. Choosing standard cabinets will save you a lot of money, but shop carefully for quality and value. Be sure you've read and absorbed the information on cabinets in Chapter 3.

Here's another idea: Consider giving your old cabinets a cosmetic facelift. You may have perfectly good cabinets right now, especially if they're solid wood. But the look may be old and tired. Remember the likes and dislikes you listed in Chapter 1? If the appearance of good cabinets is your only objection, then explore options such as refacing laminates (see "Quick Fixes" later in this chapter), or refinishing wood. I've seen kitchens take on a whole new look by simply painting dark, drab wood cabinets with high-gloss paint and adding decorative door handles. And refacing laminate cabinets can make it look like you purchased new ones, as long as the refacing job is top-notch.

Economical cabinet solution: The landlord painted the old wood cabinets with high-gloss white paint, added new doorknobs, and voila! An amazing transformation, isn't it?

This poor kitchen was the victim of a bad tenant. The landlord really had her work cut out for her, but she didn't have a big budget to take care of it. Fortunately, there was no major structural damage, or damage to the solid wood cabinets, and the job basically came down to a typical kitchen remodeling.

 Bang for the Buck

If you can't afford to have an all-wood cabinet, many manufacturers will give you the opportunity to upgrade the drawers to wood. This is a good value, because you can have your wood and the upgraded glides that come with it. Since the drawer is a functioning part of the cabinet, the added quality can make them last.

This homeowner kept old wood cabinets, but gave them a fresh look with bead board on the doors. Colorful paint completed the tropical island look.

Counter Intelligence Measures

Solid surface countertops are wonderful, but expensive. If you're remodeling on a tight budget, you may have to opt out of this option, and that's the bottom line.

But you don't have to sacrifice style for cost. If you're especially handy, consider tile countertops that you can install yourself. It's a good in-between solution for those who don't want laminates, but can't quite fit solid surfaces into the budget. Even the least expensive tiles can give a high-style look to a kitchen. Remember, though, that tile countertops means dealing with grout joints. Even well-filled joints don't leave a completely smooth surface, and working on them can feel a bit bumpy. You also need to keep grout clean, which can be an added chore. Colored grouts are available, which can be more forgiving than white when it comes to looking clean. You can also investigate epoxy grout and grout sealers to keep stains from penetrating.

Don't eliminate laminate from your choices just yet, either. Once again, today's materials are vastly improved, and you can find terrific laminates that look like more costly solid surfaces such as granite and marble. Today there are also more choices for edge details, such as beveling, which will eliminate the black line you see on a simple square laminate edge.

This countertop looks like expensive granite, but is actually laminate. Doing this allowed the homeowner to put more money into other aspects of his kitchen.   (Katie Deits)

This homeowner opted for Silestone countertops. They're more expensive, but the kitchen is small and didn't require much counter material, so the cost fit into his budget. If he had a larger kitchen, he admits he probably would have chosen a less expensive material.

Bang for the Buck

Do you love granite for counter-tops and backsplashes, but the price tag turns you to stone? You can still have your granite and save some money by choosing a less-expensive backsplash material that matches the granite. You won't sacrifice function for aesthetics—and you won't hurt your bottom line.

Floor Bored

Once again, the advice is this: If your current flooring is sound and will fit with your design, keep it (assuming you're not totally, utterly bored with it). Flooring costs can really get out of control if you get into imported tiles, mosaics, bamboo flooring, and other trendy options. If you are replacing the flooring, you must consider your budget to rein in the costs.

You may already have some solutions in hiding. If your house is old, take a quick peek underneath that ratty linoleum—you just might find a wood floor. If it's in good shape, refinishing it might be the ticket rather than taking on the expense of installing an entirely new floor.

If your budget doesn't allow much for flooring, there's always the vinyl option. This isn't as bad an option as it used to be. Today's vinyl flooring is sturdy, durable, and can be quite beautiful. Often, it can even fool the eye. Some vinyl flooring looks so much like wood that a casual observer wouldn't know the difference. I've seen vinyl that I would have sworn was stylish stone, until I got down for a close-up look.

The beset-upon landlord used inexpensive vinyl tile squares to replace the damaged floor. It looks terrific!

Remember when choosing flooring that some materials are harder on your feet than others. This is important if you spend a lot of time working in the kitchen. Thick cushiony vinyl, wood, and cork are easier on the feet as opposed to tile and stone.

Condo (Floor) Boards

Do you live in a multi-story condominium? If you plan to replace your flooring, check with your condo board before finalizing your remodeling plans. Most multi-story condos require you to install a cork soundproofing layer under your flooring to keep others from hearing your heels clacking as you walk. Be sure to budget for cork if you need it.

Is it parquet, or is it vinyl? Visitors to this home frequently compliment the homeowner on her nice wood floors, and she smiles politely. Her secret is that she paid 31 cents per vinyl tile on sale to get this great look!

I was fooled by this vinyl tile. It looks so good, I want some of this myself! It's known as luxury vinyl, which is high-quality, made from thicker materials, and offers many color and pattern choices.

Faucet Facets

The selection of kitchen faucets is vast—and so is the price range. You can spend as little as $10 for a kitchen faucet (though you probably shouldn't), or as much as $1,300 (you *definitely* don't want to do that). Deciding which faucet to get comes down to style, function, quality, and price. To avoid buying a budget buster, review all the different faucets and options in Chapter 9. Then shop, shop, shop until you drop—or, preferably, until you find the perfect faucet for you!

This stylish faucet cost only $59.95. It's made by a reputable manufacturer and is good quality. At the home improvement store where it was purchased, another nearly identical faucet cost more than twice as much!

Bang for the Buck

Don't let your money go down the drain when purchasing a kitchen faucet. Be sure to check for quality, as well as price. A more expensive faucet with internal parts that are replaceable can be a cost-effective investment, since you wouldn't have to replace the entire faucet if something breaks.

Lighting the Way

It's often easy—and budget-conscious—to leave your lighting the way it is. Unless you simply don't have enough good light or your house is so old that the original fixtures pose a danger, you can save money by not adding any new fixture boxes or moving the existing ones.

An inexpensive way to give yourself more light is to add under-cabinet lighting to supplement your current lighting. You'll still need to hire an electrician, but if you're already hiring one, it won't cost much more to have him run the wires for these lights. The light fixtures themselves are economical, especially the new and improved no-flicker fluorescent models.

Light up your kitchen life with under-cabinet lighting, an economical way to add more light without changing your overhead lighting fixtures.

Remedies for Sticker Shock

Okay, so maybe you did get a little case of sticker shock when you started looking at remodeling costs. You can still spruce up your old kitchen, but pare down the costs in several ways. Let's look at a few.

Get Phased

Consider completing your remodeling job in phases. While you may want it all and want it all now, working in phases can be the way to go for the cash-cautious remodeler.

Examine your priorities. Maybe your refrigerator is about to go and your dishwasher is already kaput. New appliances are a likely candidate for phase one of your kitchen remodel. Next, project exactly how long it will take over time to come up with the funds for phase two, phase three, and so on. Your planning could look something like this:

> Phase I: January—New appliances
>
> Phase II: April—New flooring
>
> Phase III: August—New cabinets and countertops
>
> Phase IV: October—Lighting, wallpaper, and backsplash

As you estimate phase costs, don't forget to include any labor you anticipate using. Also, note that some things do tend to go hand-in-hand. For example, you'll have to include money for the electrician and plumber when you do the cabinets in Phase III. Countertops should also be partnered with cabinets, but backsplashes can always be added later.

Quick Fixes

If you just can't live with that tired old kitchen anymore, but need some more time to raise the necessary funds for a top-notch remodeling job, consider these quick fixes to get you through the waiting period.

1. Add molding to existing cabinets. Molding can bring more pizzazz to your kitchen by adding a finished look to simple, boxy cabinets. You may have pretty good cabinets that you like, but perhaps the builder just didn't spring the extra bucks to add molding. All you need is some space above your cabinets to add crown molding. You can also add molding under the cabinets to complete the look, and to conceal under-cabinet light fixtures. Typically molding used in this way runs from 1½" to 3" thick.

2. Redo your countertops. Again, let's assume you kind of like your cabinets, but would probably like them a lot better if your countertop wasn't so worn and torn. You might upgrade from laminate to tile, or simply install new laminate in a different color, or a pattern that looks like granite.

3. Be creative with the backsplash area. Utilize the entire backsplash area with tile or material that looks like granite. Another economical option: Faux painting, or *trompe l'oeil*, which means "fool the eye." Creating a stone or brick look is a great quick fix. Hiring someone to paint it is cheaper than doing tile, or you can try your hand at painting it yourself. You might even try some stenciling.

4. Paint old wood cabinets. As described earlier, good wood cabinets can be refinished or painted and look brand new. A glass door or two can complete this quick fix.

5. Try new and interesting hardware. You'd be amazed how much difference new doorknobs and drawer handles can make. Old knobs and pulls look, well, *old*. Choose something new, modern, colorful, even daring.

6. Use freestanding furniture for function and looks. Sometimes builders try to save money by installing fewer cabinets than there is room for. The result can be storage space problems. If you have an empty wall, you can get some style and storage space with a Hoosier-style hutch, or an antique pie safe. In general, a freestanding piece of

furniture will be less expensive than a built-in cabinet, especially if you're hitting thrift shops and garage sales. Plus, whatever you get is going to be unique.

7. Reface cabinets. Old cabinets that are sound can become fresh again with new doors and laminate refacing. The cost is much lower than purchasing new cabinets, including professional installation. You can try to reface cabinets yourself, but it's a precision job that is best left to professionals. Shop for refacing options at home improvement stores.

Is it stone, or is it *trompe l'oeil*? This outstanding faux painted backsplash fools everyone who sees it.

Molding makes the difference. A little molding goes a long way toward a new look.
(Masters Kitchen Gallery)

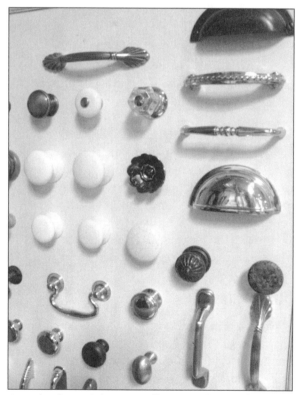

New knobs and drawer pulls can make you feel like you have new cabinets.

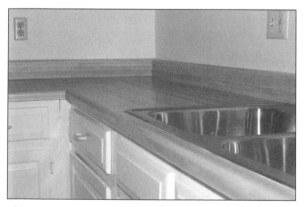

New countertops can give old cabinets a new look.

Hoosier hutches and cabinets were used by bakers to store everything they needed for baking. They were commonplace in kitchens until built-in cabinets grew in popularity in the 1930s and 1940s.

Pie safes are aptly named—they were used to store pies. These antiques make great freestanding storage cabinets in today's kitchens.

The Least You Need to Know

◆ Determine your total kitchen remodeling budget based on the value of your home.

◆ Break down the budget into major categories.

◆ Further break down the categories into kitchen elements.

◆ Purchase elements considering quality, value, and cost.

◆ Shop smart for economy. Take your time to find the best values on high-quality merchandise.

◆ Consider economical quick fixes for smaller budgets, or plan remodeling in phases over time.

In This Chapter

- ◆ Kinds of contractor help you may need when remodeling the kitchen

- ◆ How to find qualified, competent contractors

- ◆ All about electricians and plumbers

- ◆ The business side of hiring contractors

- ◆ Elements of a good contract

Chapter 6

Help!

Just because you bought this book doesn't mean you signed on to go it alone. Even handy do-it-yourselfers may decide that some aspects of a kitchen remodeling job are best left to a qualified professional. And, let's face it: For some jobs, you may simply want to have the help. So unless you or your brother-in-law is a licensed electrician, or if the thought of hanging wallpaper makes your eyes glaze over, you need to know how to find qualified help.

Who Do I Need?

Good question. The answer partly depends on what types of work you like and don't like to do on your own. You may love to saw wood, paint walls, hook up a garbage disposal, or connect a faucet, but you absolutely loathe the thought of spreading adhesive and laying tile in straight lines. Even if you've done it before and did it well, jumping into that particular job just doesn't float your boat. So you'd rather let someone else do it. That's okay. You don't have to do it if you don't want to—and if you can afford to pay someone else.

You should also consider your own do-it-yourselfer strengths and weaknesses. You know your own skills and capabilities, and what you're willing to try. Think about the various aspects of your remodeling job and rate them according to how difficult you think they might be for you. This will help you decide which contractors you would want to hire.

Here are some of the contractors you might consider hiring to help you:

◆ Electricians—Very important. More about electricians later in this chapter.

◆ Plumbers—Also quite important, and I'll discuss them further.

- Painters—For those who don't like getting splattered with Desert Mauve and Nutmeg Brown. Can be tedious and painstaking, and a sloppy job will detract from the finished product.

- Building Contractor—If you plan to knock out, add, or move walls, but don't consider yourself to be a wall mover and shaker.

- Tile Setters—For those who gripe about grout.

- Cabinet Installers—If you're not nimble with a saw and cherish your digits. May come with your cabinet purchase anyway, so why not? The supplier then assumes responsibility for the entire job until the last knob is screwed on.

- Wood Floor Refinisher—For most people, do-it-yourselfer or not. It's a specialized, messy task requiring proper tools, equipment, and expertise in applying finishes, or you'll get bubbles in your floor. Use of dangerous chemicals is involved.

Searchin' for Contractors

Let's go back to the brother-in-law who's an electrician—if you've got one, use him. End of problem. But you might not have relatives who make their living in all the trades involved in remodeling your kitchen, so you'll have to find help in other places.

There are several ways to find qualified, trustworthy contractor help, including:

- The phone book—Look for listings displaying a contractor license number, and that say "bonded and insured."

- Trade associations—Many contractors are union or trade association members, and must meet certain standards and requirements to become members. Such groups also maintain a Code of Ethics that members must adhere to, and any complaints

against a contractor member are generally registered with the organization.

- Licensing boards—Most contractor disciplines are regulated by state governments. It's easy to check on a contractor's license, and you can also learn if there are any complaints against the person.

- Building supply stores, hardware stores, and appliance dealers—These businesses may employ contractors to work with them. Generally such businesses are careful whom they recommend, since it can reflect back on them.

- Word-of-mouth referrals—The best way by far to find the right person for your job.

You can find licensed, bonded contractors in the phone book. Many include their license number in their listing, so you can get a head start on checking them out with your state licensing board.

Talk It Up

The number one proven method for finding the right professional for any remodeling service is through word-of-mouth referrals. You probably know a friend or family member who recently had some work done in their home. Maybe you know someone who knows someone who knows someone who's a plumber, carpenter, or electrician. Even that's a good start.

Talking to others about the pro you're looking for, and letting the word out that you're actively seeking a competent contractor, can lead you to qualified candidates. Most people will be happy to share their experiences—and their contact lists—with you.

When getting recommendations from people you know, it's a good idea to ask about the contractor's personality and how he interacts with people. This is an important consideration that is often overlooked. It can be stressful enough once remodeling work starts in your home, and if you can get along easily with the people who are helping you, it's a big plus for keeping your sanity. Ask the referrer a few questions like these:

◆ Does the contractor take time to explain things clearly?

◆ Does the contractor readily answer any questions you have, no matter how simple they might sound?

◆ Does the contractor treat you with respect?

◆ Does the contractor keep appointments with you, or let you know if he's going to be late for any reason?

◆ Does the contractor focus on the job at hand, or is he constantly being interrupted with other matters, or shortchanging you on the time spent on your job?

◆ Does the contractor take steps to minimize disruption while he's working?

◆ Does the contractor clean up after himself when he's done working?

In this way, you can determine if the contractor is someone you can feel comfortable working with.

Mike "Mr. Personality" Jones is an example of a friendly, competent, licensed and bonded contractor who works well with people, is courteous, punctual—and always busy because of these qualities.

When you determine that a referral sounds promising, ask the person making the recommendation to let you see the work that the contractor performed. If you like what you see, you've moved one more step in the right direction.

The Must-Have Contractors

There are certain contractors you must use for code and safety reasons, as well as for their skills and experience. You might hire an electrician for extensive electrical work such as moving or installing new lighting fixtures or relocating 220-volt outlets for stoves. A plumber might be in order if you're moving your sink location or planning to add a vegetable sink. Let's look closer at these two important contractors.

Electricians

I promised you more information on electricians, and for a good reason. They're at the top of the list of contractors you need. Unless you personally know a good electrician who is willing to help you out, you'll need to hire one for your job. Not only can you and your house *really* get burned as a result of faulty wiring, but poorly designed circuits can result in flickering lights, damaged appliances, and blown fuses. If you are moving or adding any major electrical appliances that require 220-volt receptacles, this also must be done by an electrician. Some other tasks that require this service include installing high hat lighting, and bringing in electrical feeds for under-cabinet light fixtures.

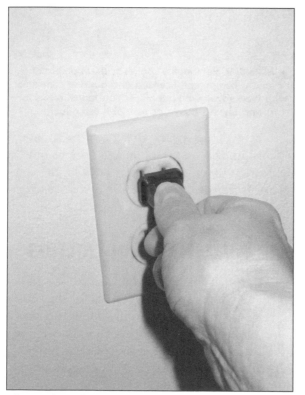

This is about the extent of electrical work you should do on your own. A licensed electrician is a must for safety and code reasons.

Fortunately, it's not difficult to locate a qualified electrician because the pros are licensed and regulated by your state.

Pro Lingo

Don't be shocked, but there are three grades of electrician you should know about.

◆ Apprentice electrician. This one is still in training and isn't licensed, so you're more interested in the next two.

◆ Journeyman Electrician. This electrician is also licensed by the state and can be qualified to do your job if it involves only installing wiring and equipment. He can't design electrical systems, and hasn't necessarily passed the required exam or met the field experience qualifications of a Master Electrician. In some states, journeymen are required to work alongside master electricians.

◆ Master Electrician. This contractor has passed a standardized exam indicating that he is thoroughly versed in the National Electric Code, including local modifications. He must have a minimum of two years' experience under his tool belt. If he specializes in residential projects, he will help you design a lighting plan if you need it. He'll also evaluate your current electrical system to make sure it's updated and adequate for the changes you plan to make.

Where can you find an electrician? Sources for referrals include the Internet, your local homebuilders' association, or an electrical supply house. Electricians generally specialize in either commercial or residential projects, and in new construction or remodeling. Those who are well-versed in home remodeling projects will know the ins and outs of adapting an existing structure, such as working within finished walls or adding additional service panels to handle an increased power demand.

Once you find potential electricians, see if you can get an opportunity to look at some of his work. A good tip for judging it is to look for neatness. A neat-looking job likely indicates that he took time to make the job safe. Look for wires that run to the service panel in a tidy, organized manner. Check that light switch and outlet plates are installed level and flush to the wall.

Plumbers

Forget the plumber cracks—you need this contractor if you're doing any major work involving the pipes. Moving a sink can be a big deal, as you may have to install a new main drain and vent stack to the roof. Adding a prep sink in addition to your regular sink is cause to call a professional plumber as well.

You might feel capable of handling some basic plumbing. After all, what's a little water, right? Well, it can turn into a *lot* of water all over the place if you don't have at least *some* idea of what you're doing. Even if you plan to attempt a minimum amount of plumbing work, like disconnecting the dishwasher, the supply and drain lines at the sink, and removal of the sink, faucet and dishwasher, you may wish to find a plumber to call just in case you run into problems.

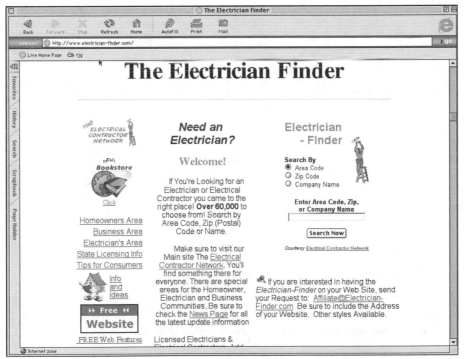

You can find an electrical contractor on the Internet on sites such as The Electrical Contractor Network at www.electrician-finder.com/. This site helps you locate licensed electrical contractors, electricians, and their suppliers across the country.

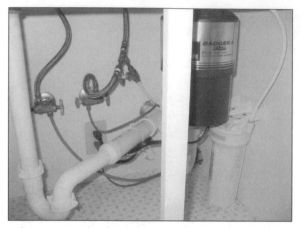

This is more plumbing than usually found under the sink. You may not want to deal with all this on your own, so a plumber can be a big help.

To find a good plumber, the same advice applies with regard to asking for referrals, checking insurance, looking for business stability, and obtaining multiple quotes. A good resource for plumber recommendations is your state or local chapter of the National Association of Plumbing, Heating and Cooling Contractors (NAPHCC).

Most plumbers are generally required by states to be licensed, although there are no uniform national licensing requirements. There is a national Uniform Plumbing Code, and most states' licensing exams will test the applicant's knowledge of the code. But not all states have actually adopted the code. Yes, it sounds confusing, but the lack of uniform requirements makes it all the more important that you do your homework when hiring a plumber.

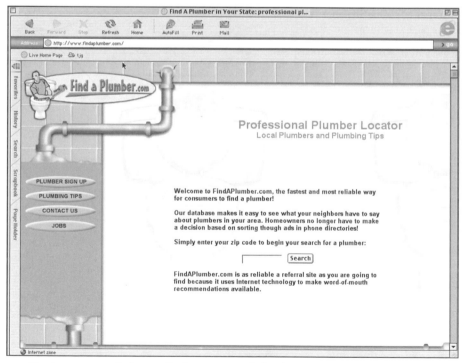

The Internet can help you find a registered plumber on sites such as this one, www.findaplumber.com.

Reasons to Hire a Plumber

Besides extensive work, you may wish to hire a plumber for these tasks, which can be difficult. Or, you may simply not want to do them:

- ◆ Installing tubing for a refrigerator ice maker.
- ◆ Installing an extensive water filtration system.
- ◆ Replacing pipes under the sink if your new sink is deeper or more shallow than your old one.
- ◆ Updating antique pipes.

Just as there are apprentice, journeyman, and master electricians, there are three grades of plumbers. Most states require only registration for apprentices, while journeyman and master plumbers must be licensed.

Evaluate a potential plumber by checking out his pipes. Visually inspect past jobs, keeping an eye out once again for neatness. Are exposed copper water lines straight with neatly soldered joints? Supply tubes should also be cleanly bent and without kinks (a kinked joint is a weakened area that could result in a leak). Drain lines, fixtures, and drains should be wiped clean of excess pipe dope and plumbers' putty. These are all telltale signs that indicate the quality of work you can expect. Also, when checking referrals, ask about how efficiently the job was completed. See if there were any problems that popped up after completion of the project, and how the plumber responded to them.

Bang for the Buck

Plumbers are expensive. That's a fact of life. And when you need one, you probably *really* need one. But you can save some money if you do your scheduling in such a way that the plumber has to come to your home only once. If that's possible, you can save money on trip charges and set-up time. (In fact, this is generally true of all contractors.)

Business Is Business

Once you've decided on what help you'll need, the next step is to check the business practices and professional credentials of your contractor candidates. Requirements may vary depending on where you live, but generally you should look for an occupational license, general liability insurance ($500,000 minimum), and proof of Worker's Compensation insurance or exemption.

Examine a potential contractor's business practices by asking these questions:

- ◆ How long has the contractor been in business? Statistics show that if someone has been in business for more than three years, it's a good chance the person is stable and reliable.
- ◆ Does the contractor have a business office and a staff, even if it's only one person who answers the phone? The person doesn't have to have a suite in a high-rise building and 25 people on staff, but even a small business presence is another stability indicator.

- Does the contractor carry adequate insurance coverage? Worker's Compensation, property damage, and personal liability coverage are the big three to look out for.

- Is the contractor well-versed in all state and local regulations that pertain to remodeling? Compliance with local laws is a must.

- Does the contractor pull the permits? Generally, the contractor is the best person to obtain all the necessary permits, since, of course, he's well-versed in state and local regulations. In some places, *only* a licensed contractor can obtain the permits.

Pro Lingo

If you can "pull the permits," can you also push them? Not really. "Pulling the permits" means going through the process of applying for and obtaining the necessary permits for remodeling work. Contractors usually do this because they know all the regulations involved, and the ins and outs of the process. They probably know the people in the permitting offices, too, which can grease the skids of the process and make it go faster.

Face-to-Face

At this point, you probably are left with a few good candidates. Now it's time to meet with them face-to-face. This is where the rubber meets the road, so to speak. You can determine firsthand if the person is someone you'll be comfortable working with.

It's important at this time to trust your intuition. If you get a bad feeling when you meet the person, then don't go there. Even if you don't understand the reasons why you're feeling the way you are, it's not worth the risk. Keep searching. It's said that there's someone in the world for everyone, and it's also true that there's the right contractor help out there for you and your remodeling job.

Hopefully, you will find a choice of contractors that give you a good feeling. Then you can get down to bid-ness.

Getting Down to Bid-ness

It's a good idea, and common practice, to obtain two or three bids for your job. Select two or three contractors from your search and meet with them to discuss your project. Ask each one to submit bids, making sure you give all of them the same requirements for the job. You should set a date and ask that all bids be received *in writing* by that date. Then sit back and wait to see what you get.

Be sure to let each contractor know that he is bidding in competition for your job. It's the honest thing to do, and it might give a bit of incentive to really work the numbers. Be wary of any contractor who objects to bidding in competition with other contractors—it could indicate that he's not even sure of his own bids! There's a downside to such competitiveness, however: Contractors may be tempted to "lowball" the bid in order to win it, assuming you'll automatically take the lowest bid (which you shouldn't—more on that next). There's a possibility of receiving a low bid that's low because of cutting corners, and you certainly don't want that. Ideally, you hope to find a low bid that was arrived at properly.

Keep in mind that the lowest bid isn't necessarily the best, even where your budget's concerned. You must consider the quality of the contractor's work, his references, and how his schedule works with yours—along with the bid—before making a decision. It may be that the best bid for you is a higher one. That's not an uncommon occurrence. Just remember that in the end, the *right* bid can save your budget.

CAUTION **Don't Get Burned!**

Don't ever pay a fee to receive a bid or estimate! Reputable contractors don't charge for such things. If someone says you have to pay for it, say "Thanks, but no thanks!"

The Dotted Line

Wait—don't sign anything yet! You need to negotiate the contract. This important piece of paper is often supplied by contractors. You can use one of your own design, but you would need to do a lot of research to make sure you cover all the important points. If you've done your research about the contractor and found someone who's licensed, bonded, stable, and trustworthy, there shouldn't be any problems with the contract he uses.

And speaking of important points, here's what they are in a good contract:

◆ Describe the construction documents. This includes your layout and any other relevant items.

◆ Scope of work to be performed. All work that's to be done should be clearly defined in detail, cross-referencing to drawings and/or spec list.

◆ Materials and products to be used. If your contractor is providing any of your products, refer to your spec list. A plumber might provide your sink, for example, so list manufacturer, model number, color, and any other identifying information. Note if you're providing any necessary equipment, and what equipment the contractor is providing.

◆ Work schedule. Specify the start date and the estimated completion date.

◆ Changes in the work. Delays or unforeseen circumstances, product substitutions, and corrections of work should be handled with a Change Order Request.

◆ Proof of insurance. You've probably already seen proof of insurance, or you wouldn't be hiring the contractor. But the contract should call for it anyway. Ask the contractor to supply you with the necessary documentation.

◆ Warranties. The written warranties for any products supplied by the contractor should be given to you. This part of the contract should also state the contractor's warranty on his work.

◆ Resolution of disputes and claims. State the form of arbitration to be used in case of disputes that can't be resolved.

◆ Agreed-upon cost for the work to be performed. State the flat price, or the hourly/daily rate, including any overtime provisions.

◆ Payment Schedule. How and when you pay generally depends on the type of work and length of time involved. You'll customarily pay a deposit at the start of work to give the contractor money for any expenses he might incur, and to give him something to live on. For smaller jobs, 50/50 is typical. Larger jobs are usually paid 50 percent up front, 40 percent at the end, with 10 percent reserved until your final approval.

If you don't understand any portion of a contract, don't sign it until you *do* understand.

CAUTION **Don't Get Burned!**

Don't rely on oral agreements. Period. No ifs, ands, or buts.

Change Order Request

This is an agreement between homeowner and contractor to approve and carry out work that is in addition to or different from the scope of the original project. Both parties understand and agree to the changes or additions specified below, and understand that these changes may affect the cost and schedule of the project.

Contractor will provide the following work:

_____

_____

_____

_____

_____

_____

_____

_____

_____

_____

Materials and Cost:

_____

_____

_____

_____

_____

Labor Cost: _____

Total Labor and Materials Cost: _____ (+/-)

Does change affect schedule? Yes/No

New estimated completion date: _____

_____

Approved by Homeowner Date

_____

Approved by Contractor Date

Sign and Sign Again

If everything about the contractor and his contract meet your approval, then sign the contract, and sign the check. But remember the payment schedule you agreed to. After the deposit, you'll pay the final balance of the money according to your schedule. Remember, agree to everything ahead of time, and *put it in writing*.

The Least You Need to Know

- Ask friends and neighbors for contractor referrals. People are happy to recommend workers who did a good job for them.
- Ask the contractor to see past jobs. Be wary of anyone who won't accommodate your request.
- Check for up-to-date professional licensing and insurance. Most states have easy consumer access to this information.
- Get two or three bids. Consider them carefully and make your choice.
- Read, negotiate, and thoroughly understand the contract. Don't sign until you do.
- Don't make the final payment until the work is completed to your satisfaction.

In This Part

Part 2

Designing Your New Kitchen

Creating a design for your new kitchen takes time, research, a lot of thought, and a vision of where you want to go. But it doesn't have to be difficult. In fact, it can be a lot of fun! From ceiling to floor and everything in between, this part takes you step-by-step through the designing process. You'll learn how to take what you learned in Part 1 and use it to design your dream kitchen. You'll learn how to measure your kitchen the way professional designers do it. Then you'll explore the basic shapes of kitchens and their variations, and learn how these layouts can be efficient and beautiful at the same time.

Then you'll pick up pencil, paper, and ruler to start designing your own kitchen. Add an island, place a wine rack, move your washer and dryer—do whatever you like. It's all on paper for now, and you can change things to your heart's content until you find the perfect kitchen layout for you. Let the designing fun begin!

In This Chapter

- ◆ How the pros measure a kitchen
- ◆ Tools you need for accurate measuring
- ◆ Making a sketch of the kitchen to record measure-ments
- ◆ Taking measurements, step-by-step
- ◆ Checking measurements for accuracy

Chapter 7

Measuring Your Kitchen

Measuring is an important step in the kitchen design process. The goal is to measure correctly so you can install the appropriate cabinets for the space and end up with a functional kitchen that's also aesthetically pleasing.

This chapter outlines the process you'll take to accurately measure your room. All you need is a couple of simple tools and a friend to assist you. It won't take long, but it's important to take your time and be thorough.

The Game of Inches

Kitchen design is all about space—inner space. No, it's not a Zen thing. In this case, the "inner space" is the room you're redesigning. Trying to lay out the components of your ideal functional kitchen can be a frustrating endeavor if you don't correctly measure your room. You could make mistakes that can be costly later, and that can hurt your entire budget.

Even if you have the architectural drawings for your home, you must measure the kitchen yourself rather than use the dimensions on the drawings. Why? Because how the real kitchen turned out versus how it was planned on the drawings could be quite different. This is where the familiar phrase "It sure looked better on paper" comes from. Not only that, but if you have an older house, settling of building materials and shifts in the foundation can affect wall, floor and ceiling measurements. You might not think there could be enough movement in the house to matter, but you'd be surprised what a difference a fraction of an inch can make in a kitchen remodeling job.

Relying on the original drawing dimensions could leave you short in some places or with gaps in others. You simply don't want to take any chances. You must know how much actual space you have to work with. Be thorough when measuring, and take your time to insure accuracy. Check and recheck your numbers, because the measurements you take can make or break your remodeling project.

Pro Lingo

For greater accuracy in measuring, **"burn an inch."** This means you ignore the first inch on the end of the metal tape measure and start all measuring at the one-inch mark. Why? Because the metal tab attached to the end of the tape can make reading difficult and lead to inaccuracies. But don't forget to subtract one inch from your final measurement!

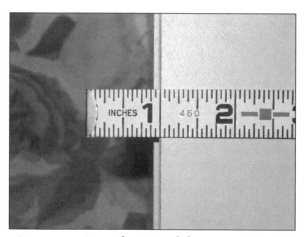

Start measuring at the 1" mark for more accuracy.

The Kitchen Scale

You will use the measurements you take to sketch your kitchen layout on graph paper to correspond to real life. This is called *scale*. Designers designate one square of the graph paper to equal a particular life-size measure-

ment. For example, one graph paper square could equal one foot in reality—or one inch, or ten feet. To avoid confusion in the world, there are standards for scale drawings and sketches. It's best to work with the standards that professional kitchen designers use.

Standard architectural blueprints are drawn to a scale of ¼" = 1 foot. But measurements are so important in kitchen design that the scale used is much more accurate. The standard scale used by kitchen pros is ½" = 1 foot. This is due to the amount of detail involved in placing kitchen elements within the allotted space, and the critical nature of "making it fit."

The kitchen window and cabinets shown here are drawn to scale.

If you don't measure properly and come up a little short in a dimension, there are remedies to compensate for the error. However, your installation may not look as nice as you had hoped. Erring in the other direction is much worse. If you exceed your planned dimensions by even ½", you may be in for a costly cabinet replacement or modification.

Yes, I'm putting a lot of emphasis on the need for accuracy in measuring, because there can be costly consequences for not being careful. But at the same time, don't be afraid of the measuring process. You can measure up to the pros and do it as accurately as they can if you take your time.

Measuring Tools

You don't need a lot of tools for measuring. A good tape measure or rigid ruler and a pencil pretty much covers the basics. If you need reading glasses, don't forget those, too.

The drawback to a tape measure is that the tape is flimsy and can bow or twist. Not a problem with the folding rigid ruler, which is a common item in a contractor's toolbox. It's easier to keep straight when measuring across longer spaces. But it has drawbacks, too. Most folding rules are only six feet long, and your walls may be longer than that. Your ceiling height is definitely past this range. Plus, rigid rulers are difficult to use in smaller spaces because they won't bend. What to do? Deciding which measuring tool to use can come down to this: Work with what you have on hand, or whichever type of measure makes you more comfortable.

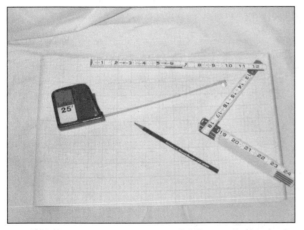

All you need is a good tape or folding measure and a pencil to measure your kitchen. A buddy is a good idea, too.

Designer's Notebook

Record all your measurements in inches, not feet and inches. Write 78" instead of 6'6".

Preparing to Measure

You can insure accuracy in measuring with a little help from your friends, and by taking a few simple steps before you start. Follow these tips:

◆ Get a buddy to help out. You can measure more accurately with someone's help, especially when measuring across long spaces. A friend can help you keep the measuring tape in a straight line, and make sure the tape doesn't twist, bend, or buckle.

◆ Make a sketch of the walls of your kitchen as seen from above. You will use this sketch only to record your measurements, so it doesn't have to be to scale. Indicate doors, windows or other obstructions, the sink, and a gas line if you have one.

◆ Clear off all countertops to make measuring easier and ensure accuracy. Trying to measure around the flour and sugar canisters or the bread box can lead to inaccurate measurements.

◆ Observe your kitchen space. Look for the location of light switches, air conditioning vents, electrical outlets, light fixtures, and the possible presence of an electrical panel. Mark these on your sketch. Your new design may require moving some of these items, so you need to measure with the possibility in mind.

◆ Plan to measure all walls in the room, even if you don't think you'll make changes on a particular wall. The fact is, you don't know where your creative design process will lead you, so be prepared with all the information at hand. Besides, you need to see the whole space when considering certain furnishings, such as a table in an eat-in kitchen.

It helps to measure in the daytime. If not, make sure you have plenty of light in the room so you don't have to struggle to read the measuring tape. Anything that could cause inaccurate measurements can cost you money, time, and hassle!

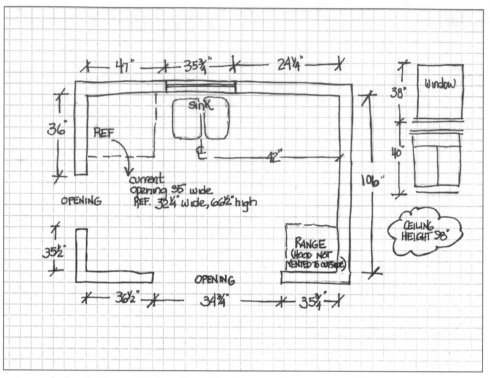

A rough sketch of your kitchen floor plan is a good way to record your measurements.

Pro Lingo

Your kitchen can be represented in several ways when you sketch it on graph paper.

- **Elevation** isn't how high you can go—it refers to the vertical view of the space, as if you were standing in front of the wall.

- **Floor plan** is the horizontal view of the space, as if you were hanging on the ceiling looking down at it. The drawings are two-dimensional, and everything is represented in scale by flat shapes.

- **Isometric** and **perspective** views are three-dimensional, but don't worry, you don't have to draw those. You can, however, work with drafting programs on your computer, which will print these difficult-to-draw views

How to Measure

You're ready to roll, and unroll the measuring tape, when you're faced with the question: Where do I begin? Start at the top by measuring the ceiling height. You'd be surprised how easy it is to forget to measure the ceiling if you don't do it first. Then pick a wall, any wall, and begin measuring clockwise around the room until you end up where you started. This is a good plan to follow to avoid missing any measurements.

Ceiling Measurements

Ceiling height can vary from one point in the room to another. So it's important to take floor-to-ceiling measurements at several places in the room, preferably around the perimeter, or wherever you're going to place upper cabinets. Whether or not your ceiling is level can affect the installation of your cabinets if they are to be placed flush with the ceiling.

It's easier on the eyes to measure the ceiling height by dividing the wall and taking two measurements, especially if you're using a nonrigid tape measure. Here's how to take accurate ceiling measurements:

1. Mark a point on the wall at eye level to divide the wall for easier measuring.

2. Measure from the ceiling to the marked point, placing the end of the tape at the ceiling so you're reading the actual dimension at eye level. Record the number.

3. Measure from the floor to the mark on the wall in the same manner, this time placing the end of the tape at the floor and reading the dimension at the marked point.

4. Add the two dimensions together. This is your ceiling height measurement. Using this method, take ceiling measurements along every wall in your kitchen.

Measure again, this time from the floor to the mark.

If cabinets are on the wall that you're measuring, make the countertop your dividing point. Simply measure from the floor to the countertop, then from the ceiling to the countertop, and add the measurements.

If there are variations in ceiling height measurements, use the smallest number in your planning. This is your worst-case situation. You'll deal with the variation at the time of installation.

For vaulted ceilings, record the smallest and largest dimensions on your drawing where they occur. You may wish to sketch this wall not in floor plan view, but in side elevation.

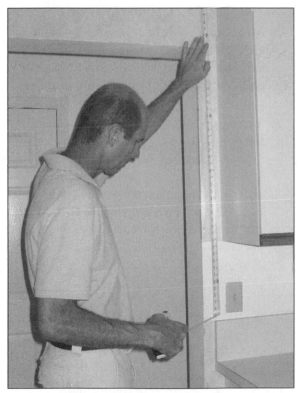

Measure from the top down first.

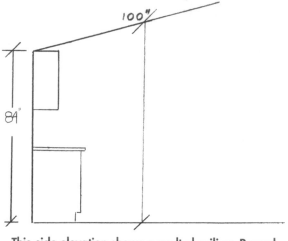

This side elevation shows a vaulted ceiling. Record ceiling heights where they occur.

If your ceiling has soffits, you must account for them in your measurements. A soffit is a space projected from the upper wall for architectural appeal, or for function, such as to house ventilation ductwork. Cabinets will sometimes touch the soffit, so you need to measure the height and depth. You need the depth measurement only if you plan to keep the soffits. If you're removing them, you can omit this measurement, but you still need to include the height dimension in your total ceiling height measurement.

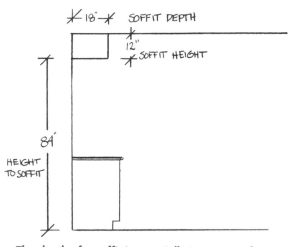

The depth of a soffit is especially important if you plan to use crown molding on your upper cabinets. The molding projects about two to three inches beyond the cabinet, so you must make sure the soffit is deep enough to accommodate it.

Wall Measurements

Start with one wall and work around the room in a clockwise direction until you've covered all walls in the kitchen.

Horizontal wall measurements can be a bit trickier to take. For one reason, you have to work with cabinets in the way. This is why it's helpful to have someone working with you when measuring. You may have to bring the tape forward from cabinets in order to get accurate measurements.

Just as you took ceiling measurements in several locations, you must also measure walls in at least three locations. Walls generally aren't perfectly straight, especially in older homes.

Here are the steps:

1. Measure at floor level, about halfway up, and at ceiling level. Use the smallest of the three dimensions in your planning, but take note of all the variations.

2. Measure in front of cabinets, as well as along the wall if possible. You may see variations due to walls not being straight, and this will affect your cabinet installation.

3. You also need to measure at least two feet out from each wall, just in case the walls aren't square, but veer slightly at an angle. Use the smaller measurement when ordering cabinets, but take the larger measurement into account for the total width. You'll take care of the gap with fillers.

It would be difficult for one person to try to measure this long wall.

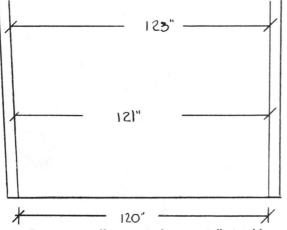

Walls can veer off at an angle, especially in older homes. This can cause problems at installation time if you haven't discovered the problem.

Measuring Doors and Windows

Windows with frames, windows without frames, doorways with doors and open doorways—all of these require special attention when measuring. Here's how to do them.

1. First, measure the windows. Do so from the outside of the left casing or trim to the outside of the right casing. Cabinets to be installed on either or both sides of a window shouldn't be flush against the casing. Plan to leave at least an inch clearance in your layout.

2. Measure the window height above the floor to make sure the window and/or casing will clear the cabinets and the backsplash. You can measure from the floor to the top of countertop, then from countertop to bottom of windowsill.

3. Measure the height of the window itself, from the bottom of the windowsill to the top of the casing. You may need this dimension if you're considering placing a shelf over the window to connect cabinets.

4. Measure walls with windows and doors in sections. First measure from the wall to the window or door's casing. Then measure from the outside edge of the casing on the other side to the opposite wall.

Add these two dimensions to your window or door width, and the total is the length of that wall.

5. Finally, locate the centerline of your window. First find the exact center of the window by measuring the window width and divide that number by two. Put a piece of masking tape on the glass and mark the exact spot with a pencil line. Next, measure from the closest wall to the centerline mark. This dimension is your window centerline, which you'll use in your layout (see Chapter 9).

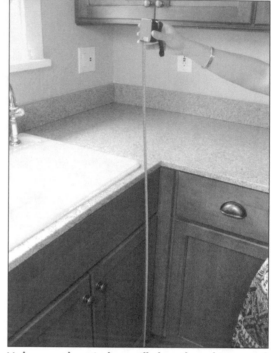

Make sure the window will clear the cabinets and backsplash.

Windows with casings must be measured from the outside edge of the casing. If there's no casing, measure the inside width of the window.

🔨 **Pro Lingo**

Here's some revealing information: The empty space between a window casing and a cabinet or a door and a cabinet is called a **reveal**. It's also used to describe the space from the edge of a cabinet door to the end of the cabinet.

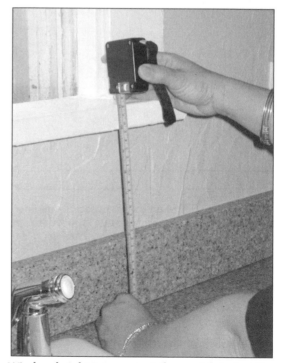

Window height is important if you wish to install a valance or shelf above the window.

Walls with obstructions should be measured in sections. It's similar to dividing the wall to measure ceiling height.

Place a piece of masking tape on the glass and mark the center of the window. Then take the centerline measurement.

Measure doorways in the same manner as windows. Take the inside dimension of doorways without door frames. If there's a frame, measure from the outside of the left frame to

the outside of the right frame, just as you measured a window with casings.

Does your kitchen have a door to the outside or to another room? Note the direction of the door swing and indicate it on your sketch.

Like windows, casing width must be included in a doorway measurement.

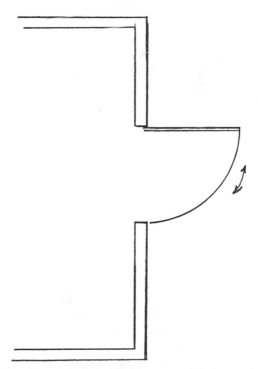

Note door swing directions on your sketch, or you might forget about the door and find yourself bumping your cabinets!

Designer's Notebook

When noting the location of air-conditioning and heating vents, it's handy to sketch an elevation view of that wall. You can show the exact placement of the vent and easily note the dimensions.

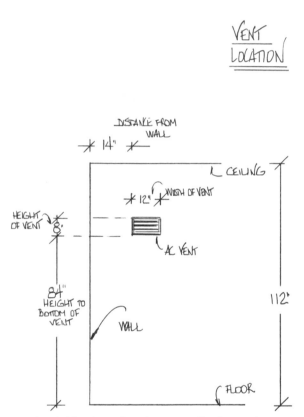

A sketch like this is handy, especially if you plan to move a vent.

Other Important Measurements

You may be anxiously awaiting the day you can dump the old dishwasher or give the heave-ho to the Harvest Gold fridge. But if you don't have a problem with your appliances and plan to keep any of them, you need to measure them so you can work them into your plans. Record height, width, and depth measurements of refrigerators, stoves, trash compactors, dishwashers, range hoods, and above-the-stove

microwave ovens. If you happen to have the owner's manuals for your appliances with specifications listed, use those measurements and record them on your sketch. They're the most accurate.

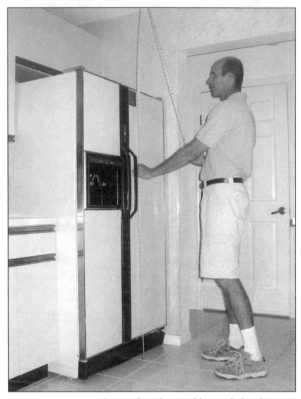

Measure appliance height, width, and depth.

CAUTION **Don't Get Burned!**

Refrigerator door swings can be a problem when placing the fridge up against a side wall. Open the door and measure how much space the door swing takes. Some refrigerators open on themselves, which means they don't require any additional space beyond their width to open the doors. Others need extra space to obtain enough door swing to pull vegetable and deli meat drawers out fully. The manufacturer's literature should list these specs. If you don't have the manual, you might find it on the Internet, or contact the manufacturer.

Another crucial and often overlooked consideration is your sink and all the plumbing underneath it. Open your sink cabinet and take a look at what's inside. At the very least, you have one drain pipe if you have a single-bowl sink, two for a double-bowl—and that's it. Or, you might have lots of pipes, a water filter, garbage disposal, even a hot water dispenser. Whatever you have, you must know at least the approximate width of all the plumbing so you can purchase a sink cabinet large enough to contain it. Many a kitchen design has been significantly modified, at some expense, because the under-sink plumbing dimensions were overlooked. You don't need an exact measurement. Just run your tape measure from the left side of the pipes to the right side and record the length. Your sink cabinet must be larger than this number.

Generally the width of the sink you're using will require a cabinet that will be large enough to contain all your plumbing. So you should be okay, but it pays to check, since the plumbing could vary from the centerline considerably.

You can see that this supply line valve barely made it inside this cabinet. This is why it's important to check the centerline plumbing measurements.

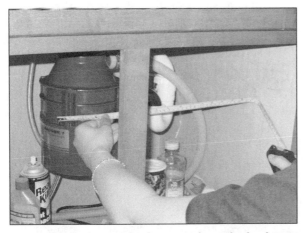

An approximate width of your under-sink plumbing will suffice to help you choose a sink cabinet large enough to hold it all.

Does your kitchen sink have a view? If so, there's one more measurement you need to take. Designers generally strive to center the sink perfectly with a kitchen window. This won't always be possible, but you want to give it your best shot. While you can easily place the sink cabinet centered under the window, the plumbing might not be located dead center. You must find the centerline of your plumbing.

Look inside your sink cabinet again. Does the plumbing appear to be centered in the cabinet? If so, measure from the closest wall to the center of the sink. However, if the plumbing does not look like it's centered, measure from the closest wall to where the plumbing starts, and record that dimension. Then measure from that same wall to where the plumbing ends, and record that dimension. You know that the plumbing must fall between those two points.

You have flexibility to move the sink cabinet an inch or two either way, as long as the plumbing fits inside. Even if the cabinet isn't centered with the window, it should look fine.

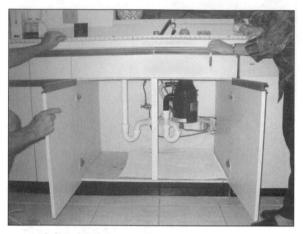

Even if the plumbing is off-center in the sink cabinet, you need to find the centerline. Measure from the closest wall to each end of the plumbing.

This is my kitchen sink cabinet. It's not perfectly centered with the window, but it looks fine, and I'm okay with it.

> **CAUTION Don't Get Burned!**
>
> If you're ordering cabinets from a home or design center, they may take their own measurements. Let them. If something is wrong, they're liable to correct it at their expense.

Check Your Measurements

After you've completed measuring, check the numbers to make sure everything is equal.

◆ Compare total measurements for opposite walls. They should be equal.

◆ If you've measured a wall in sections, add those numbers together. Now measure the complete wall. The two numbers should be equal.

If you find discrepancies, measure, measure again. You've probably heard the saying, "A miss by an inch is as good as a mile." In kitchen design and layout, a *half* inch is as *bad* as a mile when it comes to ensuring that everything fits for function and looks terrific.

> **CAUTION Don't Get Burned!**
>
> Are you planning to install new flooring? If so, you must account for it in your ceiling height measurements. It's best to install cabinets on top of your flooring. Otherwise, you'll have to cut and install flooring around everything in the kitchen, which is more difficult and time-consuming. Thus, it's critical to account for the flooring thickness in your measurements or your cabinets might not fit, particularly tall cabinets like pantries or oven cabinets. Remember, a half inch is a big deal in kitchen design and installation.

The Least You Need to Know

◆ Take your time to measure your kitchen thoroughly and accurately.

◆ Record measurements in inches on a sketch of your kitchen. The sketch doesn't have to be to scale.

◆ Start with ceiling height, then measure walls, working clockwise around the room.

◆ Measure existing appliances if you plan to keep them. Use specs from the appliance manuals if you have them.

◆ Check and double-check your measurements! Every fraction of an inch counts in the kitchen.

In This Chapter

- ◆ Explaining the six basic shapes of kitchens
- ◆ Modifications of the basic shapes
- ◆ The pros and cons of various kitchen shapes
- ◆ Tips for efficiency in each shape

Chapter 8

Kitchen Shapes

You may wish to change the shape of your kitchen when remodeling. Or, if you like the current shape, you might relocate kitchen elements within the current shape for more function and efficiency. In either case, you should know about the most common kitchen shapes, their pros and cons, how they're used best, and ways to modify the standard shapes.

Let's look at the six basic kitchen shapes: L, U, double-L, G, single-wall, and galley. I'll note some typical variations on these layouts, but there are many variations that can be done. It's important to not limit your thinking when doing your own layout. Rely on what your needs are and the architecture of your room and home when creating your layout. Consider the shapes that are possible for your space, but make your choice based on what the best design solution is for you.

The L-Shape

A common configuration, the L-shape is fitted on two adjacent walls. It's a popular style for open designs that incorporate a family room or dining area.

L kitchens have an open, airy feel, and are generally step-saving, easy to work in and to move about. The adjacent counter spaces provides plenty of work room without having to walk much around the kitchen.

On the downside, space for cabinets is limited to the wall space, which may be small. To add more cabinets, you can modify the L with a peninsula or an island.

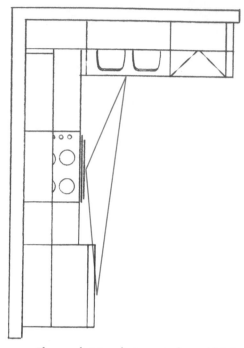

The work triangle in an L-shaped kitchen.

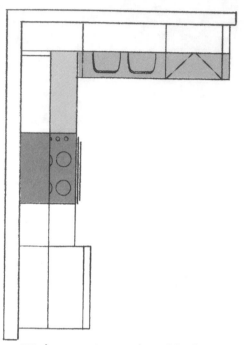

Work centers in an L-shaped kitchen.

This simple L-shaped kitchen is small, but it packs a lot of functionality and efficiency in its space. Not only that, but it's visually pleasing.   *(Masters Kitchen Gallery)*

Adding an island to this L-shaped kitchen helped define the room and control traffic into it. It also provides additional work surface. *(Masters Kitchen Gallery)*

Bang for the Buck _____

Is your own private island too expensive? Get a personalized, custom look and save money by using a wonderful table as an island, or a moveable cart, which can perform double duty as a serving car. Both are more affordable than a permanent island. Best of all, they can be taken with you if you move.

The Double L-Shape

This kitchen layout has lots of cabinet space, because you can place them around the entire perimeter of the room except for where it's broken by two or more openings. Because of this, however, you may have traffic flow issues. One way to restrict traffic from crossing the work areas is to do an island modification, if you have the space. This keeps the work areas on the Ls.

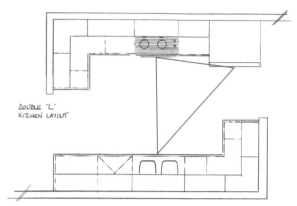

DOUBLE "L"
KITCHEN LAYOUT

The work triangle in a double L-shaped kitchen.

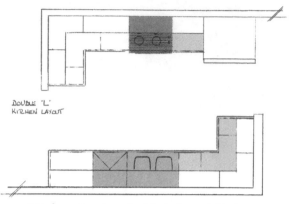

DOUBLE "L"
KITCHEN LAYOUT

Work centers in a double L-shaped kitchen.

This kitchen is a double L. When the homeowner remodels, he plans to keep the shape, because it works best for this space.

The U-Shape

This layout can be a real step-saver, and offer plenty of cabinet space because you have three walls to work with. The problem is that many builders don't make use of the corners with cabinets such as blinds, diagonals, or square corners. So many U kitchens have dead corners. Luckily, this can usually be remedied in a remodel, as long as you have enough space to use such cabinets.

Placement options for the refrigerator are limited in a U-shape. Generally, you must place it along the end of one of the two legs. A U-shape can be modified with an island or peninsula, if you have enough space, to form a G-shape. Doing this narrows the opening into the kitchen.

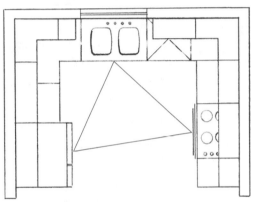

The work triangle in a U-shaped kitchen.

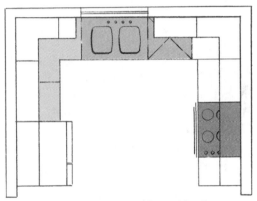

Work centers in a U-shaped kitchen.

An efficient U-shaped kitchen. It's easy to work in, and this one offers plenty of storage space. *(Masters Kitchen Gallery)*

Designer's Notebook

How many steps does it take to prepare a meal in your kitchen? You may not want to count, but studies at Purdue University did. It was discovered that a meal prepared for a family of four in kitchens of different shapes required 450 steps in a U, 490 steps in an L, and a whopping 760 steps in a single-wall kitchen. Conclusion: The U was most efficient.

The G-Shape

A G-shaped kitchen is simply a U with a fourth leg added, either by using a peninsula, or by taking advantage of a fourth wall area. It's worth noting because it's a good modification for large U-shaped kitchen spaces that can provide more storage, countertop space, and possibly an eating surface.

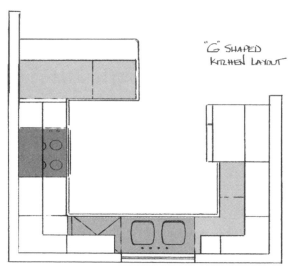

A U becomes a G with the addition of a fourth leg.

The Galley

The galley is a common layout in condos and apartments, and found less often in houses. Cabinets are located on opposite walls, and often one end of the kitchen is closed off. It's a step-saving design, but if both ends of the kitchen are open, you can have traffic issues. You can easily remedy this by closing off one end of the kitchen from other rooms with a pocket-door (a sliding door that slides into the wall to open) or other closure. If one end is closed by a wall, it's not really usable for anything except perhaps to hang pictures.

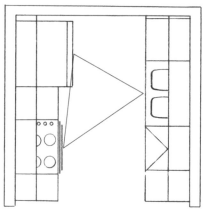

The work triangle in a galley kitchen.

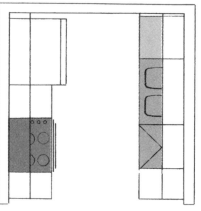

Work centers in a galley kitchen.

This is one side of a galley kitchen in a condo. You can see the cooking center.
(Masters Kitchen Gallery)

This is the other side of the galley. It holds the food prep and cleanup work centers.
(Masters Kitchen Gallery)

Designer's Notebook

If your galley kitchen has a wall that closes off one side, use that wall to tie the two sides of the galley together visually. One way is to use wainscoting on the wall. It gives a unified visual feel without taking up any space. Nice wallpaper can also serve the purpose.

The Single Wall

The single wall kitchen is found most often in efficiency or studio apartment situations. The entire kitchen is built along one wall. It's definitely space-saving, but since all elements are on one wall, the cabinet and countertop space is restricted. This isn't a step-saving design, either, since you must walk back and forth along the one wall as you work.

A good way to develop more space is to add a freestanding storage unit such as a hutch for dishes, located in the dining area. You can also gain space by going with taller wall cabinets, taking them all the way to the ceiling.

Adding an island to a single wall kitchen can actually provide you with a work triangle. So can attaching a peninsula to form an L-shape layout.

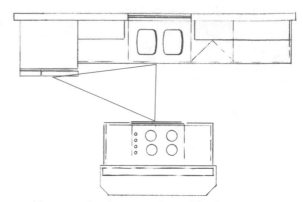

Adding an island to a single wall kitchen gives you a work triangle.

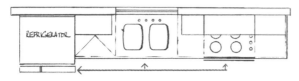

The work triangle in a single wall kitchen isn't really a triangle at all, but a line.

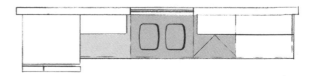

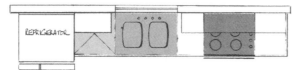

Work centers in a single wall kitchen. Because there's only one wall to use, your work centers can overlap.

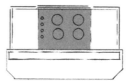

A peninsula added to a single-wall kitchen gives you an L, and once again, an actual work triangle.

![Pro Lingo]

Pro Lingo

What's in a name? Sometimes a kitchen shape by another name is still the same shape. Single-wall kitchens are also called **Pullmans,** because such kitchens were used on railroad Pullman cars. **Galley** kitchens are often called corridors (though I've never heard a ship's kitchen called a corridor).

The Least You Need to Know

- Study the standard kitchen shapes and possible variations.
- Consider what shapes are doable within your kitchen space.
- Change your kitchen shape, or relocate elements for more efficiency using your current shape.
- Remember to consider placement of work centers in your chosen shape.

In This Chapter

- ◆ Tools you'll need for drawing your design, and how to use them

- ◆ Working with the architecture and room shape as you design

- ◆ Drawing your basic layout

- ◆ Adding cabinets and other major kitchen elements

- ◆ Adding accessories to your kitchen layout

Chapter 9

Your Kitchen Layout

Now that you have your measurements, you can have some real fun: Designing the layout of your new kitchen. Here's where you can play within the parameters and choose the cabinets that fit your plan, as well as your needs and wants. First, let's discuss the tools you'll use for drawing.

Tools of the Trade

Since you'll draw your layout to scale, you want to be more accurate. Instead of doing a freehand sketch like you did for recording measurements, you'll need to use a few drafting tools for your layout drawing. Here's what you need:

- ◆ Graph paper—Use standard ¼" paper. For kitchen scale, two squares will equal one foot.
- ◆ Triangle—For drawing horizontal lines and 45-degree angles.
- ◆ Scale ruler—Use to convert your measurements to half-inch scale.
- ◆ Pencil and eraser.

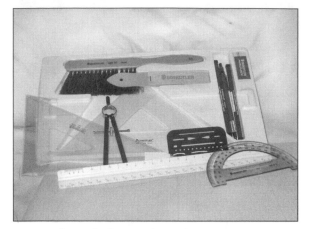

Using basic drafting tools can help you create an accurate layout drawing of your new kitchen.

Some additional items you may find useful are a T-square, straight edge, triangle and circle templates, and drafting tape. All items are inexpensive at office supply stores.

Drawing with these tools is easy. To make lines that are vertical or at a 45-degree angle, line the bottom of the triangle up with the horizontal line of your graph paper. If you're using a T-square, rest the bottom of the triangle on it. It's important to keep your lines straight. If they're crooked or slanted, your scale will be off. As a result, your cabinet sizes may not fit.

If you feel you can't draw a straight line even with a ruler, and you're comfortable with computers, you may wish to use a computer program to do your layout, such as 3-D Architect (for Windows only, about $30 at software outlets), or Home Depot's Home Improvement 123 for Windows and Mac (about $19.99).

Considerations to Keep in Mind

Before you get started, keep in mind that your layout needs to work *with* the architecture of the room. Take a look at your current kitchen. Is the room *symmetrical*? This means you would have an equal amount of space on each side of a door, or a window located dead-center in a wall. This lends to symmetrical placement of cabinets, so you'll want to think about sizing cabinets and doors equally on each side of windows and doors.

Is the room *asymmetrical*, meaning openings aren't centered? The layout can be a bit more difficult in an asymmetrical room, but this doesn't mean that your elements can't be visually balanced. Asymmetry is simply another design look. Even if your window isn't right in the middle of the wall, which dictates an asymmetrical cabinet placement on that wall, you can still create visual balance.

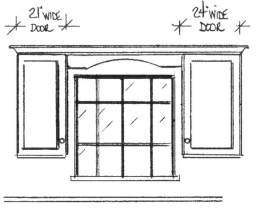

An asymmetrical room dictated that this window have a 21" cabinet on the left side, and a 24" cabinet on the right side. Using one door on the 24" cabinet rather than two doors gives a sense of balance to the wall, even though one cabinet is larger than the other. The reveal is equal.

In this asymmetrical kitchen, the reveal isn't equal on both sides of the window. However, people generally won't notice this unless it's pointed out to them. Other elements in the room help provide visual balance, but it's still preferable to avoid uneven reveals at a window.

Another important point: Function. Remember to consider work centers as you plan so you can increase efficiency by reducing the amount of steps taken as you work. Refer back to Chapter 2 for discussions on work centers.

It's time to get started. So grab the graph paper, pick up the pencil, or fire up the computer, and let's get on with the design.

Designer's Notebook

Some design tips for function and efficiency:

◆ Plan for some counter space next to the refrigerator, if possible, for convenience.

◆ Counter space next to a wall oven is a good idea for safety reasons, so you don't have to carry hot bakeware any distance.

◆ Plan counter space next to a range so that your pot handles don't bump into a wall or tall cabinet, and so you have plenty of space to work.

◆ Locate the fridge where it's accessible to people working in the kitchen, but also so others in the household can get in and out without crossing into the kitchen work area. This may take some thought, but you'll be glad later on that you took the time now to do it right.

◆ Avoid placing tall cabinets right up against a stove. Codes dictate that wood cabinets can't be that close to a cooktop. And you don't want to damage your cabinets from heat and steam.

Step One—Draw Your Layout

Referring to the sketch you made when measuring, redraw the layout on graph paper using the kitchen scale of ½'' = 1 foot. For convenience, you may wish to mark the ½'' scale side of your scale rule with a small piece of tape, so you don't have to hunt for it every time you pick up the rule. Remember, on standard ¼'' graph paper, two squares will equal one foot. Mark your dimensions, including any variations in wall width you might have found when measuring the kitchen. Ceiling height variations will be taken care of during installation (Chapter 13). But you'll account for wall variations now, as you do your layout drawing. Fillers will fill the bill—and close the gaps.

Don't forget to note window and door locations, including casing or trim. Also, be sure to note the centerline of any windows.

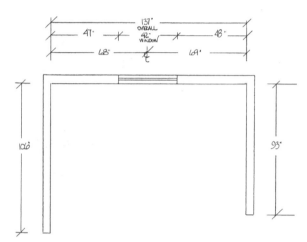

I'll use a U-shaped kitchen to demonstrate the steps in drawing your design.

Designer's Notebook

Don't be afraid to use your eraser! I use mine all the time. Design is an evolving process. That's why you're using a pencil instead of a pen.

Step Two—Cabinet Depths

Start by lightly drawing a line 24" out from the wall. This will be the base cabinet depth. Lightly draw another line 12" out from the wall to represent the wall cabinet depth.

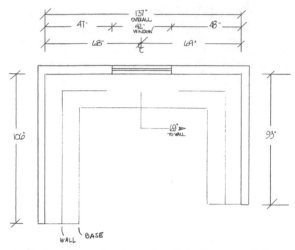

Indicate cabinet depths with a light line—you'll have to erase the line when you place other items, such as the refrigerator. It's a general guideline for now to indicate where the base and wall cabinets will be.

Step Three—Working the Base Corners

It's a good idea to place corner cabinets first. We'll begin with your base cabinets. Be sure to note the direction of door swing for all single-door cabinets.

There are three options for the corners:

1. The best corner solution is an *easy reach* or *diagonal cabinet*, because they allow full access to the corner (see Chapter 3). *Lazy Susans* may be installed into either of these cabinets. Use of these corner cabinets requires 36" in both directions for base cabinets, and 24" in both directions for upper or wall cabinets.

2. If you don't have the space, you can use a *blind corner cabinet* to get the storage space you need. But the downside is that they're awkward to use. They are available in widths from 36" to 48". Remember, the door size on a 36" cabinet will be only 12", as the rest of the cabinet is *blind*.

3. If you're tight on money and space, you may opt to *kill the corner*. This means that you won't use the corner at all, and it's dead space. If you've met your storage requirements, this could be your best choice. Even if you kill the corner, you still need to give clearance to the two adjacent cabinets, so don't forget your fillers. Note that blinds on the wall have the same requirements—you must use fillers to ensure that doors can open properly.

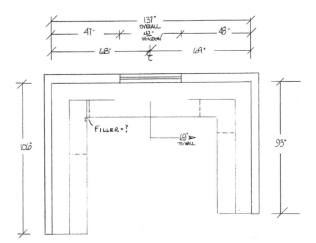

I placed an easy reach base cabinet in the right corner, and a blind base cabinet in the left corner. I don't have enough room to use another easy reach in this corner. I don't know the filler dimension for that cabinet until the sink and dishwasher are placed.

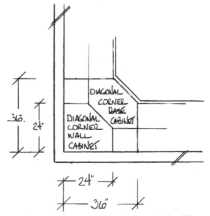

Here's what a diagonal cabinet looks like on a layout drawing.

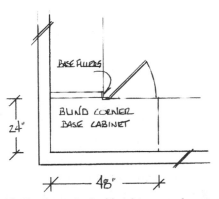

A blind cabinet looks like this on a drawing.

Some cabinet companies offer a half lazy Susan for blind cabinets, which greatly increases functionality.

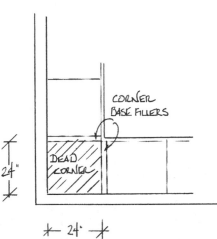

You won't go to jail if you kill the corner. Ideally you want to make use of all available space, but sometimes, killing the corner is unavoidable.

Bang for the Buck

The fewer cabinets you use, the more economical it is. So it's best to use larger cabinets when you can, such as a 36" rather than two 18".

Designer's Notebook

When using a 36" blind corner cabinet, you will have up to three inches for adjustment. You must use a filler between the door and where the perpendicular cabinets meet the blind cabinet to allow the door or drawer knobs on the adjacent cabinet to clear the door on the blind cabinet. A good guideline: Handle depth plus ½" = filler width. But it can be more if necessary.

Ideally, you want the blind cabinet filler to be the same size as the one on the cabinet adjacent to it, for visual balance.

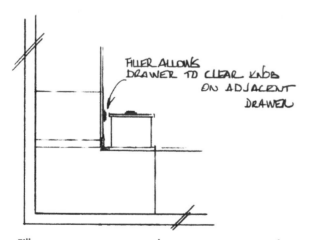

Fillers are necessary to make sure you can open the drawers and doors next to a blind cabinet.

Step Four—Placing the Sink

You must place your sink before you can locate your dishwasher. Draw that now, placing the correct cabinet size in first, then center the sink in the cabinet, using the dimensions of the sink you plan to install. Represent the sink bowls—one or two—with rectangles. Remember that the plumbing under the sink must fit within the cabinet size you've chosen.

Here's where you may be trying to center the sink cabinet with a window. As I said earlier, being a bit off-center won't necessarily look bad. So if you have to go off center, one to two inches shouldn't harm your look.

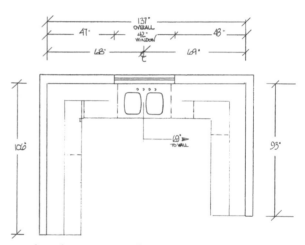

Kitchen designers round the corners of their sink rectangles to look more like a real sink. We have lots of cool templates to do this elegant kind of drawing.

Step Five—Locate Major Appliances

Begin drawing the appliances on your layout. Remember that electrical outlet location is important here. You can probably move appliances an inch or two either way, but if you go farther than that, you may need to relocate an outlet. This is particularly important in regards to your range, which operates on 220-volt electricity and uses a different type of plug. An electrician is required to move a 220-volt plug.

Don't forget to plan for a ventilation hood. Cooking surface appliances are required to have a ventilation system with a fan rated at 150 cfm (cubic feet per minute). Ventilation can be to the outside, or it can be a recirculating fan, which filters the air and recycles it back into the room.

CAUTION Don't Get Burned!

You can't put a range or cooktop under an operable window, unless the window is 3" or more behind the appliance, and/or more than 24" above it. Otherwise, it's a fire hazard!

Standard Appliance Sizes

Fortunately, appliances come in standard widths. The dimensions of European model appliances and some high-end brands can vary, so if you're going for the gold and buying the high-end stuff, check measurements carefully. Here are the standards:

Refrigerator: 36" (may vary slightly, but leave 36" in your plans and you'll be covered) by 70" high (remember to measure the top of the hinge!)

Dishwasher: 24"

Range: 30" width.

Microwave/range hood: 30" wide by 15" high

These appliances will normally fit into standard depths except for refrigerators, which vary (see Chapter 3, "Refrigerator Standards" sidebar).

Standard base cabinet height before counter tops is 34½". Under-counter appliances are compatible with that dimension.

Your dishwasher is usually located next to the sink. Which side of the sink you choose is up to you. There's always a lot of discussion about which side of the sink to locate the dishwasher. Often the topic of being right-handed or left-handed is brought up, but I don't think it really matters. I usually ask people what side they would like to have it on, because there simply aren't any hard and fast rules. I've known left-handers who wanted it on the right, and right-handers who preferred it on the left. The bottom line is, whatever makes you comfortable is how you should do it.

One thing I do recommend, however, is this: Trash, sink, dishwasher. No matter which direction this process flows, placement of these elements should allow the flow to occur in this order for optimum function. Even if you simply place a trash can in your sink cabinet, it should be located on the opposite side from the dishwasher. You clean the plate into the trash, move (right or left) to the sink to rinse, then continue to move (in the same direction) to the dishwasher.

The only times you wouldn't install a dishwasher right next to the sink is if you don't have the space, or if your sink is installed in a corner. In this case, you should place a small cabinet (at least 12") between the sink and the dishwasher to allow you room to stand when loading and unloading with the dishwasher door open.

Be sure to include at least 21" of standing space between the dishwasher and adjacent counters. Also, be careful not to place a dishwasher and range opposite or closely adjacent to each other, where the door openings will interfere with each other.

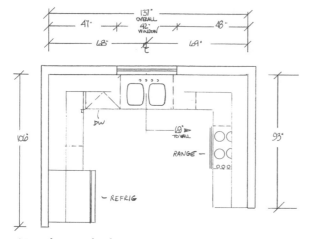

Note the standard representations for various appliances when placing them in your layout.

Refrigerators have some special considerations regarding layout. Depth can be an issue with today's large refrigerators, so don't forget to check the depth if you're buying a new refrigerator. Many attractive, reasonably priced models look great in catalogs or by themselves on the showroom floor, but can be an eyesore once you get them home because they can protrude from 6″ to 9″ into your kitchen! They might block walkways and render adjacent light switches useless. If this is a real issue in your design, look for counter-depth or semi built-in models. These are 24″ deep, excluding the door, so they only project the depth of the door, which is normally only 2″ or 3″. True built-in models are also available, but these are the most costly. They are generally 84″ in height to compensate for the shallower depth.

If you must have a refrigerator that's deeper than normal, you might consider other options for placing it.

My kitchen is so small that when I redesigned it, I opened up a lot of space by setting the fridge into its own little alcove. Fortunately, I had an extra closet in the adjacent room that I appropriated in order to do this.

Stove placement will be dictated by two things: Either you'll keep it where it is because it's already well-located and you don't want to move your 220-volt outlet, or you may be creating a different cooking work center and will need to move it.

CAUTION   Don't Get Burned!

If you choose Thermofoil cabinets and place them next to a self-cleaning oven, be careful! When you use the self-cleaning feature, you must open the cabinet doors or they will de-laminate. Another option: Install a heat shield on each side between the stove and the cabinets.

Notes on the Fridge

Here are a few more tips to consider about refrigerators:

◆ If you have or are buying a top-over-bottom refrigerator, make sure you note the directions of the door swing on your layout drawing, as well as the refrigerator depth.

◆ Leave 15" of counter space on the side of the refrigerator opposite the door hinge. This way, you can take items out of the fridge and easily place them on a counter without having the door in the way.

◆ If you're getting a new fridge and are placing it close to a wall, check the fridge specs for the door swing clearance. Make sure to leave space in your design to open the door (or doors if a side-by-side) a complete 90 degrees in order to fully access interior drawers.

Step Six—Fill in Base Cabinets

If necessary, fill in the rest of the base cabinets in your design. Remember that standard base cabinets are 24" deep and 34½" high. My example design doesn't need any more base cabinets. When I located the appliances, sink, and corner units, the spaces left over determined the rest of the base cabinets. Remember to think about work centers as you plan, and to include some drawers instead of just doors. It's nice visually to break up the ol' door monotony.

When all base cabinets are in place, go back and add up your total dimensions. The cabinet dimensions should equal your total wall dimension. If not, it's back to the drawing board for you! You need to figure out where the discrepancy is and why you have it. You may have

placed the wrong size cabinet somewhere, or left out a measurement, especially on a wall you had to measure in sections.

CAUTION **Don't Get Burned!**

When you come up to a door casing or opening, make sure to allow a minimum of one inch extra space between the cabinet and the casing or opening. You need to account for your countertop, which hangs an inch over the side of the cabinet.

If you haven't found actual mistakes, see if you can remedy a discrepancy with fillers. Remember to use fillers against walls and in blind corners. Fillers are available in three-inch widths and are meant to be cut down as needed on site. The ideal size to use in planning is about 1½". This size isn't visually objectionable, and you still have the flexibility to cut it down further if necessary, or to go with the full three inches if needed. Using fillers is your *fudge factor*. It's really how you make it all fit.

Talk About Tall Cabinets

Tall cabinets such as pantries or oven cabinets are generally placed at the time you fill in the base cabinets. If you have a very long wall, you could locate a tall cabinet in the center to break up the monotony. But usually tall cabinets are placed at the end of a row of cabinets.

Step Seven—Upper Cabinets

In kitchen layout, as in so many other things in life, you start at the bottom and work your way to the top. Begin placing your upper cabinets, and start again with the corners. If you want to use easy reach or diagonal cabinets, the uppers require 24" both ways.

Next, place the cabinets over the range, refrigerator and sink if you have one planned for there. These cabinets should line up with the elements they're placed above.

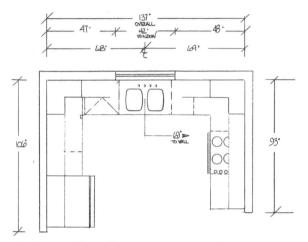

My layout allowed me to use easy reach cabinets in both corners, which is a real luxury! And it maximized the usable space.

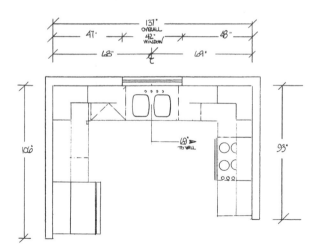

Cabinets made for use above the stove and refrigerator are sized to line up perfectly with standard-width appliances.

Now fill in the rest of the cabinets as determined by the space you have left over. If your layout has a window, try to have equal reveal on either side of the window. You may have to use a filler between the wall cabinet and the

adjacent cabinet to make this work. It will look fine. A filler between the cabinets is less noticeable than an uneven reveal at the window.

Here's an important item from a design perspective: If you plan to use glass doors on any of your upper cabinets, you should locate them so they can be seen from any dining, breakfast, or living areas adjacent to the kitchen. This is where you get the most from the extra money you spend on this visual detail. There's no point in having glass doors if they're not going to be seen.

That's it for the cabinets! If the upper cabinets line up with base cabinets, that's great. But this won't always be the case, and that's okay, too.

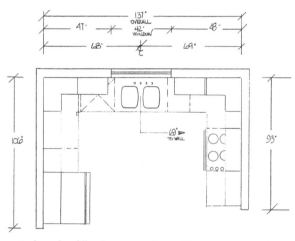

I placed a filler between the cabinets on the right side of the window so I could have equal reveal at the window.

Designer's Notebook

If you need to place a wall cabinet filler in the same location where a base cabinet filler exists, you should strive to make them about the same size. It wouldn't look good to have a one-inch filler on the wall cabinets above a three-inch filler on the base below it, for example.

After you've placed all the wall cabinets, total the dimensions. They should equal the base dimensions *and* the wall dimensions. Everything should jibe.

Let's check my example design:

> Sink wall uppers:
> 24"+21"+2"+42"+2"+21"+1"+24" = 137"
>
> Sink wall bases:
> 24"+2"+24"+36"+15"+36" = 137"

Now check the centerline measurements. Start at the centerline of the window/sink and work your way to the right. In my design:

> Uppers: 21" (half the window width)+2"+21"+1"+24" = 69"
>
> Bases: 18" (half the sink cabinet width)+15"+36" = 69"

Since the right sides checked out, it's not necessary to calculate the left side. We know they'll be equal as well.

Now, go through this procedure for all walls in your layout. If the numbers on the top don't equal the numbers on the bottom, find the mistake and correct it.

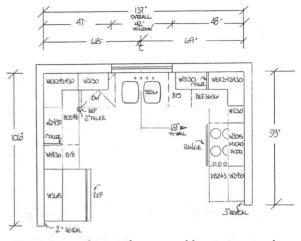

Name your cabinets! If you use abbreviations, make sure to create a key so others know what you mean.

> ┌─────────────────────────────┐
> │ **CAUTION** **Don't Get Burned!** │
> │   You can't cover an electrical │
> │ panel box due to code restrictions. If your │
> │ panel box is in the kitchen, you must leave │
> │ it open. │
> └─────────────────────────────┘

Step 8—Add Accessories

At this point, you can call out any accessories in your design, such as wine racks, spice racks, roll-out shelves, tilt trays, cutlery trays, and so on. Then, indicate the type and size of each cabinet, and show location of those accessories. Don't forget to call out any starter strips you may need if your wall cabinets go all the way up against the ceiling.

Placing accessories so they're functional takes a little thought. Here are some tips to help you out:

◆ Locate built-in silverware trays in drawers right next to the dishwasher or sink.

◆ A pull-out trash bin is best located in line with the sink and dishwasher. However, avoid placing it between the sink and dishwasher, or last in line after the dishwasher. Again, think "trash, sink, dishwasher," meaning you scrape plates, rinse them, and load them in the dishwasher, in that order.

◆ Locate spice racks on doors within your cooking work space. It's great if you can place them on cabinet doors located right next to the stove.

◆ Place tray dividers convenient to the range or oven, since you'll store cookie sheets in it.

◆ Use a tilt-out tray in the "useless" area of your sink cabinet to hold sponges. You must specify this when you order your cabinets, or the false front will be fixed.

◆ Consider lazy Susans and half lazy Susans in blind corner base cabinets to make them really accessible.

Designer's Notebook

Consider using space that isn't readily accessible for showing off collections or decorative items. The higher areas over the refrigerator or microwave, for example, can be harder to reach, but make for great visibility. These are good locations for an open bookshelf or glass cabinet doors.

Step 9—Indicate Countertops

Draw a solid line one inch out from the base cabinet depth. This is your countertop depth.

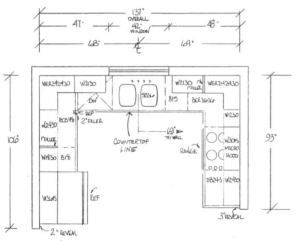

Remember, countertops extend an inch past the cabinet edges.

Step 10 (Optional)— Islands and Peninsulas

If you're designing an island or peninsula in your kitchen, remember that there are space requirements. Islands require 36" of access space all around. This means the distance from wall to wall needs to be at least 12 feet. Here's a tip: Put some chairs on the floor where you plan to have an island. Live with them there for a few days. Does the space feel adequate? If so, you can have an island.

If you can't make an island work due to space limitations, a peninsula could fill your needs and give your kitchen some character as well. Peninsulas can provide a place for seating that's not in the way of the kitchen, as long as you still can provide 36" of clearance to walk around it. In fact, if the peninsula juts into a major kitchen thoroughfare, consider leaving more than 36" if possible.

Designer's Notebook

Wouldn't a cooktop on a kitchen island or peninsula be great? You can do it! Ventilation is your only concern. You can't use a standard range hood, so you must include an overhead hood made specifically for this use.

In this drawing, the island has plenty of access space all around it. *(Masters Kitchen Gallery)*

A peninsula can serve as a boundary between the cook and family or guests.
(Masters Kitchen Gallery)

That's it! You've completed your layout, and now you have a scale design you can take to cabinet suppliers to obtain exact pricing. Remember that final check measurements should be done by your cabinet supplier. This way, they are liable for errors.

Now it's time to get down to work. In Part III, you'll schedule your job and do the installations. Before you know it, you'll have your new kitchen.

The Least You Need to Know

- Obtain basic drafting tools, including scale rule and graph paper.
- Keep function and room architecture in mind when designing.
- Draw your layout, step-by-step.
- Remember standard appliance sizes. If you're reusing appliances, check the specs in the owner's manuals.
- Add up your dimensions. Check and double check for accuracy.

In This Part

Part

3

Getting It Done

For the do-it-yourselfer or the handyperson who's using a little help, this is the hands-on part of kitchen remodeling. In this part, you'll essentially learn how to be your own kitchen contractor. You'll start with scheduling, ordering products, obtaining permits, and preparing to live with disruption in your house. Then you'll move on to putting on your work gloves and getting down to the real business of remodeling.

You'll learn the methods, tips, and tricks of professional kitchen installers as you remove your old kitchen elements and install the new stuff. When you're finished, you'll have a kitchen you can be proud of. So dust off those work clothes and get ready to get dusty all over again. Let's get it done!

In This Chapter

- ◆ The importance of scheduling for a smooth-running project
- ◆ A timeline checklist to help you with your scheduling
- ◆ The process of obtaining permits and getting inspections
- ◆ Preparations to make before you begin remodeling
- ◆ Setting up a temporary kitchen
- ◆ Deciding what time of year to remodel

Chapter 10

Scheduling, Permitting, and Preparation

You've made all your decisions regarding kitchen elements, materials, and how much of the remodeling job you're doing yourself. Now we'll discuss constructing a schedule for getting the work done, obtaining permits, and the final preparations before beginning construction work.

Scheduling

You tear out your old kitchen cabinets and are horrified to discover that your new cabinets haven't arrived yet! What a nightmare! Don't let this happen to you. Preparing a schedule for your remodeling job is an absolute necessity to minimize household disruption, and to keep your budget intact.

Unfortunately, there's no magical rule of thumb to tell you how long a kitchen remodeling job will take to complete. Every situation is different, so you need to make time estimates and create a schedule based on the details of your particular job.

How do you begin creating a schedule? Take a look at your overall project, and read through the following chapters on demolition and installation. You'll see that there's a logical flow to both phases of the job, and that certain aspects go hand-in-hand. For example, you can't use the water again until you install the sink, which can't be done until the countertops are in place, and you can't put in the countertops until the cabinets are installed. You can see how important scheduling is to keep the work flowing.

The countertop connected to the base cabinets, the sink connected to the countertop—just like the bones of song, kitchen elements are connected, and installation is a logical process. You must think about the order of things when preparing a schedule.

Good planning with realistic scheduling will ensure that your job is completed with minimum frustration, within budget, and in a minimum amount of time without a working kitchen.

Ordering Order

The first item of business on your schedule is ordering new kitchen elements, beginning with cabinets. Generally, they take the longest time to receive. From date of ordering, expect delivery to take anywhere from four to twelve weeks. That's a wide range, which is why it's important to try to get the best delivery time estimate possible from your cabinet supplier. One rule of thumb: The more custom-made the cabinets, the longer the production time.

Designer's Notebook _____

When scheduling, be aware that when your cabinet supplier quotes "lead time," it may not necessarily include shipping time. Often the supplier quotes production time only, and shipping time could add another week to that. Always ask to make sure.

After you've ordered your cabinets, you can order other elements such as flooring, appliances, plumbing fixtures, and anything else you'll need to make your kitchen complete. If you don't actually purchase the products at this time, make sure they'll be readily available when you need them.

Special Delivery

Does your cabinet supplier deliver products directly to your house, or do they use a receiving warehouse where they can safely store your cabinets and schedule a delivery at your convenience? It's important to ask your supplier this question. If you're to have a jobsite delivery directly from the manufacturer, it should be cheaper, but you'll likely have to wait around for the delivery truck, and will have to provide assistance in unloading. You'll also need to make sure your street can accommodate a massive semi-truck with trailer, which is usually how the factory ships.

If your cabinet supplier receives into a warehouse, they schedule the delivery to you, generally on smaller trucks, with their own people to unload, and at your convenience. Their employees will often unbox and unwrap the cabinets for you and dispose of the packing materials, which can be substantial. Many suppliers build the cost of all this service into the cost of the job. It can be well worth it.

Work Schedules

With materials ordered, you can now determine how and when you'll get the work done. Once you've pinpointed delivery dates as closely as you can, you can decide on a date to begin removal of your old cabinets.

It's best to leave your old kitchen intact as long as possible. If you're doing most or all of the work yourself and hold down a full-time job, try to take an adequate amount of time off from work to avoid dragging out the amount of time to complete your job.

Mike's Installer Notebook

Not having everything you need, when you need it, can bring installation to a grinding halt. Bad planning can delay the work, cost you money, and prolong your inconvenience. Be sure that cabinets, moldings, panels, trim, hardware such as doorknobs, drawer glides, etc., and anything else you need to complete your job are on hand before you begin your installation. Big items need careful scheduling, too. Arrange for appliances to be delivered by the second or third day of work.

Use this handy timeline checklist to help create your work schedule and stay on track. How long will each item take? Again, every remodeling project is different, and the size of the kitchen is a big factor. With this in mind, I've placed a "guesstimate" time frame beside each item, with a small- to medium-size kitchen in mind. Use these numbers as a guideline *only*. You need to examine your own situation carefully and make determinations about how long each step might take you.

1. Empty kitchen cabinets, box and store items. (1 day)

2. Assemble temporary kitchen. (1/2 day)

3. Remove and dispose of existing cabinets and countertops. (1–2 days, depending on size of kitchen)

4. Dispose of old appliances or store the ones you'll keep in a safe location. (1/2 day)

5. Have new electrical and/or plumbing work done, or modify existing. (A couple of hours to 1 day)

6. Remove existing flooring, if replacing. (1/2–1 day)

7. Perform any necessary wall repairs to make them ready for new cabinets. (A couple of hours–1 day)

8. Install new flooring. (1–2 days, depending on type of flooring, tile requiring the longest time)

9. Install new base and tall cabinets. (1–2 days)

10. Template for solid surface or laminate countertops and order (1/2 day, note that you need to allow one to two weeks for delivery of either type of countertop), or install tile countertops (1–2 days, allow for contractor scheduling).

11. Install upper cabinets. (1–2 days)

12. Install laminate or solid surface countertops and backsplashes. (A couple of hours–1/2 day, allow for contractor scheduling). Install decorative backsplashes if applicable (1+ days)

13. Install sink, plumbing, faucet, dishwasher, and icemaker line if applicable. (1/2–1 day)

14. Install hardware, accessories, moldings, base boards, and do finishing touches such as caulking. (1–2 days)

15. Install appliances and light fixtures. (A couple of hours–1/2 day, depending on type and number of light fixtures)

16. Perform wall work—paint, or apply wallpaper. (1–2 days)

And the final step: Rest, admire your work, and start enjoying your new kitchen.

Plot out the steps of your remodeling project on a calendar. This helps you to schedule any contractor help you might be using. Remember Murphy's Cushion in your budget? You should also have some padding in your schedule, in case the unexpected decides to pay you a visit. For example, say your cabinets are scheduled to be delivered on Wednesday. You should schedule the installation to begin on Thursday, in case the cabinets don't arrive until late in the day. You may expect a 9 A.M. delivery, but you could just as easily end up with a 4 P.M. knock at the door, and you'll have lost a day.

CAUTION **Don't Get Burned!**

Expect the unexpected when thinking about your schedule. Allow some time padding in case something pops up that you didn't count on. Typically, unexpected problems that occur when remodeling a kitchen include:

- Floor or wall damage under the sink due to leaks you might not have known were there.
- Electrical wiring that's not up to code.
- Plumbing that's not up to code.
- Wall repairs as a result of work to plumbing or electrical wiring that you didn't expect.

With a bit of extra time scheduled in, you won't feel panicked if the unexpected occurs. If all goes well, you can be a bit ahead of schedule, and feel good about that, too.

Take note that in the next section, permitting, we discuss how permits and inspections can affect your schedule, so take this information into account when creating your schedule, too.

Permitting

Part of the process of getting ready to remodel involves obtaining the proper permits. By definition, remodeling a kitchen is building construction. Most cities, towns, or municipalities require homeowners to obtain permits before doing building construction—some require them for almost *any* type of construction, and some deem it necessary for electrical and plumbing work only. Even more complicated, some burgs won't issue permits directly to homeowners, requiring licensed contractors to obtain them, while others will. There are no blanket laws in this area, so codes and requirements vary by location.

Permission to Remodel, Please

It's important for you to find out exactly what is required for kitchen remodeling in the area where you live. However, you may be thinking, "But I helped Uncle Albert build a deck, and we never got a permit," or "My buddy Joe did his kitchen without getting permits." That may be true. It doesn't mean, however, that Albert or Joe's hometown didn't have code regulations requiring permits. The truth of the matter is this: Many homeowners don't obtain permits when doing their own work. Some don't even obtain them when hiring contractors. While not passing judgment, we'll explain to you the pros and cons of getting—or not getting—permits for your remodeling job.

Pros of getting permits:

- If your community requires permits, obtaining them complies with the law.
- All work done under permits is inspected and blessed by a third party as being in compliance with local codes. And the number one reason for this is *safety*.
- Your homeowner's insurance carrier likes the above fact when it comes to paying claims for a fire, water damage, or other

calamity that may befall your household. If the remodeling job is found to be somehow at fault, it may not pay your claim.

Cons of getting permits:

◆ Along with permits come inspection schedules, putting you on a schedule other than your own.

◆ Delays and work stoppages can occur as a result of inspections.

◆ If work isn't approved, it can cost you money in lost time, rescheduling of any contract help, and costs to fix the problems.

Find out exactly what is required from you in order to obtain permits for remodeling. Generally, this is the procedure:

1. Visit the building or planning department and fill out an application.

2. You may need sketches or drawings of your job, including floor plans and elevations, especially if you're taking down or moving walls.

3. You may also need a specifications list that includes materials and fixtures you'll be using.

4. As long as everything you want to do complies with codes, you'll be issued the proper permit(s). There will be a fee, usually not too expensive.

Your building department will explain which codes relate to your work and outline the requirements. But it's up to you or your contractors to perform the work to meet the codes.

Inspections

Your permits will outline a schedule of inspections according to the phase of the job. For example, electrical and plumbing work are inspected after they're completed, and if new

wiring is being done by your electrician, it's inspected before being covered up by walls. So you'll need to estimate when those jobs would be done in order to have the inspections performed in a timely way.

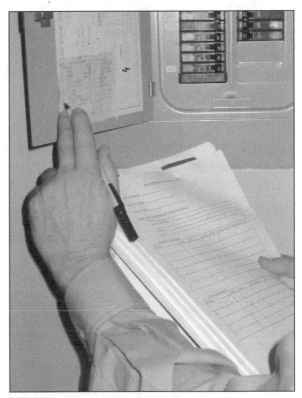

Electrical and plumbing work generally require inspections. The reason is safety, and it's a good reason.

Other jobs that typically require inspections include:

◆ Rough plumbing

◆ Framing if you're adding walls

◆ Duct work and anything involving gas lines

◆ Window glass if you're adding or changing windows

Again, your requirements may vary, so find out exactly what pertains to your project in your location.

But Who Will Know?

Yes, you and Uncle Albert built the deck and did so without permits. But you could have been found out, and if you were, it could have cost you a bundle. Is taking the chance of remodeling your kitchen without permits worth it? You decide. Here's what could happen:

♦ You could get caught by code enforcers, plain and simple. Some towns can afford to have code people drive around looking for unpermitted construction. One big clue they look for are those large rental construction Dumpsters. They run the address against the permits list, and if you're not on it, they'll come a-knockin', with fining authority and possibly punitive permit fees in hand.

♦ Your neighbors could turn you in. Maybe the noise bothers them, or they never got over you accidentally cutting limbs off their favorite tree on the property line. In any case, they can exact revenge with one phone call.

♦ It comes back to bite you when you sell your home. In the course of routine pre-sale inspections, the fact that work was done—and done without permits—can be discovered, and put a giant roadblock in your home sale process. You might even have to tear up old work and have it redone to satisfy inspectors.

♦ Nondisclosure of unpermitted remodeling work can become a legal issue in a sale. You could even be sued for damages by a buyer who backs out of the sale—and would have a right to do so because of nondisclosure.

Renting a Dumpster for construction debris is a good idea, but it advertises the fact that you're doing construction. Code enforcers look for these Dumpsters.

So there you have it. Permits cost money and can drive your schedule, but you must weigh the pros and cons when deciding what's best for you to do.

Preparation for Disruption

It's difficult for most people to imagine being without a kitchen for even one day, let alone a week or more. Unless your kitchen is simply there as a showroom, you use it—and you'll miss it when the remodeling work begins!

You probably can't afford to move out and live somewhere else while your remodeling work is going on. So you'll have to live with it. But don't worry, you can take steps before you start tearing the old kitchen out that can make life easier, or at least tolerable, while you're remodeling. Hopefully, it will be a brief period of time that you'll be without a kitchen.

What a mess! This is what you'll have to put up with when remodeling. But you can plan ahead and make living with this easier. Remember, too, that the new kitchen makes it all worth it.

Storing Your Stuff

You need to empty your kitchen completely, and that requires places to store your stuff. If one of the reasons you're redoing the kitchen is because you have too much stuff for your space, finding places to keep it in the rest of the house may not be easy, and will take some time and thought.

You'll need to pack away items you won't be using during remodeling, and put things you will be using in your temporary kitchen (see the next section). You can box up less-used kitchen items well ahead of time, taking a few seconds to clearly mark the boxes so you can easily locate items later. You might even inventory the contents, making a list on a sticky note or taping a sheet of paper to the box. Store as much as you can in sealed boxes, because you'll have less to wash when you move things back into your new kitchen.

Store as much stuff as you can in boxes, which can be stacked to save space. Good tip: Organize box contents according to where they'll be stored in the new kitchen. This makes emptying boxes quick and easy when you move back after remodeling.

This could be a good opportunity for downsizing. As you pack, think about items you rarely, if ever, use. If you don't really need it, consider getting rid of it. That means less stuff to put back into the kitchen, plus you'll be more organized and more efficient when you do move back in.

Once your base cabinets are installed, you can begin moving some items back into the kitchen. Don't place items in top drawers until after the countertops have been installed, since that process will likely create more dust.

Your Temporary Kitchen

You can still eat at home, even cook, with a temporary kitchen. You'll be roughing it a bit, but for the sake of a new kitchen, you can do it.

Where to locate your temp kitchen depends on available space in your house, though the prime consideration is proximity to water. A dining room could do the trick. A dining area that's sort of connected to the kitchen might not work as well because of construction dust and debris. In that case, consider a guest bedroom, den, or home office area.

Your temporary kitchen should include convenience foods you like, alternative means of cooking, and your must-have items, such as coffee and tea.

The most difficult aspect of living with the temporary set up is dealing with cleanup. If you're fortunate enough to have a laundry room with a sink you've got it made. Otherwise, you can make do with a bathroom sink. Consider using disposable plates and eating utensils so you can keep the bathroom dishwashing (two words that probably shouldn't even be in the same sentence) to a minimum.

Here are some tips on what to include in a well-stocked temporary kitchen:

◆ Alternative cooking method, such as gas grill, camping stove, toaster oven, and microwave, your best friend during remodeling. (Note: Your over-the-range hood will still work safely even when un-installed. Just use a table or an old cabinet for a temporary microwave stand.) Small appliances such as steamers, crock pots, rice cookers, even an electric skillet can be life-savers at a time like this.

◆ Refrigeration. Move your fridge to another temporary location so you can still use it.

◆ Table or old cabinet for storing temporary kitchen items.

◆ Table for eating surface. A fold-away card table could do the trick. If it's summer, you might use an outdoor picnic table.

◆ Dishes and utensils, or disposable dishes and utensils. Don't forget paper cups, including thermal ones for hot coffee, even soup.

◆ Microwave dishes and utensils.

◆ Paper towels and napkins.

◆ Dishcloths or sponges, dishsoap, garbage bags.

◆ Alternative washing/food prep location, such as a bathroom sink.

◆ Canned, boxed, and microwaveable food items.

◆ Condiments.

◆ Coffee- or tea-making essentials (coffee or tea pot, sugar, creamer, filters, coffee, tea bags, and so on).

Be sure to include your sense of humor. Don't pack that away, because you'll really need it. Keep your chin up, your attitude upbeat—and keep that vision of your new kitchen in your mind—and you'll make it through the mess in good spirits.

Keep your sense of humor by keeping in mind a vision of your new kitchen. You'll have it soon!

Remodeling Season?

Another important decision to make: When is the best time to do a remodeling job like this? Of course, your lifestyle is the driving factor. You have to consider if your household has a busy time of year, a slow time of year—or is it happy household chaos all the time? Naturally you'd consider the slow time of year for remodeling, but thinking about the seasons might be the way to go when scheduling the work.

Summer time is traditionally the "remodeling season," and it's not a bad idea. You can use the nice weather outdoors to your advantage and cut down on disruptions to your household schedule. You need somewhere else to cook since the kitchen is under destruction and construction, so summer works in your favor by allowing you to cook outdoors on your grill.

You don't have to sacrifice much in the way of meals, since you can make a lot of your favorites on the grill. Further utilize the great outdoors by cooking on a camping stove, which fills in nicely for your regular stove. Pastas, soups, stews, and anything else you cook on the big stove can be done just as easily on a good camping stove.

Coping with Remodeling

Your household will be disrupted, there are no two ways about that. Here are some tips to help you better cope with the disruption:

- Scale down on your grocery shopping in the weeks prior to beginning your project.
- Freeze meals, casseroles, and other favorite foods for easy microwave preparation.
- Go out to eat! Remember, you included this expense in your budget. Clip restaurant coupons in the weeks prior to remodeling to help save money. At the very least, have take-out menus handy.
- Consider household pets. They'll be disrupted, too. For scaredy cats and dogs, prepare a place for them in the house that's removed from the noisy construction work. Cover fish bowls and tanks to keep them dust-free, or move them away from the work.
- Don't get freaked out by the dust. It's easy to get into a cleaning frenzy before the remodeling work is complete, but that's a battle you simply won't win. Accept that life will be dusty until the work's done, then you can launch an all-out attack on the dust.

Not only that, but the picnic atmosphere can let you "get away with" using paper plates, plastic utensils, and paper cups. So the need for dishwashing is minimized.

Remodeling can be a picnic if you do it during the summer months. You can save money by still eating at home, just do your cooking outdoors—and have a picnic.

On the other hand, a family might be tempted to think that summer is a bad time. With the kids not in school, the idea of a houseful of people at the same time remodeling work is occurring might be, well, a terrifying thought! Still, it's also a time when kids are more active, going places, traveling, perhaps visiting out-of-town relatives for summer vacation. So think again if that's your concern.

Summer is relative, however. Depending on where you live, summer can be the time of year you live for (the land of four distinctive seasons, the North), or it could be the time you're hot to escape to somewhere else (the steamy, muggy South and the blistering Southwest). So your geographical location comes into play. But as you can see, the idea here is to consider how you might work your household lifestyle around the remodeling work. So whatever time of year is conducive to outdoor living for you, that's probably your best bet.

One reason to consider the off-season: If it's the best time for you to remodel, it's also the best time for everyone else in the world. So contractors will be busy, prices may be higher, and scheduling can be more difficult. In the end, you simply have to add up the pros and cons as they relate to you and your household, then choose the best time, even if it might mean paying a bit more for the contractor help you need.

The Least You Need to Know

◆ Order your cabinets and other kitchen elements. Try to get the best delivery date estimate possible, but remember: The more custom-made the cabinets, the longer the production time.

◆ Create a schedule for work based on delivery of items, contractors you may be using, and time required to complete each phase of the job.

- Apply for and obtain necessary permits for the work. Integrate the inspection schedule into your work scheduling.
- Pack things you won't need into boxes to keep them dust-free. Group items in boxes in terms of where they'll be placed in the new kitchen to make moving back in easier.
- Set up a temporary kitchen in another location in the house. Include your favorite convenience foods and must-have items, along with an alternative means of cooking.
- Begin the remodeling work!

In This Chapter

- ◆ Preparations for demolishing your old kitchen
- ◆ Disconnecting and removing appliances
- ◆ Disconnecting all pipes and plumbing under the sink
- ◆ Removing old cabinets
- ◆ Removing countertops and backsplashes
- ◆ Taking up old flooring

Out with the Old: Demolition

It's time to get hands-on and put all that planning, scheduling, and preparation to work. So get ready to kiss those ugly old cabinets, worn countertops, and boring flooring good-bye!

This chapter takes you step-by-step through the process of removing your old kitchen elements. Go through the information carefully before you pick up the first hammer or crowbar. The steps presented here are in a logical order that makes demolition of your old kitchen easier, efficient, and less damaging to your room and any items you might be keeping. Reading through it first and relating the information to your own kitchen can help your demolition phase go smoothly—and safely.

Get Ready to Rip!

Wait—if you're thinking you can let 'er rip, literally, and just rip everything out quickly, think again. A little more preparation is in order first. You need to slow down and take your time doing demolition work. There are lots of reasons for this:

◆ Minimize dust in your home. You can't eliminate it, but you can keep it from really flying.

◆ Minimize wall damage. You'll have to perform some wall preparation and repair work before you install your new cabinets. Being careful during demolition can save you more work later.

◆ Safety first! You don't want to get conked by a cabinet or mangled by a microwave and not be able to finish the project.

◆ You don't want to damage anything you're keeping.

So read on to learn about the final preparations to take before work begins.

Designer's Notebook

It's a good idea to have all your new cabinets either on hand or ready to deliver before you demolish your old kitchen. This will minimize the disruption time in your household and allow you to work continuously to get the project completed as quickly as possible.

Don't Get Dusted

Let's deal with dust first. You may or may not have much of a dust problem once you get going, but it's a good idea to prepare as if you will. The best way to slow down dust's progression into the rest of your home is to seal off the kitchen with clear plastic sheeting. You can buy it in rolls from four feet in width up to 20 feet or more. Simply hang the sheeting across doorways and other openings to keep dust corralled in the kitchen. Make sure you get plastic that's thick enough so it will hang nicely and not rustle around every time you walk past it.

Must-Have Tools

It's demolition time! Do you have all the tools you'll need? Use this checklist.

- Power drill, cordless if possible
- Screwdrivers, both Phillips and slotted
- Wrenches—adjustable and pipe wrenches
- Wire snippers
- Crowbar
- Ladder
- Circular saw
- Hammer
- Carpet knife or razor

- Trash can
- Handcart, useful for moving things
- Shop Vac for cleanup
- Helper (optional, but often quite useful)

Some of the tools necessary to begin removing old kitchen elements. Larger, more costly items can be rented, such as a Shop Vac, handcart— even a helper.

Safety First!

Working with tools and demolishing a room can be dangerous business, so it pays to take some safety precautions. It's a good idea to have and use the safety equipment listed here:

- Lumbar support belt—A good idea when you're lifting, pulling, tugging, and moving things like heavy cast-iron sinks, ranges, and cabinets. You'll see these belts being worn by most of the employees at home improvement stores.

- Ear protection—Power tools can be loud, so give your ears a break. Wear safety ear muffs or foam ear plugs.

- Eye protection—Safety goggles are a must if you're sawing, chipping away old tile, pulling down drop ceilings, or doing any other work that raises dust, debris and sharp objects that could get into your eyes.

◆ Foot protection—So you love to wear sandals. Don't! Put the Birkenstocks away and don a pair of sturdy, closed-toe shoes in case you drop something or step on sharp objects. If you have work shoes or boots with steel toes, all the better.

◆ Breathing protection—A good dust mask is in order if you're taking up tile, or doing any work where you might end up breathing in dust. Not a bad idea if you're painting, either, and tend to be bothered by paint or paint thinner fumes.

You can buy the listed safety equipment at any home improvement store at economical prices. It's well worth the investment to protect yourself!

This small L-shaped kitchen in a condominium building is past due for updating. We'll show you how to turn it into a modern, efficient kitchen.

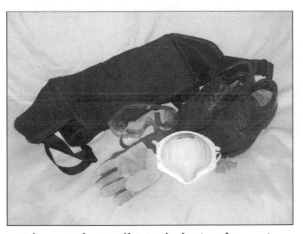

Take care of yourself—get the basic safety equipment shown here, and use it!

Now you can get down to work! The next sections take you, one step at a time, through the demolition phase of your remodeling project. To show you how to do it, we're actually going to demolish and remodel a kitchen for you. Take a look at this 1960s-model kitchen. You'll be amazed at the final result of this job.

This kitchen does have new appliances, so we'll keep those, and add an over-the-stove microwave.

Because the kitchen is so small, the fridge, dishwasher and sink will stay in the same location. We're going to move the stove to the center of the wall it's on, however. A stove should never be located right next to a wall like this one is.

Step One—Ceilings

Always start at the top. Any ceiling work you require should be done first, including removal of any hanging light fixtures and fans. You could end up hitting such fixtures if you're carrying ladders around the room, or pulling down the wall cabinets. And that ugly old cove ceiling? Here's where you get to take your revenge and rip it out, so have fun!

Here are the steps:

1. Remove ceiling fans and light fixtures that are to be changed, eliminated, or are hanging in the way of your work.

2. Carefully remove drop ceiling panels and frames. Wire snippers are handy to snip off wires holding the frame.

Don't forget to turn off the power before removing light fixtures and ceiling fans.

If you plan to reuse your old cabinets, take care when removing doors and drawers so you don't damage them. It's a good idea to put hinges and other hardware in a plastic zip bag, then tape it to one of the cabinets so you don't lose them.

Take care when removing ceiling panels so the whole kit and caboodle doesn't crash down on top of you. Here's where a helper can be valuable.

Step Two—Cabinet Doors and Drawers

The next step is to remove all cabinet doors and drawers. This makes it easier to handle the cabinets when you take them down, especially wall cabinets. It's also for safety reasons—doors and drawers won't swing or slide out, causing injury or catching your fingers.

1. Remove doors and hinges that might cause injury when you pull down the cabinets.
2. Pull out all drawers.
3. Remove any adjustable and nonfixed shelves from the cabinets.

Step Three—Sink and Appliances

You must disconnect and remove all appliances and the sink before you can remove cabinets and countertops. Remember, if you're saving any of these items, be extra careful so you don't damage them.

Everything Including the Kitchen Sink

Time to get down to the nitty gritty of your sink and the plumbing. The first step is to disconnect all the pipes and any other plumbing in the sink base cabinet so you can remove the sink.

1. Unplug the garbage disposal and the dishwasher—both are usually plugged in under the sink.
2. Turn off the shut-off valves attached to the supply lines, then disconnect the water supply lines to the faucet. If you're replacing your faucet, you can simply cut the lines with wire cutters, but if you plan to reuse it, disconnect the lines with pliers.

3. Disconnect the sink drain traps and remove the pipes. If the pipes are corroded and won't budge, you'll have to use a hacksaw to cut through them.

Using pliers, disconnect supply lines at the shut-off valves. Unscrew the nut in a counterclockwise direction to release the line. You may want to lay down some shop rags to absorb any excess water coming out of the lines.

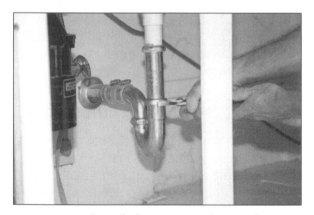

Disconnect the sink drain traps at the nut, shown here. Use an adjustable wrench or a pipe wrench to loosen it. PVC pipes can often be loosened by hand.

Mike's Installer Notebook

If your house is old, the shut-off valve may not turn off completely. If that's the case, you will have to cap the shut-off valve to prevent dripping. A ⅜" cap costs about 25 cents. It screws onto the valve where the supply line was removed.

Now turn your attention to the garbage disposal, if you have one. As you look at this strange creature, you'll probably have no idea how it comes undone! But it's really quite simple once you know the secret: All you do is twist the flange that holds it to the sink drain. But before you do, disconnect the dishwasher drain line, which goes into the disposal. You'll see it going into the side or back of the disposal. It's held in place by a screw clamp.

This shows the back side of a garbage disposal and the dishwasher drain line going into it. Remove the line from the disposal before taking the disposal out.

Examine the connection closely—you'll see how the flange holds the disposal to the sink drain. Twist it by hand to remove the unit.

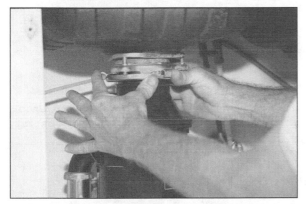

You may have to tap a bit on the flange with a hammer to loosen it.

Mike's Installer Notebook

If you're buying a new garbage disposal, get it before you remove the old one. You can use the manual that comes with the new disposal to help you discover how to remove the old one.

The next step, removing the sink from the cabinet, could take some ooommmph on your part—or not, depending on what kind of sink you have, and how strong you are! If it's stainless steel, it's fairly lightweight, so you can usually

leave it in place and simply carry it out with the countertop. But don't bite off more than you can chew. If you think it's too heavy, or if you plan to keep it, then remove it from the cabinet.

If your sink is porcelain on cast iron, you definitely have to remove it from the countertop first because it will be quite heavy. In either case, leave the faucet attached for now.

1. Using a razor or carpet knife, score the caulking all around the sink so you can loosen it from the countertop.

2. Find a corner where the sink is loose from the countertop. Insert a small screwdriver under the corner and gently begin working your way around the sink to loosen it further. If you're going to reuse a porcelain sink, be careful not to chip the porcelain as you work your way around.

3. When the sink is separated from the countertop, pry it up far enough for you to grab it. Lift the sink from the countertop (or you and your friend lift it), and set it aside for safe storage, or disposal.

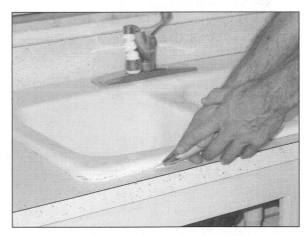

After scoring the caulk, press down on the countertop around the sink with the heel of your palm to help separate the sink from the countertop.

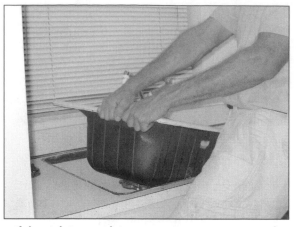

If the sink is porcelain on cast iron, you may need help lifting it out of the counter because it's really heavy!

That's it for the sink and plumbing! Nice job. Now rest a bit, or jump right into the appliance removal phase.

Dishwashers

Now you can unplug all appliances and remove them. Depending on where your refrigerator is located, it may not be in the way and can possibly stay put for now. If it will be more convenient, move the fridge out of the way, but leave it accessible and plugged in.

Let's start with the dishwasher.

1. Disconnect the water supply line. To do this, you have to find the plumbing, which is hidden, but accessible from the front of the dishwasher. Remove the panel just under the door and above the floor to reveal the plumbing. The water supply line is a ⅜ inch copper tube. You'll see it running into a small right-angle fitting located on the left side of the dishwasher.

2. The dishwasher is attached to the countertop with two screws. Once all the water lines are disconnected, you can take out those screws and pull the dishwasher out from under the counter.

3. As you pull the dishwasher out from under the countertop, you may have to lift it and jiggle it a bit to get it going. Once it starts moving out easily, be sure to guide the drain lines and electrical cord with it.

4. Store the dishwasher in a safe place if you're planning to reuse it, or set it aside for disposal or donation.

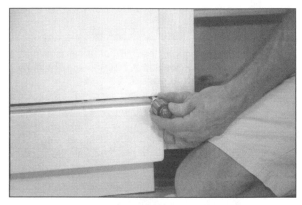

Four screws generally hold this panel in place. Undo them to remove the panel.

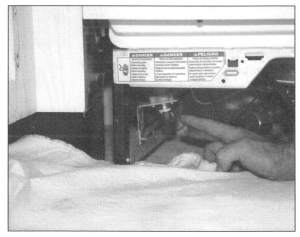

The water supply line to the dishwasher is behind this panel. Disconnect it.

Open the dishwasher door and look under the countertop rim. The dishwasher is attached to the countertop with two screws. Remove these to release the dishwasher.

Pull the dishwasher away from the wall. If you aren't replacing your flooring, take precautions to avoid scratching your floor. You can lift the front of the dishwasher onto a rug, then slide it out on the rug.

That wasn't too difficult, was it? But the next step, the range, is even easier.

Ranges

Be sure to remove the broiler pan, and any pots or bakeware you might store inside the range.

1. Throw the breaker switch in your electrical panel to turn off the power to the stove. If you have a gas stove, consult your gas company about how to disconnect the gas safely.

2. Begin pulling the stove away from the wall. When you can reach it, unplug the cord, then fully remove the stove.

3. Store it safely if you'll reuse it, or set aside for disposal or donation.

This one's a breeze—just pull the stove out from the wall. It helps to open the oven door slightly and grasp the top of the stove to pull it out.

Mike's Installer Notebook

If you've never seen a 220-volt outlet, this is what it looks like. Stoves, air-conditioning units, and dryers use 220-volt. It's twice the voltage, and if you tried to run a stove or dryer off a 110-volt line, it would overheat the wires inside the wall and start a fire. So the wire for 220-volt is a larger gauge to handle the greater amount of voltage flowing through the lines. Be extra careful when unplugging 220-volt appliances—don't touch the prongs of the plug while they're still in contact with the outlet. The higher voltage is more dangerous than a 110-volt outlet.

Microwaves and Range Hoods

Let's move to the microwave hood unit or range hood mounted over the stove. It's generally a good idea to have someone to help you with these items, especially with a microwave.

The plug for a microwave mounted above the stove is generally located in the cabinet directly above it. Before you tackle this removal, let's see how these microwaves are typically mounted.

Eighty percent of cabinet-mounted microwaves have two screws that hold it to the cabinet toward the front of the microwave unit. But that's not all that holds it in place. A U-clip mounted firmly into the wall holds the back of the microwave via a mounting bracket.

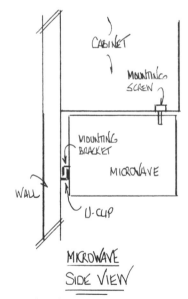

The mounting bracket rests in the U-clip, holding the back of the microwave to the wall.

To remove the microwave:

1. Start loosening the mounting screws. The front of the micro begins to drop, but the back is still being held by the U-clip.

2. At this point, you must lift the back of the unit upward to move the mounting bracket off the U-clip (this is where a buddy is a big help). Then it can be freed.

3. Slowly lower the microwave. Store for reuse, or set aside for disposal or donation.

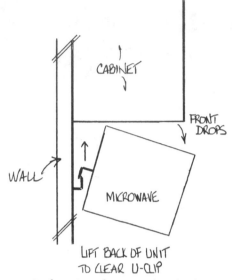

As you tip the micro downward in the front, you need to lift the back so you can pull the bracket out of the U-clip and fully release the micro.

Range hoods are next, and they require some patience. First note that there are many types and styles of range hoods—and they're all a bit different from one another. So you may have to explore the inner workings of yours a bit to find the access panel to the fan motor, which is your first step.

1. The range hood is hard-wired rather than plugged into an outlet, so you must shut off the electricity to the hood at the breaker panel first.

2. Find the access panel to the fan motor, remove it, and look inside for the box that holds the wiring for the fan and lights.

3. Make sure you did indeed turn off the electricity to the hood! When you find the hot wires, disconnect them.

4. Begin to disconnect the mounting screws. There are several, and they'll be in different locations depending on the particular model hood you have.

5. Be careful, and work slowly. As you back out the screws, the hood will begin to drop. You have to hold on to it because the wires you detached are still running from the wall through the hood and into the box. Keep your helper around long enough for this step, too.

6. This part gets a bit tricky. Slowly bring the hood forward until you can see how the wires are fed into the wall. Undo them, and remove the hood. If you're not saving the hood, you can simply cut the wires.

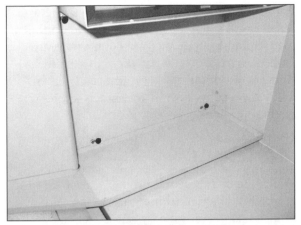

Look against the back of the unit to find the mounting screws. Remove them carefully.

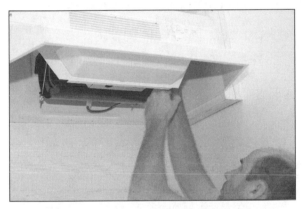

You'll have to explore your hood to find the access panel. They look different from model to model.

Hang on to the hood as it begins to lower, until you can see how the wires feed from the wall. Disconnect or cut them, and fully remove the hood.

How are you doing so far? You're about half-way through! Now you're going to take the cabinets and countertops out, and then your demolition is done.

Step Four—Cabinets and Countertops

This part of the job can be easier than it sounds at first. Often, the most difficulty can occur if your home is older and the cabinet mounting screws have been painted over, making them difficult to find.

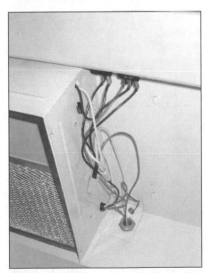

Removing the access panel reveals the box with the light and fan wire. Open it to disconnect the wire.

You'll start this phase by removing the wall cabinets. It's generally a good idea to do this while the base cabinets and countertops are still in place. You can use them to set your tools down while working, or even kneel on the countertops for more leverage and better access to upper cabinets.

Wall Cabinets

Your line of cabinets is probably made up of several individual cabinets fastened together. This makes removal easy, since each one by itself, with doors and shelves gone, should be pretty light, even if they're solid wood.

However, in older homes, you'll often find one big long cabinet covering an entire wall (this was the case in our example photos). With doors and shelves gone, however, this monstrosity should be fairly light as well. But it can be a cumbersome operation to take down a long cabinet. Here's where another pair of helping hands can again save the day.

Don't Get Conked!

Be sure to check the tops of wall cabinets thoroughly before you start to take them down. The hiding place of more than one long-lost dish or piece of pottery has been discovered the hard way by professional installers and handy do-it-yourselfers alike!

Here are the steps:

1. If you have one long cabinet, go right to the next step. For individual cabinets attached in a row, start by removing the screws that attach the cabinets to each other. Sometimes cabinets will also be caulked together—if that's the case, use your razor to score the caulk. Score any caulking along the wall.

2. Find the screws that mount the cabinet to the wall. Sometimes you'll find them behind the shelves you removed earlier.

3. Begin removing the mounting screws. Even if your cabinets are individual, it's a good idea to have that friend around to assist in catching cabinets as they're released.

4. If any cabinet won't come loose after you've removed the screws, start looking for a hidden screw. All it takes is one to hamper removal.

5. If you can't find the hidden screw, then you'll have to resort to brute force. Grab the cabinet and pull on it straight toward you. Tug a couple of times, and you should be able to pull out that pesky screw.

6. Set cabinets aside for disposal or storage if reusing.

Mike's Installer Notebook

You may have to go on a hunting expedition to find the cabinet mounting screws. If your cabinets are old and wooden, and have been painted several times, the mounting screws may have been painted over! Look for them along the top of cabinet interior. You can probably spot the screws, even under several layers of paint. Use a razor to scrape off the paint, then remove the screws.

Score any caulking where the cabinet meets the wall.

Remove the screws that hold individual cabinets together.

Even this single long cabinet is light enough for Mike to handle by himself, once the doors are removed.

Mounting screws can be found inside the cabinet, near the top on the back.

The empty wall. The wall shows no significant damage, even though Mike had to use brute force to pull the long cabinet off.

Backsplash and Countertops

You've cleared the walls and are headed into the home stretch. Next up: The backsplash and countertops.

Here's how to do it:

1. The backsplash is probably caulked to the wall. Score the caulking with a razor or carpet knife.
2. Insert a crowbar between the wall and the backsplash and gently pry it loose from the wall.

When the screws are removed, take them down from the wall. This one had a hidden screw somewhere, which Mike didn't find, so he had to tug it off the wall.

3. If it won't come cleanly off the wall, it's probably screwed into the counter at the bottom. If so, just pry the backsplash loose from the wall and remove it with the countertop. If you're discarding the counters and there's no need to be careful, insert the crowbar into each corner, hammer it in, and lift to pop the screws.

4. If you're saving the counters, look for the screws inside the base cabinets, remove them, and take off the backsplash.

5. Find the screws inside the cabinets that fasten the countertop to the cabinet, and remove them.

6. Lift the countertop off the cabinets and remove.

Score the caulking between the backsplash and the wall. Work slowly so you don't slice the wall—or yourself!

Tool Tip

When you pry at the backsplash with a crowbar, place a shim or a small piece of wood between the bar and the wall. You'll pry against the shim and reduce wall damage that would have to be repaired later.

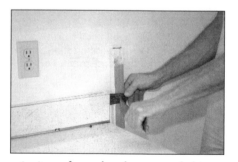

A piece of wood makes a good shim to prevent wall damage when prying with a crowbar.

Insert a crowbar between the backsplash and the wall ...

... then pry the backsplash loose.

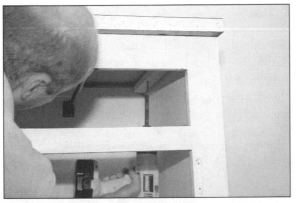

The countertop is attached to the base cabinet with screws. Remove them to free the countertop.

Lift the countertop off the cabinets and set aside for disposal or saving.

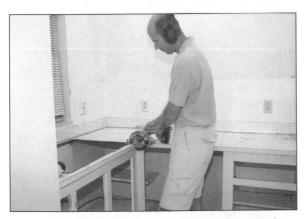

You can simplify removal of the sink countertop by cutting it with a circular saw. Don't forget to wear ear protection when operating machinery.

You may have a countertop/backsplash that's preformed as one unit. In this case, you obviously can't take the backsplash off first, since it's connected. You must remove the whole preformed unit at once. If your kitchen is L-shaped, preformed countertops are joined at the corner of the L with a nut and bolt located underneath the counter.

Here's how to remove preformed countertops:

1. Score the caulk at the wall.
2. If you're dealing with an L-shape, check the corner where the L is joined with the nut and bolt, if possible. If that corner is a dead corner, you may not be able to get underneath to see it. If you can, try to disconnect the joint.
3. Now go under the cabinets and find the screws that attach the countertop to the cabinets. Remove the screws, then lift and remove the countertop.

Mike's Installer Notebook

If you're tossing the countertops, you don't necessarily have to be careful removing them. You can take a crowbar, insert it between the cabinets and countertop, and tap it with a hammer to loosen the countertop. Wiggle it a bit and pull—it's just particleboard, so it should come right off. Do the same for a preformed L-shape countertop. If you can't get to the nut and bolt at the joint, just pound the joint firmly with a hammer and break it loose. If all else fails, just saw the countertop off and leave the joint in place.

Base Cabinets

The base cabinets are the easiest to remove. All you have to do is this:

1. Undo the screws holding the base cabinets to the wall.

2. Pull base cabinets away from the wall and remove.

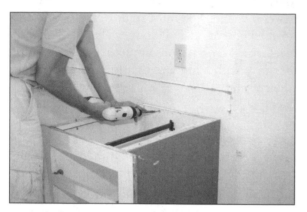

With the countertops gone, it's easy to find the screws that attach the base cabinets to the wall.

Pull the cabinet from the wall and haul it away.

And that's it! You've cleared the room. If you're keeping your flooring, you're done—congratulations. Otherwise, you're almost there, and can move on to the last step.

Step Five—Flooring

The last step is to remove old flooring. Flooring removal can be a difficult task, especially if your old floor is linoleum or vinyl. Tile, which most people would think is hard to remove, can often be the easiest.

If you have a wood plank floor and are thinking of removing and replacing it, you should ask yourself this question: Why? These days, a lot of homeowners strive to save and refurbish wood floors. If you don't like wood floors or if yours is damaged beyond repair, we'll tell you how to remove it.

> **Mike's Installer Notebook**
>
> Because different building techniques are employed in different areas of the country, it's a good idea to ask questions about flooring removal at your local home improvement center, or tile and flooring dealer. They will be familiar with the techniques and materials that are used in your area, and can help you select the proper setting materials and bonding agents for your job.

You should consider the possibility that you may not have to remove your old flooring to install a new one. If it won't significantly impact your cabinet height, you can often install new flooring over old. If you think this is an option for you, we'll cover the details of how to do it in Chapter 12.

Let's look at how to remove different types of flooring.

Tile

There are several ways to remove tile flooring. An important factor driving how difficult the job may or may not be is what type of sub-floor the tile is laid on top of.

In general, tile comes up easier if it's laid over a wood sub-floor. The wood "gives" and breaks the adhesive bond more readily. Plus, wood and the mortar adhesive aren't compatible and don't really form a good bond to start with.

Tile laid over a cork soundproofing layer generally comes up easily, too, especially if the cork is on concrete. The most difficulty in removal usually occurs if tile is laid directly onto concrete slab. Concrete and mortar form the best bond.

Here's the rundown on your tile removal options:

1. Hire a tile contractor to take up old tile by whatever means necessary. It's certainly the quickest and easiest way for you. Expect to pay for at least a half day for removal, maybe a full day.

2. Remove it yourself with a demolition hammer. This is a smaller, less powerful version of a jackhammer, and it's not as intimidating to use as you might think. You can rent a demolition hammer at rental centers and most home improvement stores. Caution: Use this method only if your tile is laid over concrete slab. Demolition hammers cause too much vibration for plywood or hardwood sub-floors. You could damage the sub-floor, loosen nails that hold the sub-floor to the floor joists, and even damage walls, especially plaster.

3. Use a chipping hammer. This is a smaller, hand-held demolition hammer that makes chipping away at tile easier, but without the heavy-duty force of a demolition hammer. It can be used when wood sub-flooring is involved, or to remove stubborn, leftover adhesive after the tile is taken up. They're easy to use, and you'll receive instruction when you rent one.

4. Take it up the old-fashioned way, using a large hammer (like a small sledge hammer) and cold chisel or a crowbar. This is the quickest, low-tech way to go. How you use the hammer depends on what kind of sub-flooring you have. More on that later.

The first option is easy—use it if you want and if your budget can handle it. If you want to go the demolition hammer route and your structure allows it, choose the right size for your job based on tile size and thickness and room size. Demolition hammers aren't difficult to learn to use. You'll get all the instruction you need at the rental center. The same goes for chipping hammers.

Chipping hammers are simply hand-held demolition hammers. They make tile removal quicker, and are safe for use with wood sub-floors. Once again, place the bit at an angle against the tile and start chipping. *(Bosch)*

You definitely need to wear your ear and eye protection when removing tile. Also wear work gloves, long pants and long-sleeved shirts to protect yourself from flying debris. A dust mask might be necessary if conditions get dusty. If you think your removal method will cause a lot of flying debris, it would be a good idea to stand some plywood sheets up against the walls to box out the area where you're working.

Now we'll discuss tile removal using the ol' hammer and chisel (or crowbar) method. This is the most economical way to remove tile because there's no heavy equipment to rent or buy, and you do it yourself. Depending on how well the tile is bonded, this can also be quite time-consuming and labor-intensive. But it's the best method because the power, weight, and force of the hammer blows create a good separation effect between the sub-floor and the tile setting material. Contractors call it "breaking the bond," and it sends the message through the tile that it's not welcome here anymore. In fact, a large hammer creates more of a separation than a demolition hammer does and removes a lot of debris quickly.

Here's how to do it:

1. If there's a loose or broken tile, start there. If not, tap the tiles lightly with the hammer and listen for a hollow sound that indicates a tile that's lightly bonded. Start with that tile.

2. Bang the center of the tile with the hammer. You'll need to use some force, but probably not much. Pound away at a small area.

3. Use a crow bar to lift tile pieces and chip away at mortar. If the adhesive is stubborn, use the chisel by placing it at an angle against the tile or mortar lump and hit it soundly with the hammer.

4. Clean up the area you've worked on, then start again until all tile is removed.

5. Chisel up any remaining adhesive on the floor. You can also use a large razor scraper on a long handle for this chore.

One problem you can face with concrete sub-floor is not being able to remove all the tile adhesive if the bond is strong. In this case, you may want to use some floating material to make the floor level. The material is like concrete—it's poured on the floor and leveled with a large trowel. You must get it smooth so the floor is level for the new flooring. In fact, people often choose to float the floor anyway. It can be easier than chipping up remaining setting material, and the time and effort spent trying to remove it isn't always worth it. If you do use floating material, note that your new floor could be as much as ¼" higher than the old floor.

It's best to float the new floor right after removing old tile. Get it nice and level right away. The next day, after the floating material has set, but isn't completely cured, take a three-inch or five-inch razor blade scraper on a long handle and level off any little bumps and rises on the new floor. If you wait too long and the floating material completely cures, it becomes too hard to level out.

Locate a hollow-sounding tile. This means it's not well-bonded to the floor, and it's a good place to start hammering away.

Break up a few tiles with the hammer. Be sure to use eye and ear protection when doing this.

Use a crowbar to lift tiles and to chip away at the mortar bond. The crowbar is good for larger tiles. If tiles are small, a cold chisel may work well enough.

Chip away mortar bumps and lumps to smooth out the floor.

Vinyl

Of all the flooring jobs, removing old vinyl or linoleum can be one of the most labor-intensive—and frustrating. If the stuff pulls up nicely in one sheet, or tiles lift in a snap, congratulations. You've won the old flooring lottery! We wish we could say that this is the case more often than not. However, don't count on it.

Old vinyl or linoleum usually breaks apart, and once you do get it up, the floor is covered with old adhesive. These adhesives can cause problems when you lay new vinyl, because they can react with new flooring materials and turn

them yellowish. So it's important to remove all old adhesive, and that takes patience.

So there's the hard truth. If you need to remove old vinyl, the hard truth could become your reality. If so, here are your choices for dealing with it:

1. Don't remove it at all. Decide to lay new flooring right over top of the old. This is a good alternative if the old flooring is smooth, or you can easily smooth out the rough spots with a fast drying patching compound. Here are two options: Lay a ¼" plywood base over the old floor, then install new floor on top of that; or use floating material over the old stuff and install the new floor over it. In any case, don't forget to consider the new floor height, which could be considerable if you're using a plywood base.

2. Remove old vinyl or linoleum the slow but sure way—cut it up with a razor or utility knife a little bit at a time. With this method, which is effective and often used, you'll also need a hammer, putty knife or cold chisel, and maybe a heat gun. This method works no matter what kind of sub-flooring you have (concrete, plywood, or hardwood). Let's look at the details of this removal method.

For sheet or tile vinyl and linoleum, cut the flooring into strips about six inches wide. Use the hammer to tap a stiff putty knife or chisel under the old flooring to help loosen and break it. Take up the strips, then scrape away the old glue with a paint scraper or razor knife. If you have trouble loosening the strips, a heat gun can help by softening the glue. You can also soften the glue to assist in scraping it up. This will work with the old tar-based adhesives, too.

Slow but sure gets the job done. Removing vinyl can be tedious, but keep reminding yourself how terrific your new flooring will look!

A special note about hardwood sub-floors: Take extra care when removing old vinyl to not damage the hardwood underneath. You should pull up enough vinyl so you can see which direction the hardwood planks run, then cut the old linoleum in the same direction. It's best to use a utility knife for this job, because you can set the blade depth to just deep enough to slice through the vinyl. To minimize scraping damage, use a heat gun to soften old glue, and scrape carefully so you don't scratch the wood.

Clean the floor as best you can. At this point, you can bring in a hardwood floor professional to sand and refinish the floor, or you can sand away the remaining glue yourself.

Wood Flooring

If you want to remove wood flooring, it's fairly elementary, and pretty much brute force. Old wood flooring is generally nailed, while newer flooring may be glued.

For nailed wood, insert a crowbar between the boards and begin prying up individual planks. You can do this with newer glued floor as well, but may need to chip between the planks and the sub-floor to break the adhesive bond, just as you would when removing tile.

When you've removed the old flooring, you're done! You can relax, but not too long. You have to get that new kitchen installed. But first, get rid of the junk you have left over from your demolition.

To the Dump!

You should have decided your disposal options at this point. If you're having others haul your junk away, they should be on hand when you're done with demolition to take the stuff off your hands. Or, if you've worked your schedule to take advantage of your community's bulk pickup day, then all you need to do is take the junk to the curb for pickup.

Here's a tip: If you have a smaller kitchen, and a garage or basement to store junk, you can put out a few pieces at a time for your regular trash pickup. It saves you the effort of hauling it to the dump yourself, and maybe the cost of renting a trailer or paying someone else to haul it away. Even cabinets can be disposed of in this way if you break them apart into flat panels. This is good, too, if you're doing your own hauling, as you can load a lot more into your trailer or pickup truck.

The Least You Need to Know

- Isolate the rest of your house from dust and debris by hanging clear plastic sheeting across doorways and other openings.
- Assemble tools and safety gear. Remember, a helper can be one of your most valuable "tools."
- Perform ceiling work first to eliminate possible overhead hazards as you progress with the demolition.

- Remove cabinet doors, drawers, and moveable shelving to make the cabinets lighter, and easier to remove.
- Disconnect plumbing and remove the sink. Take extra care if you plan to reuse your sink, especially if it's porcelain, which is susceptible to cracking.
- Take out all appliances. Use drop cloths to protect your flooring from being scratched or gouged when pulling dishwashers and ranges from their places.
- Take down wall cabinets. Mounting screws may be harder to find in older homes, as they may have been painted over more than once. Find as many as you can to make removal easier.
- Remove backsplashes and countertops. Simplify sink countertop removal by cutting it into pieces with a circular saw.
- Remove base cabinets. They're the easiest to remove—just unscrew the screws holding the cabinets to the wall and haul them away.
- Take up old flooring. Wear safety gear, gloves, and shirts with sleeves if you're smashing old tile.
- Discard trash and store any "keeper" items.

In This Chapter

- ◆ Preparing for installation
- ◆ Installing base cabinets, doors, and drawers
- ◆ Installing wall cabinets and doors
- ◆ Installing countertops, sink and plumbing
- ◆ Installing flooring, appliances, and light fixtures
- ◆ Performing remaining touchup and finishing work

Chapter **12**

In with the New: Installing Your New Kitchen

You've got an empty room, and are probably missing having a kitchen already! Let's get right to the job of installing your new kitchen elements. So grab your tools, lay out your layout drawings, uncrate those new cabinets, and let's get started.

First Things First

You've got a big job ahead of you. To do it properly, and make your work a bit easier, you should have the right tools and safety equipment ready.

Tools of the Trade

You'll need the following tools. You can purchase, borrow, or rent any items you don't already have.

- ◆ Levels, preferably two—24" and 48" in length
- ◆ Assorted-length screwdrivers with Phillips and slotted heads, preferably an electric screwdriver or drill with screwdriver bits
- ◆ Drill, preferably cordless, with bit set, including hole saws and/or wood bores
- ◆ Tape measure
- ◆ Table saw or skill saw

- Carpenter's square
- C-clamps with rubber tips (to hold adjacent cabinets together during installation)
- Stud finder
- Ladder
- Touch-up kit or wax stick to match cabinet finish (available with cabinet purchase, used to fix nicks and drilling mistakes)
- Wood shims (for adjusting cabinets to be level and square)
- Wood glue
- Some 2 × 4s or 1 × 4s (for temporary supports for upper cabinets during installation)
- Screws and nails, including finishing nails
- Handcart for moving large items
- Drop cloth
- Razor knife
- Pencil

CAUTION Don't Get Burned! _____

First things first—as soon as your cabinets arrive, unbox them and check them out. Take inventory to make sure you've received everything you ordered, then measure each one to double-check the sizes. If you're missing something, determine whether or not it affects the start of the installation process. Some missing baseboard, for example, shouldn't delay you, but not having your sink base definitely would! Missing or incorrect critical items should be dealt with immediately. Call your supplier and work out the problem.

Safety Equipment

Installation is no different from demolition in that you should use safety equipment to prevent injuries. The same list applies, and is worth repeating:

- Lumbar support belt
- Ear protection
- Eye protection
- Foot protection
- Breathing protection

As you work, it's helpful to keep your job site as clean and clear as possible so you're not tripping over things. It's a safety issue, certainly. But also, staying organized and minimizing environmental confusion will help keep you from making mistakes, like installing a cabinet in the wrong place.

Let's Get Started!

Remember our outdated kitchen we demolished? How could one forget! Well, it's time to install the new kitchen, and we've made a few changes in the layout and types of cabinets. We've kept the appliances, as they were fairly new. Here's a rundown of the changes and additions:

- Installed new cabinets—the upper ones are taller and reach to the ceiling with crown molding on top.
- Moved the range from beside a wall to the middle of the row of cabinets.
- Added an above-the-range microwave/hood combo.
- Relocated the dishwasher to the left side of the sink.
- Installed deep-drawer base cabinets.
- Cut back the top half of a wall (across from the range, not visible in the "before" photos) to make a small bar on the dining area side of the wall. On the kitchen side, added base cabinets with two drawers on top, and roll-out drawers behind doors on the bottom.
- Used refrigerator panels to give a more finished look to the fridge location, and to bring the over-the-fridge cabinets forward.

- Made use of the upper corner with an easy-reach corner cabinet (the corner wasn't utilized before).

- Installed a single-bowl under-mount stainless steel sink, and thus a narrower sink base cabinet.

- Installed a wine rack above the sink.

- Installed an upper cabinet with glass doors.

- Installed granite countertops.

- Installed hardwood floor.

- Removed cove ceiling, and installed track lights and under-cabinet lighting.

In many ways, this is a "typical" kitchen. It's L-shaped, not very large, has a window on one wall, and two doorways. On the other hand, the room did provide a few design challenges, so in that regard, this kitchen has "issues." Many people will find at least one difficult issue in their own kitchens. You might find your particular issue described in detail here.

Here are some of those special issues:

- We had to kill a base corner.

- Optimum layout led to placing two appliances right next to each other—the refrigerator and the dishwasher.

- The range was relocated from an undesirable position (right next to a wall).

- We installed an over-the-range microwave where none was before.

- We also widened the doorways and partially cut down a wall to make a bar. As these are basic construction matters, we won't cover them in detail.

So, let's get started and build this kitchen!

Ceiling Repair Work

If you're planning to paint your ceiling, you should repair the ceiling before you do any other installation work. In our case, we had removed a cove ceiling, and simply had to fill cracks and sand the joint compound to prepare the ceiling for paint.

There was a little repair work to do after removing the cove ceiling. Sanding the joint compound smooth was all the work we needed to prepare the ceiling to be painted.

Find the Studs

It's a good idea to find all wall studs before you start placing cabinets. This little detail can cause you a big headache if you don't do it now. You could find yourself later on holding up a heavy cabinet, ready to attach it to the wall, and suddenly realize that you don't know where the studs are!

If you've taken out old cabinets, you should be able to easily find the studs—simply look at the holes where the screws held the old cabinets. But don't assume the screws were in a stud. Check them out anyway by poking a screwdriver into the hole to make sure there's wood back there.

For areas where there are no existing screw holes, you'll have to look for the studs. Use an electronic stud finder, if you have one. If not, use the old-fashioned kind: Your knuckles and your ears. Knock along the wall with your knuckles and listen carefully to the sound. Most people can hear the stud location, as the sound changes from a hollow tone to a solid sound. If you think you've found a stud, test it by tapping a nail into the wall at that point. Then mark the wall at the base cabinet and wall cabinet level.

An electronic stud finder is easy to use, and they're inexpensive to buy. Otherwise, tap on the wall and listen for the hollow sound to change, indicating the presence of a stud.

Check Ceiling Height

If you have cabinets going to the ceiling, or are using crown molding, you need to verify that your dimensions are going to be correct. This dimension should have been figured out in your layout, but you should check it anyway. Here's how:

1. Start at the ceiling and measure your crown molding or starter strip distance (in our case, 2¼" crown molding).

2. Add the height of your upper cabinets (ours are 36").

3. Add the backsplash dimension (we designed for the standard 18").

4. Add your countertop thickness, and the height of your base cabinets (1½" and 34½" in our case).

5. Total the dimensions—this should equal your ceiling height measurement.

Ours totaled 92¼", which matched our ceiling height almost perfectly.

Hopefully, you won't find a problem in your dimensions. The worst case scenario is that your ceiling is "too short." If that's the case, you can reduce your backsplash height to accommodate the cabinets. Ideally, the backsplash should be between 17" and 19". This leaves some room for fudging if necessary. If you plan for 18" and have an error of up to an inch either way, you can then adjust the backsplash height. For that small amount, it won't be noticeable, nor will it affect functionality.

The odds of having an error greater than an inch are pretty small if you've measured carefully and checked your measurements back in Chapter 7. An error larger than an inch requires detective work. Perhaps the cabinets are the wrong height, or there was a serious miscalculation somewhere along the way. If so, you'll need to find the problem and correct it. A really bad error could mean having to exchange cabinets, which would be costly, and underscores the fact that care in measuring and design is essential!

Let's get to work!

Install Base Cabinets

Demolition starts at the top, but installation begins at the bottom. Installing base cabinets is pretty easy. The key to a good installation is to set the cabinets level with the floor, and square with the walls. (You can install flooring before or after you install cabinets—but if you install flooring first, be sure to account for it in your cabinet heights. See "Floor Installations" later in this chapter.)

Check Floor Levels

Base cabinets must be level so the countertops are level. If the floor isn't level, you'll need to adjust the cabinets by placing shims under them. Note that if the floor is off by ¹⁄₁₆" or less across a six-foot span, you generally won't need to shim the cabinets.

It's really a good idea to have a long level to perform this check, preferably 48" long. If you've leveled your floor after removing old flooring during demolition, you're one step ahead of the game. Otherwise, here's what to do:

1. Lay the level parallel to a wall where you'll install base cabinets. If the floor is level, go to each remaining wall where you'll install cabinets and do the same.

2. If you find the floor isn't level, note where the higher point is. You'll need to shim the cabinets up to meet this higher spot.

3. For L, U, Double-L, and any other kitchen layout that has cabinets meeting at an angle, check the floor level diagonally across the angle to see if you'll need to shim cabinets along an adjacent wall to meet the higher point.

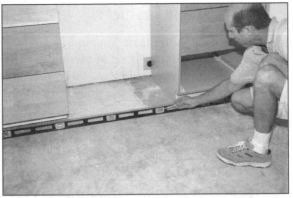

Check floor levels along all walls where cabinets will be installed.

Check diagonally across the area where cabinets will meet at a corner.

Mike's Installer Notebook

Shims are wedges of wood. I use cedar shims that measure from ½" thick down to, well, nothing. Here's what they look like.

A shim is a wedge-shaped piece of wood used to raise cabinets to make them level.

Place and Square Cabinets

It's okay to be square in the kitchen. In fact, it's essential. Cabinets must fit square with the walls, or they'll be tilted forward or backward, resulting in uneven countertops.

Organize the base cabinets by setting them in their approximate place. Next, you'll measure for accurate placement, and use shims to make them level and square.

1. Starting at a corner, begin measuring to place cabinets in their exact locations. Follow the layout drawing's dimensions. Carefully measure openings where appliances will be installed—these must be accurate so the appliances will fit. If you have killed a corner in your layout, start at the opposite wall and work toward the killed corner.

2. Gently nudge each cabinet against the wall, starting with the corner, unless you have a killed corner, as in our case. Check each cabinet with the T-square to see that it will be square with the wall. This is especially important where the appliances sit between them.

3. If the cabinet isn't square, lay a level on top of it from wall to cabinet front.

4. Insert a shim under the front or back of the cabinet, depending on which end you need to raise to make it level. Place it under the side that isn't square with the wall. Watch the bubble in the level, and stop when it's in the center.

5. Check the other side of the cabinet to make sure it's square, and follow the same procedure if not.

6. See if the cabinet is flush against the wall. If not, that means the wall bows slightly. Place a shim between the cabinet and the wall to keep it in place when you're screwing the cabinet to the wall. Without a

shim, screwing the cabinet into the wall would jerk the cabinet out of shape. Do this carefully and check the square again, as the cabinets can move out of square while you're shimming them. Place shims along the stud line location, since the screws must pass through the shims on their way to the stud.

7. Now place the level sideways across the cabinet. If it's not level, insert shims under the side to level it out.

8. Leave all shims in place for now.

9. Follow this procedure for all base cabinets along the wall.

10. Place a long level across the cabinets, lining it up with the cabinet faces to make sure all cabinets are straight. If not, shift them a bit, making sure you maintain the correct opening for your appliances. Do this only if the faces are really off—if they're off just a tiny bit, it won't matter and you're better off to not mess with it.

11. Double-check all measurements before proceeding.

With layout drawing in hand (or nearby where you can see it), begin measuring to place your base cabinets. Make sure you maintain the openings for appliances.

Make sure cabinets are square with the wall. Before you drive the first screw to attach cabinets, always check again to be sure they're square.

Insert shims under cabinets to make them level. Keep a level on top of the cabinet while you make adjustments. We raised these cabinets about ⅛'' in the front, and up to ¼'' on the sides.

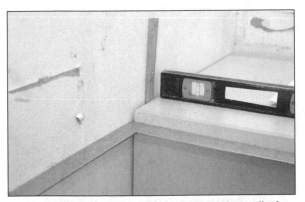

Place shims between the cabinet and the wall, if necessary, to keep the cabinets in place while you're attaching them to the wall. A bowed wall can cause cabinets to jerk out of place while you attach them.

Make sure all cabinets along a row are level with each other.

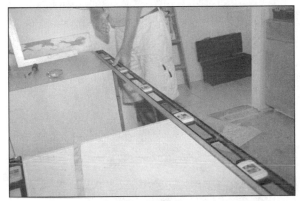

Line up a level with cabinet faces to make sure they're flush with each other. If making adjustments, take care to maintain appliance openings.

In our kitchen, we didn't need to connect any base cabinets. We had a single cabinet next to the wall, then the range opening, another cabinet, then a killed corner. Your case may be different. If so, you'll need to hold the adjoining cabinets together until it's time to insert permanent screws.

After the first cabinet is in place, square and level the adjoining cabinet, and use a C-clamp to hold the two cabinets together (see photos accompanying wall cabinet installation, next section—the use of C-clamps is the same). Do this for all adjoining cabinets. The next section describes how to attach adjoining cabinets.

Designer's Notebook

We told you to watch your 220-volt electrical outlet when laying out your kitchen, noting that you may have to move it if you relocate your appliances. But there's another situation to watch out for. In our kitchen remodeling example, a cabinet partially covers the outlet. It's not much, however, so we decided to notch out the cabinet rather than move the outlet. It was a trade-off we had to make in order to have the proper cabinet size. In this case, the cabinet is a set of drawers, so you won't ever see the notch-out, even when the bottom drawer is open. It simply wasn't worth the expense to move the outlet.

You can see that the cabinet partially covers the 220-volt outlet.

Solution: Cut a notch in the cabinet to completely expose the outlet and make it accessible for the range plug. This cutout won't be seen from inside the cabinet.

Attach Base and Adjoining Cabinets

Now you'll attach the base cabinets to the wall, and to each other if you have adjoining cabinets. Make sure you use the right length screw. It must go through the depth of the cabinet, the depth of the wall, and far enough into the stud to hold properly. If a screw is too long, however, you could hit concrete in a home that's concrete block construction. To attach adjoining cabinets, it's especially important that the screw be the right length so it doesn't pass through and out into the next cabinet.

Before you start inserting screws, make sure you know the location of plumbing lines, too. You don't need to run a screw through a pipe and have a flood on your hands!

Just to be safe, double check your layout drawing again to be certain you're putting the right cabinets in the right places.

Mike's Installer Notebook

It's helpful to obtain a special fitting for your drill, a sleeve that's magnetic and holds long screws in place. This makes attaching cabinets easier, since you don't have to reach into the back of the cabinet with both hands to hold the screw in place and use your drill. The sleeve costs around $6.

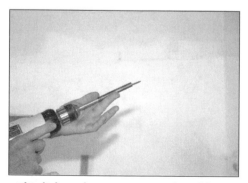

This little tool can save you a lot of frustration. It holds screws on the drill when you're working in those hard-to-reach places.

Let's start attaching the cabinets.

1. Knowing the stud locations, measure and mark where to place the screws on the inside of the cabinet so you'll hit the stud. Screw location should be through the top rail of the back of the cabinet, making sure it passes through any shims you may have placed.

2. Drill a lead hole through the back of the cabinet to guide the screw straight into the stud.

3. Set the screws into the holes.

4. To attach adjoining cabinets, drill two lead holes in the side of the front stile—one hole about 2" above the toekick, and the top hole should be about 2" from the top of the cabinet. If there's a drawer, it should be above the drawer glide. It's a good idea to countersink these holes so doors or drawers don't rub on the screws.

5. Insert and set the screws (see photos in the next section, upper cabinets).

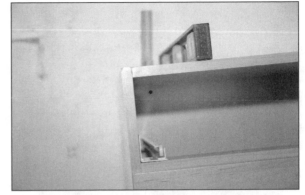

Drive screws through the back of the cabinet, through any shims you may have used, through the wall, and into the stud. Make sure screw length is adequate.

Fillers at Killed Corners

If you're working into a killed corner, you'll need to place a filler on the end of the cabinet. The outside edge of this cabinet will be unfinished.

Normally, you'll cut fillers to the exact dimension you'll need. In the case of a killed corner, you really don't have to do that. You can cut an exact size filler for the cabinet that will adjoin it perpendicularly.

Here's what to do:

1. Place the filler along the raw edge of the cabinet, making sure it's flush with the cabinet face. Hold it in place with C-clamps.

2. Drill lead holes through the cabinet front stile into the filler.

3. Insert and set the screws.

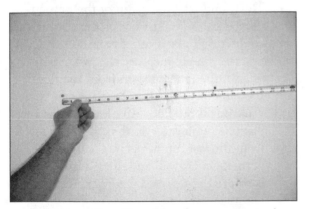

Measure wall stud locations, then measure and mark where you'll drive the screws inside the cabinets.

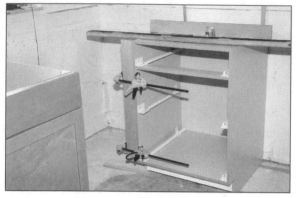

Clamp the filler to the cabinet, flush with the face. It's not necessary to cut the filler at a killed corner.

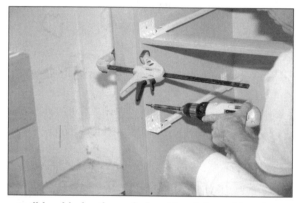

Drill lead holes through the side of the cabinet into the filler, then drive screws to attach the filler.

Perpendicular Cabinet Placement

For U or L and L variation layouts, you'll have a wall of cabinets perpendicular to the ones you just placed. If you used an easy reach or diagonal corner cabinet, you can skip this section. If you have a blind cabinet in the corner, you can simply measure off the blind for placement of the adjoining cabinet. But if you have a killed corner, as in our case, you'll have to go through the following procedure to insure accurate placement of the perpendicular cabinet. This is important to insure that doors and drawers will open properly at the corners.

1. Run a straightedge across the face of the cabinet next to the killed corner to the wall where the perpendicular cabinet will be placed. Mark this point—it's your reference line.

2. Now take measurements off this point for accurate placement of the cabinet—in our case, it happens to be the sink base.

3. Check your layout drawing. It should show the size of filler that needs to be placed at this corner to meet the filler you already attached. Measure this distance out from your reference line and mark it with another line.

4. This line is where your next cabinet starts. The space in between is filler.

5. Don't forget door and drawer handle clearance! Double-check the filler width to make sure it allows this clearance. In this kitchen, the drawer is ¾" thick, plus a 1" handle, plus ¼" extra for clearance = 2". This is the filler width that was called out on the layout drawing.

6. Next, find where the top of the perpendicular cabinet must be for the continuous countertop to be level. If your floor is level, you can simply measure the last cabinet height, then measure up from the floor the same distance along the perpendicular wall. But if the floor isn't level across the diagonal, you can't do that. Run the level from the last cabinet you placed to the perpendicular wall and draw a mark. This is where the top of the perpendicular cabinet must be.

7. Now you can accurately place this perpendicular cabinet and begin working down the line, placing remaining base cabinets.

8. Cut a filler to fit the gap between the cabinet and the filler you previously installed at the corner. Install the filler as previously described.

Place a long level across the cabinets, lined up with the faces, and run it to the perpendicular wall.

Make sure the cabinet is level with the one perpendicular to it. This is critical, since the countertop will be a continuous L-shape.

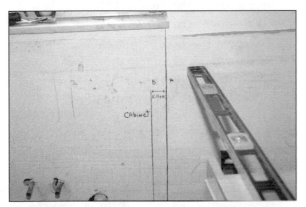

Mark this point—it's your reference line to start measuring along the wall to place your next cabinet.

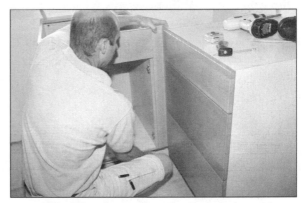

Install the filler, driving a screw through the cabinet into the filler, then through the filler into the previously installed filler (from the back).

Sink Base Placement

In our kitchen, the sink base adjoins the killed corner, so we'll go through the sink base placement procedure now. Follow this procedure no matter where your sink base is located.

If your cabinets have finished backs, you'll have some extra work to do when you're ready to set your sink base cabinet. You'll have to drill holes in the back of the cabinet to accommodate your plumbing. You may also have an electrical outlet in this location for your dishwasher and/or garbage disposal. Some cabinet manufacturers provide open-back sink bases that

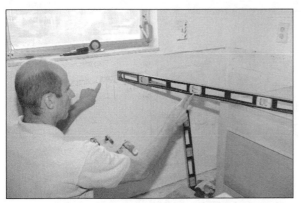

Measure from the reference line to find where your cabinet is placed. The distance between the reference line to the start of the cabinet is filler width. Now you can accurately place the perpendicular cabinet.

simply fit against the wall, and you wouldn't have to do anything to the cabinets or the plumbing if this is the type you purchased.

For sink bases with backs, you'll have to remove or cut valves off the drain and supply lines, then cut holes in the back of the cabinet to accommodate the pipes and electrical outlet if applicable, set the sink base, then redo the plumbing. This is a good time to also cut holes in the side of the cabinet for the dishwasher lines, and an icemaker line if applicable.

First, determine where you'll set the sink base. If there's a cabinet next to the sink base, just take measurements right off of it as you did with other base cabinets. In this kitchen, the corner is killed, and the dishwasher is placed on the other side of the sink base, so we had to place the sink base using the procedure just discussed.

Here are the next steps:

1. Unscrew valves and remove them. If valves are old, you should probably replace them, in which case, it's just as easy to cut the valves off with a tube cutter or hacksaw. You may have to do this anyway if you find the valves too hard to remove otherwise. If water drips from the pipes, stuff some rags into the pipes to hold the water until you get the cabinet in place and can finish the plumbing.

2. Place the sink cabinet near its location so you can accurately mark where you'll drill holes. Measure each pipe's location in relation to the side, and the top or bottom of the cabinet. Measure to the centerlines of the pipe circle. Likewise, measure the location of any electrical outlets.

3. Measure and mark the pipe and outlet locations on the back of the sink base cabinet. Clearly mark which pipe it is, and what size hole needs to be cut so you're sure to cut the right hole in the

right place. Check and check again—a mistake will leave an unsightly hole inside the cabinet.

4. Cut the holes using a hole saw or a wood bore. A good method: Start the cut from the back of the cabinet first, then finish the cut from the inside for a cleaner-looking cut. For an outlet, use a jigsaw to make the rectangular cut.

5. Measure and mark hole locations to accommodate the dishwasher lines and an icemaker line if applicable. You'll cut through the side of the cabinet that's closest to the appliance. Cut holes in the same manner as Step 4.

6. Now set the cabinet. Place it against the wall, with pipes coming through the holes. As with the other cabinets, check all levels and make sure the cabinet is square with the wall, and level with the cabinet perpendicular to it. Shim if needed.

7. Drill lead holes, then set screws into the wall.

These valves are too big and had to be cut off so we could drill holes in the back of the cabinet for the pipes only. The valves were reinstalled after the sink base was placed.

This is a good time to put the valves back on, before you install the countertop and have plenty of room to work.

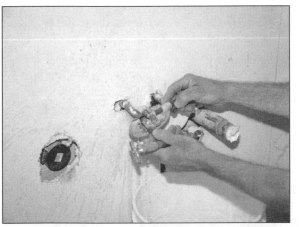

Use a tube cutter to remove valves if they're old and can be replaced, or simply unscrew them and reuse them.

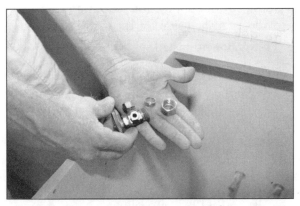

The old valves in this kitchen were one big mess. We replaced them with new brass valves.

Cut holes in the back of the sink base cabinet to accommodate pipes and any electrical outlets.

The finished product. Make sure your new valves will serve all your needs. In this case, there are fittings to attach the dishwasher and faucet to the hot water supply, and an icemaker and faucet to the cold water supply.

Dishwasher

Your kitchen layout may locate the dishwasher between two cabinets, or between a cabinet and a wall. If that's the case, you can skip this section. However, if your dishwasher is located beside another appliance, such as a refrigerator, you'll need to follow the procedures in this section.

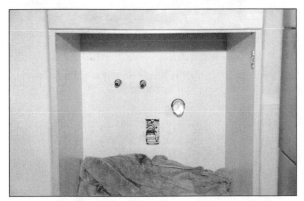

Set the sink base against the wall, inserting pipes through the holes in the cabinet.

A dishwasher that's not located between two cabinets needs a countertop support panel. This is the case in our kitchen. We have a special dishwasher panel that will be attached to the wall to provide support for the countertop, and provide a finished side for the dishwasher.

Here's how to install it:

1. Draw a level vertical line on the wall where you'll attach the dishwasher support panel at 24" width from the adjoining cabinet.

2. Mount a strip of wood brace along this line. This is to support the dishwasher panel. Make sure the brace won't interfere with the dishwasher.

3. Stand the panel up against the brace. Measure the gap to make sure it's 24" for the dishwasher.

4. Check to make sure the panel is level. If not, use shims to make it level. Check that it's square against the wall, again making sure the opening remains at 24".

5. Screw the panel into the wooden brace.

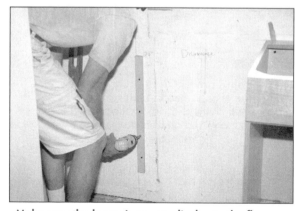

Make sure the brace is perpendicular to the floor so the dishwasher panel stands straight.

Stand the panel up against the brace.

Make sure the panel is level—insert a shim to level it if necessary.

Screw the panel into the brace.

Install a temporary brace across the opening to
maintain 24" as you continue to work.

Refrigerator Panels

If you're not installing refrigerator panels, you
can skip this section.

Our kitchen was designed with a refrigerator
panel to give a built-in look, and to allow the
above-the-fridge cabinets to be installed forward for easier access. Since our fridge goes
against a wall, we're using only one refrigerator
panel, and it goes right beside the dishwasher
panel we just installed.

In our situation, installing the refrigerator
panel is simple. We placed it against the dishwasher panel, made sure it was level and square,
shimming if necessary, and screwed it right into
the dishwasher panel.

Most commonly, refrigerator panels will
mount against a cabinet. Follow the same procedure just described to level and square the
panel, then screw it into the adjoining cabinet
in the front stile, the same location where you
attached adjoining cabinets.

The refrigerator panel mounted right against the
dishwasher panel. More typically, it will mount
against cabinets.

At this point, you should have installed all
base cabinets. If you choose to, you could install
any remaining fillers at this time. However, we
prefer to install all cabinets first, then cut and
install all fillers afterward, at the same time we
install toekick and moldings. It's a matter of
convenience, requiring table saw setup only
once. If you wish to do filler installation now,
skip forward to the section "Install Fillers."

Template for Countertops

As soon as your base cabinets are installed, you
should order your countertops. The supplier
for whatever countertop material you've chosen
will come in and measure for them, and create
a template, which is a pattern made from thin
strips of wood. The strips are placed along the
outside edges of the tops of the base cabinets
and glued together to form a template that is
used to fabricate the countertop.

Besides custom-made countertops, you can buy stock countertop from a home improvement center that you can cut and install yourself. If this is what you've done, you will install the countertop after the upper cabinets are in place. You can take measurements for the countertops yourself, but it's preferable to have the supplier do the measuring. They would then be liable for errors.

The supplier of our granite countertop made a template to the size of the countertop using thin strips of wood.

The wood strips are glued together, then the whole template is taken to the supplier's to be used to make the countertop.

Let's move on to the upper cabinets.

Install Upper Cabinets

Before you bring upper cabinets into the kitchen, lay a cloth down on the floor. Upper cabinets don't have protective legs and will rest directly on the floor, so use the cloth to prevent scratches on the cabinet bottoms that you'd be able to see when they're installed.

Take all doors off the cabinets and remove shelves so they're not as heavy and will be easier to handle. You can use a helper if you want, and having help is always a good idea. But the method of hanging upper cabinets that we'll describe can usually be done by one person if necessary.

As with the base cabinets, you should start in a corner, unless you have a killed corner, in which case you would start at the opposite end of the wall. In our kitchen, we have a corner cabinet on the wall, an easy reach, so we'll start there. But first, we'll put up stringers to help in the installation.

> **Pro Lingo** _____
>
> In the news business, **stringers** are freelancers. But in the kitchen biz, stringers are support boards temporarily attached to the wall. They're used to make sure the upper cabinets are level and at the proper height, and to make installation easier. They're especially helpful if you're doing the installation alone, since they'll support the cabinets while you screw them into the wall.

Install Stringers

Lengths of 2" × 4", or 1" × 4" board are good to use for stringers. These will be available in eight-foot lengths. Make sure the boards you plan to use are straight. Here's how to place them:

1. Go back to the section, "Check Ceiling Height." Your dimension for the top of the backsplash/bottom of the upper cabinets is where you'll place the upper surface of the stringer. In our case, it's 19½" above the base cabinets (18" for backsplash, and 1½" for countertop thickness). Mark this line on the wall.

2. Place the top surface of the board along the line and screw it into the wall with one screw at one of the studs. Don't screw it too tightly, as you'll adjust the board next.

3. Place a level atop the board and adjust the board until it's straight and level. Recheck the distance from the top of the base cabinets to the top of the board. If necessary, remove the board and remount it. Once it's at the right place and level, put more screws into it at the studs, and set them completely.

4. Place stringers along all walls where you'll install upper cabinets. Cut shorter pieces of board where necessary. Be sure to make the boards level, and check the placement dimension each time.

Place the top of the stringer along this line—the upper cabinets will sit on the stringer as you install them.

Make sure stringers are level before tightening the screws.

Start in a Corner

Our kitchen has a corner easy reach cabinet, so we started there. If you don't have a corner cabinet, you should be placing your first cabinet at a wall, either right up against it, or leaving a space for a filler, whichever is required by your layout. If you have a killed corner, start at the opposite wall and work toward the killed corner.

1. Use the same procedure you did for placing and installing the base cabinets. Begin measuring to place cabinets in their exact locations, following your layout drawing's dimensions.

Measure up the wall to find the top of the backsplash, which is where the bottom of the upper cabinets will be. Mark this line.

2. Find the stud location(s) for the cabinet you plan to install.

3. Measure and mark where to place the screws on the inside of the cabinet so you'll hit the stud(s). Screw location should be about 1″ from the top of the cabinet.

4. Pre-drill the screw holes in the back of the cabinet. This makes it easier for you to attach the cabinet since the screw will be guided into the wall, right into the stud.

5. Place a screw into the sleeve on your driver and have it ready to use. Here is where the special sleeve really helps.

6. Lift the cabinet and set it in place, resting it on top of the stringer. Adjust the position of the cabinet if necessary to set it in the exact location.

7. Screw it in, but not tight.

8. Check to see that the cabinet is level. If not, adjust it. If it's level, set the screw(s) completely.

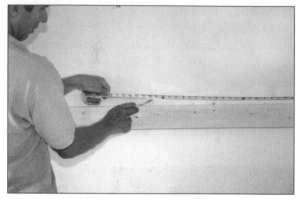
Measure along the wall to place your first upper cabinet.

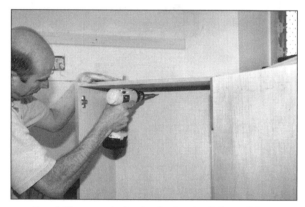
Pre-drill screw holes in the back of the cabinet, about an inch from the top.

> **CAUTION** **Don't Get Burned!**
>
> If your corner cabinet sits solo on one wall, as in our case, make sure you install it with the finished side visible. The majority of upper cabinets look the same right side up or upside down. Those designated to be at the end of a row of cabinets and not against a wall will have one side finished. Make sure you install the cabinet the right way. This is an easy thing to forget to check, but if you do, you'll find out soon enough, and have to rehang the cabinet.

Lift the cabinet, set it on the stringer, and drive the screws into the wall—but not completely. You need to check the how level the cabinet is first.

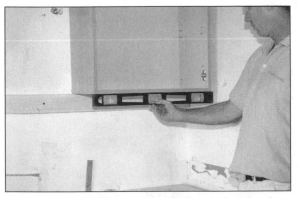

Check the level of the cabinet before tightening the screws completely.

Our easy reach corner cabinet, installed. Note the shorter stringers placed on the wall to hold it.

Go on to your next cabinet. If it's a regular upper cabinet the same size as the first one, follow the procedure outlined here. (If your next cabinet happens to be a microwave cabinet, go to the next section.)

1. Mark where you'll place the mounting screws on the inside of the cabinet. It's not necessary to pre-drill these holes, since the cabinet will be supported by the adjacent cabinet (next step), but you can pre-drill them if you wish.

2. Lift the adjacent cabinet to the wall and set it on the stringer. Attach it to the neighboring cabinet with the C-clamps.

3. Be sure the fronts of the cabinets are flush with each other. Attach the two cabinets together, making sure the screws are the right depth. For upper cabinets, attach with two screws in the front, top and bottom, like you did for the base cabinets, but also place two screws in the back of the cabinets, top and bottom.

4. Check the level, then screw the cabinet into the wall.

5. Continue to install remaining upper cabinets in this same manner, including bookshelf cabinets, wine racks, over-the-fridge cabinets, and others. The installation procedure is the same.

Designer's Notebook

The owner of this kitchen wanted a wine rack, which we placed above the sink. However, the wine rack wasn't available in a length as great as the span between the cabinets on either side of the sink. Not to worry—we used fillers on both sides to center the wine rack above the sink and close the gaps. It looks great! The moral is: Don't let a few gaps stop you from using an accessory that you want. You can usually find a way to make it fit and look good.

Continue placing upper cabinets in the same manner.

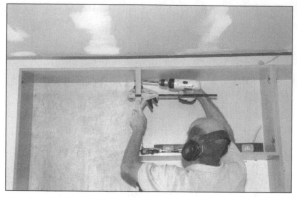

Clamp cabinets together with C-clamps until you attach them.

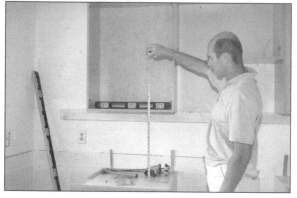

Level and attach the cabinets to each other, then to the wall. Check your backsplash height each time to make sure it's correct.

This narrow cabinet goes right up against the refrigerator panel.

This wine rack goes above the sink, on a shelf between the two cabinets flanking the sink.

Mike's Installer Notebook

If you'll be installing a microwave cabinet or a cabinet above the sink, be careful with the cabinets on either side of it. Since part of the sides of those cabinets will be visible, one side will be finished and the other side won't be. So you'll have definite "right side" and "left side" cabinets. You want to make sure the finished side is toward the microwave. Check carefully. You can even write on the back outside of the cabinet "This side up" and draw an arrow. Even the pros can make the mistake of installing the cabinet the wrong way, so be careful. This is especially important for a cabinet above the sink, since those sides will always be seen.

Our second cabinet was the smaller cabinet that supports the microwave/hood above the range, the microwave cabinet. You'll need to cut some holes in the cabinet prior to installing it, whether you have a microwave or a ventilation hood.

Microwave/Hood Cabinet

Before installing a cabinet that supports an over-the-range microwave or range hood, you must drill a hole in the back of the cabinet for the electrical wire from the wall that will connect directly to a hood, or will later be connected to an electrical outlet for the microwave plug. Cut a hole big enough to feed the wire through. You may already have an electrical outlet on the wall at this location if you had a microwave before, so in that case, you'd have to cut a rectangular hole in the back of the cabinet for it. In our case, we had a wire only because there was no microwave installed previously.

1. Measure the location of the wire coming from the wall, and mark off the place on the back of the cabinet where you'll drill a hole for it. Or, measure the location of an existing electrical outlet and mark the dimensions for the rectangle you'll need to cut in the back of the cabinet.

2. Drill the necessary holes, again from the back until almost through, then finish from the front for a cleaner cut. Or, use a jigsaw and cut the rectangular opening.

Now your microwave cabinet is ready to install.

Using a wood bore or hole saw, drill holes in the microwave cabinet as needed for power cords, electrical outlets, and so on.

In the case of a microwave cabinet, it's obviously shorter than the rest of the cabinets, and therefore won't rest on top of your support stringer. You could attach another stringer at the location of the cabinet's base, or cut a temporary vertical support and place it on top of your existing stringer to help hold the microwave cabinet in place. This is what we did. You can do this for any shorter cabinet, such as those mounted above the fridge, or a cabinet or shelf mounted over the sink.

The microwave cabinet needs to be even with the cabinets next to it, so measure from the top of the regular-size cabinet down.

Place a temporary vertical support on top of the horizontal stringer to hold the shorter microwave cabinet. Or you could install another stringer for the microwave cabinet.

Here are the next steps:

1. Mark where you'll place the mounting screws on the inside of the cabinet. Again, it's not necessary to pre-drill these holes, as the microwave cabinet will be supported by the adjacent cabinet, but you can pre-drill them if you wish.

2. Lift the microwave cabinet to the wall, and attach it to the neighboring cabinet with the C-clamps.

3. If you didn't use a horizontal stringer, cut another vertical support and prop up the opposite end of the cabinet. Don't worry about making the cabinet level yet.

4. Be sure the fronts of the cabinets are flush with each other. Attach the two cabinets together, two screws in the front and two in the back, making sure the screws are the right depth.

5. Now adjust the microwave cabinet to be level by moving the free end, then screw it into the wall.

Use a second vertical support if you didn't put up another horizontal stringer. Make sure cabinet is flush with the face of the adjoining cabinet.

Don't attach the cabinets completely until you're sure the new cabinet is level.

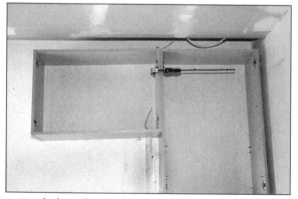

Attach the cabinet to the neighboring cabinet with rubber-tipped C-clamps.

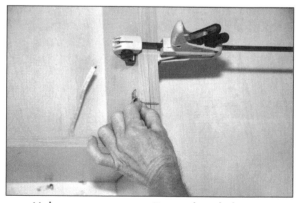

Make sure screws won't pass the whole way through the two cabinets and stick out. Simply hold them up to the cabinets to measure.

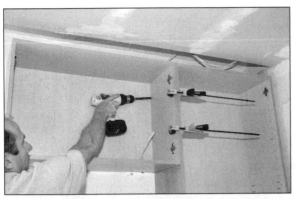

Attach cabinets in four places—two screws in the front and two toward the back of the cabinet.

Hang all cabinet doors before attaching handles or knobs.

Your upper cabinets are installed! Now you can remove the stringers, stand back, and admire the finished work. Wait—there are no doors or drawers. Let's do those next.

Doors, Drawers, and Hardware

Your cabinets will arrive with door hinges and drawer slides already in place. All you have to do is attach the doors and slide in the drawers. The doors will need adjustment, however.

Most likely, your cabinets will come with what are called European hinges. Once a "luxury" item, they're quite common now. These hinges have three adjustment screws: One moves the door from front to back; one moves it up and down; and the third adjusts it from left to right. Once you attach the door, find which screw adjusts in which direction, then make adjustments to center the door in all directions.

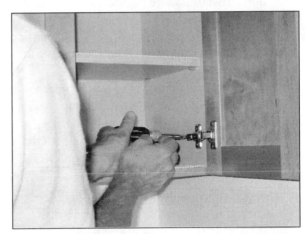

Hinges have adjustment screws to move doors up and down, from front to back, and sideways. Carefully adjust all doors so they're centered, flush, and open and close properly.

Next, install your knobs or handles. If you have knobs requiring one screw, it's an easy job. Pulls or handles with two screws take a bit more care to make sure you line up the two screw holes so that the handles will be level.

Here's the conventional wisdom on locating handles and knobs:

- On small drawers: Place the knob or handle in the center—from top to bottom, and side to side.

- On larger drawers: Place the knob or handle the same distance down as the drawer above it (when drawer sizes are different the top drawer will always be smaller). It looks better, and it requires less bending to open the drawer.

♦ On doors: Generally, if a door has a frame around it, install the handle or knob in the center of the frame opposite the hinge. However, door pull location is truly a matter of preference. Again, bring in the person who will use the kitchen most and ask their preference. Be sure it's visually appealing wherever you locate the handles. It's a good idea to avoid placing knobs or handles too far toward the bottom of the door. Install handles in the same location for all cabinets, base or uppers.

If drawers measure 27" or larger, it's recommended to use two handles, placing them roughly four to six inches in from the side of the drawer on each side. Or, you can put them on according to preference. Bring in the person who will be using the kitchen most and try different locations to see what that person likes the best.

When you pre-drill the holes for hardware, choose a bit size just a little larger than the screw to allow a little play in the handle in case it's off a bit.

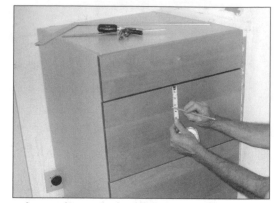

For larger drawers, place handles three inches from the top for ease of use—and it looks better than centering it on the drawer.

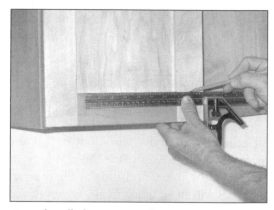

Door handle location is subjective—place them where you want them, and where they'll look the best to you. But avoid placing handles or knobs too close to the bottom of a door.

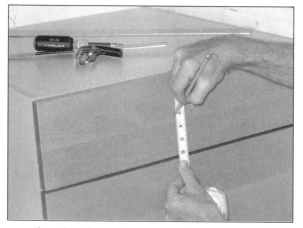

Place handles in the center of small drawers.

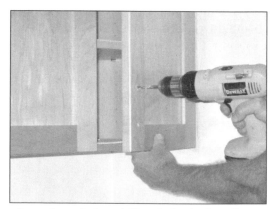

Open doors before drilling holes for handles to avoid drilling into a finished stile or a shelf. You also verify the door swing direction.

 **Don't Get Burned!**

Two important things to remember when installing handles on doors:

Check the door swing direction before marking hole locations! This is another one of those mistakes that even experienced installers can make. It just takes a few seconds to make sure you're putting the hardware in the right place.

Open the door when drilling the holes! This is to make doubly sure you're putting the hardware in the right place, but also to prevent you from drilling through a finished wood stile that might be present inside your cabinet, or even a shelf.

Better safe than sorry!

Let's install the hardware:

1. For hardware with two screw holes, measure the distance between the screw holes.

2. Measure and mark hole locations for hardware on doors and drawers. For two-hole hardware, be sure the two holes are equally located on each side of the centerline of drawers, and equally above and below the center point of the pull on the door.

3. Double check door swing directions before drilling.

4. Pre-drill holes for the hardware.

5. Attach the hardware and tighten the screws. For two-hole pieces, don't tighten the screws fully at first. Place a level atop the handle and make small adjustments if necessary as you tighten the screws.

Carefully measure the distance between screw holes to avoid making mistakes. Hole drilling mistakes can be difficult to fix—and unsightly.

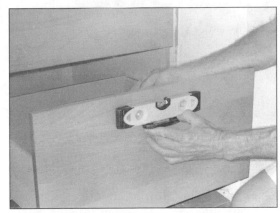

Check that handles are level before fully tightening screws.

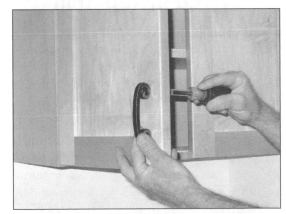

You may wish to use a hand screwdriver when attaching handles so you can make tiny adjustments to the handles and hold them more easily as you tighten the screws.

Door and drawer handles in place.

Now you can stand back and admire your complete cabinets, doors, drawers and all.

Next, you'll install your countertops, or have your countertop contractor do the work.

Countertop Installation

Actually, you'll have your countertops installed whenever they're available. Generally it's a good idea to install upper cabinets before the countertops arrive to avoid possible damage to the countertops. You won't be able to install your sink until the countertops are in, however.

In our kitchen, we chose a granite countertop. This, like all solid-surface material countertops, must be professionally installed, including the under-mount sink that's used with solid-surface countertops. To give you an idea of how a contractor installs these types of countertops, here's how it happened in our kitchen:

1. The countertop arrived in three sections for this kitchen: An L-shaped piece for the sink area, with a hole already cut for the sink; a small section for the right side of the range; and another small section for the separate base cabinet near the bar. There were also four-inch backsplash pieces for each section.

2. The installer set the pieces where they were to be installed, leveling and squaring each piece.

3. The countertop sections were glued in place.

4. Backsplashes were installed and glued in place.

5. The under-mount sink was installed, but not without a fight! The sink base cabinet was a bit too small and a notch had to be cut out. This was done on the left side of the cabinet, beside the dishwasher, so the cut out will never be seen. We knew we would have to do this ahead of time. The sink was mounted and sealed at the joint with the countertop to prevent water from leaking into the cabinet.

And that's it.

The countertop supplier places the L-shaped section of the granite countertop and measures the sink opening.

Preparing to install the backsplash on this lone cabinet.

The under-mount sink was installed by the counter-top supplier when the countertops were installed.

To properly place this sink, the cabinet had to be cut away on the side. This won't be seen once the dish-washer is installed next to the sink.

For laminate countertops, your contractor will go through a similar process, but instead of using adhesive to install the countertop, it will be screwed in place.

If you've purchased stock countertop, the easiest thing to do is have the supplier cut it to the sizes you need. If you have an L-shaped kitchen, have them cut the miter joint to the proper 45-degree angle, and clamp the two pieces together. It doesn't cost much, and is well worth it. All you have to do then is set the countertop on the base cabinets and screw it in. It's also worth it to have them cut the sink opening. If you purchased a sink at the same home improvement store, show them which one it is. If not, measure the sink carefully, then diagram it to provide them the most information.

When your countertops arrive, install them this way:

1. Pre-drill the corner brackets inside the base cabinets.

2. Set the countertop on the base cabinets. Check to see that it's level and square. If not, it's likely it won't be off by much. Use shims to make the countertop level.

3. Attach the countertop with screws. Use a razor knife to cut any shims as close as possible to the cabinet face under the countertop overhang.

Set the countertop on top of the cabinets, care-fully tapping it into place in corners and against the wall.

Attach countertops to the cabinets with screws.

Caulk countertop and backsplash edges along the wall, along cabinets, and between backsplash and countertop, if applicable. Use matching caulks. Wipe excess caulk when finished.

Sink Cutout

If you are cutting out the sink opening yourself, follow this procedure:

1. Your sink will come with instructions for making the cutout. Follow those directions.

2. If there are no instructions, mark the centerline of the sink on the countertop. Lay the sink upside down in the exact location you plan to install it. Make sure it's square, and not too close to the front of the cabinet or the backsplash.

3. Trace the outside perimeter of the sink onto the countertop. Measure ⅜" inside this line and draw a profile to match the trace. This is the actual cutout line.

4. Drill starter holes at each of the four corners large enough to insert a jigsaw blade. You'll use a standard fine-toothed blade.

5. Begin cutting. Round all corners to a ½" radius.

Your cutout is complete.

This countertop has separate backsplash sections. Use caulk to attach backsplash sections to the wall.

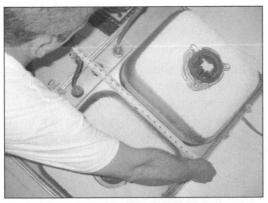

Measure the inside dimensions of the sink for the cutout in the countertop.

Transfer sink dimensions to the countertop. Place masking tape around the perimeter where you'll cut—this helps keep the laminate from cracking or getting scratched by the jigsaw blade.

Drill holes at the four corners before cutting with the jigsaw. This helps to cut rounded corners, and to insert the jigsaw to start the cut. Note: Be careful to not drill into the cabinets! It helps to lift the countertop a bit and insert blocks or some 1" × 4" board to keep the countertop off the cabinet while you drill.

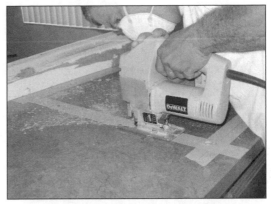

Use a jigsaw to make the cutout, again being careful to not cut into the cabinet underneath.

Tile Countertops

Did you decide to tile your own countertop? This isn't an easy task, and many people wouldn't want to tackle it. If you choose to do so, here's an outline of the procedure:

1. Measure each length of cabinets where you'll be placing a countertop. Measure the depth as well, from the front edge to the wall.

2. Check the square of the walls at corners, and check the levels. If it's not level in any place, you can use shims under the plywood base to level the countertop.

3. Cut ¾" plywood to size for your countertop base, or have it cut for you at your home improvement center.

4. Lay the plywood on top of the cabinets, extending in the front to the face of the cabinet doors, or about an inch, and extending a half-inch over the sides. Use screws to attach the plywood to the cabinet frame at least every two feet.

5. Lay ½" cement backerboard cut to the same size directly on top of the plywood. Backerboard is a rigid board used under tile to provide a smooth, even surface for installation. Verify that the sizes are accurate, then screw the backerboard into the plywood with special backerboard screws.

Don't use any other type of screw—a regular screw head will stick out, but backerboard screw heads are designed for the head to go flush with the surface.

6. Place fiberglass tape over the joints between the sections of backerboard, and apply a thin layer of mastic (an organic, multipurpose tile adhesive that's smoother than mortar) over the joints, making them smooth.

7. When the adhesive dries, clean the backerboard surface clear of dust and debris.

8. Cut out the sink hole (see previous section).

9. Draw perpendicular guide lines on the countertop to assist you in starting to lay the tile straight.

10. Without adhesive, lay tiles out to see how they'll fit. A good place to start is with whole tiles on either side of your range, and at the front edge of the countertops. This will be visually appealing. Determine what tile cuts you'll need to make. Temporarily place bullnose trim to see what cuts need to be made as well. Bullnose is a trim tile with a convex radius on one edge, used to finish the front edge of a countertop.

11. You'll install the bullnose trim first. Place a temporary tack strip, 1″ × 2″, underneath the edge of the countertop to hold the trim in place until the adhesive dries. This is similar to how you used a stringer to support upper cabinets. Spread mastic on the edge of the trim and place on the countertop edge.

12. After the trim is in place, spread adhesive evenly with a trowel on an area of the countertop—you can do a whole countertop section if you wish, but check to see the working time of your mastic so it won't dry out. Set the first tile with a slightly

twisting motion, starting at the front edge of the counter, using tile spacers to leave room for grout.

13. Lay tiles on the entire countertop in this manner. When you reach a place that requires tile cutting, it's often easier to move on to lay all whole tiles first. Then go back and make tile cuts and place those tiles.

14. If you're tiling the backsplash, spread adhesive on the wall. Place tiles on the wall, using spacers.

15. If you planned a tile design anywhere on the wall, such as behind the range or sink, find the centerline of that area and place the design first, then tile the rest of the backsplash.

16. At electrical outlets, mark tiles for cut lines, then cut and place them.

17. With a grout float, spread rubber grout into the joints, holding the float at a 45-degree angle. Make grout as flush as possible with the tile surface.

18. Let grout cure a bit according to the directions for the particular grout you're using, then remove excess grout with a damp sponge to get all the grout lines even. This is usually between 10–15 minutes after first applying grout. Then allow grout to cure fully.

19. Clean tiles with a damp sponge, taking care to not pull out any grout.

20. When the surface is dry, polish tiles with a dry cloth.

21. After the full curing time (typically 48 hours), apply a good quality grout sealer with a sponge, or paint it on with a soft paintbrush.

22. Total time involved for the entire countertop tiling job can be about three days or more.

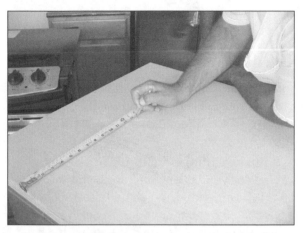

Find the center of your countertop section. In this case, we're tiling an island. Draw perpendicular lines to use as guides.

Spread adhesive evenly on the countertop area using a notched trowel. Cover the sides of the countertop where the bullnose trim will attach.

Dry lay the tile to see where you'll need to make cuts.

Begin placing tiles, using whole tiles at the front edge of the countertop. In the case of this island, we placed whole tiles on the side that will be seen the most from a kitchen counter and from other rooms, and placed cut tiles on the back edge.

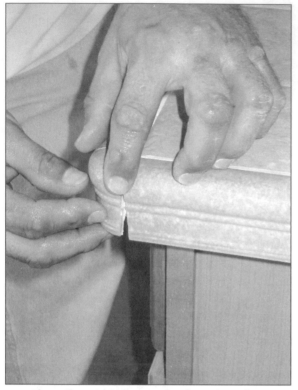

Place tiles and bullnose edge first, then place corner pieces.

Spread grout with a grout float held at a 45-degree angle, forcing grout into joints, then wipe excess and let cure according to directions. Wash tiles with a damp sponge.

Next, we'll install fillers, moldings, and toe-kick.

Fillers, Moldings, and Toekick

You can now finish off the cabinet installation with the finishing touches. Fillers fill the gaps, as we've said, and moldings and toekick polish off the entire job.

It can save time and effort if you measure for and cut your fillers, moldings, and toekick all at the same time. You should use a table saw, if possible, for the best and most accurate cutting of these items. If you do them with a hand saw, you'll need a miter box and a fine-toothed saw. In any case, doing them all at the same time requires you to set up for cutting only once.

Let's start with the fillers.

Fillers

You've already installed fillers, at the corner where two strings of base cabinets met. Let's look at the procedure for placing fillers in the remaining gaps in the cabinet.

1. Measure the gap where you'll place a filler in several places, at least three. In this case, between an upper cabinet and a wall, we measured at the top, the bottom, and in the middle. This helps account for slight variations in size from top to bottom. If the difference from the top to the bottom is ⅛" or less, don't be concerned. You'll fill the remaining space with caulk to match the cabinets or the wall later.

2. Mark the width dimensions on a length of filler (remember, fillers come in the same length as your cabinet heights). Draw a line where you'll cut the filler.

3. Using a table saw or a fine-toothed hand saw, carefully cut the filler along the line.

4. Insert the filler in its place. In our case, there was a tiny gap at the bottom, so we placed a shim in there just to hold the filler in place until attached.

5. Attach the filler to the cabinet in the same way you attached adjoining cabinets, with screws through the front stile, this time in three locations.

6. Fillers placed between a cabinet and a blind corner cabinet are cut and attached the same way.

7. Cut and place all fillers.

8. Run a thin line of caulk where fillers meet the wall, or where a cabinet meets the wall. Wipe the excess with a moist sponge or cloth.

9. Let the caulk set. You can then paint over it if you wish.

Mike's Installer Notebook

It's preferable to use white caulk along a wall, which you can then paint when you paint the walls. Or, if you're hanging wallpaper, white should also look fine. You can also get caulk in a color to match or close to a color you plan to paint the walls. If you need to caulk at a filler between a cabinet and an adjacent blind corner cabinet, however, you should get some caulk to match the cabinets, or some special touch-up paint from your cabinet manufacturer to paint over the caulk after it sets.

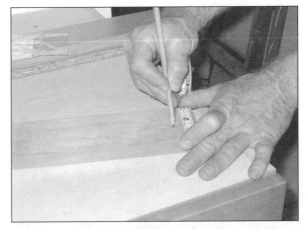

Mark the filler dimensions and draw the line, then cut the filler to fit.

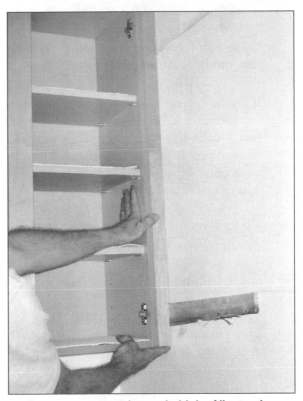

If necessary, use a shim to hold the filler in place while you attach it.

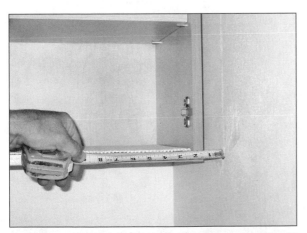

Here, we measure for a filler between an upper cabinet and the wall. Measure at the bottom of the cabinet, in the middle, and at the top.

Moldings

Moldings such as crown molding and under-cabinet light rail are options, and not everyone will be using these items. If you've chosen not to, you can skip the first two parts of this section and go right to toekick.

In this kitchen, we're installing both crown molding and under-cabinet light rail to conceal under-cabinet lighting. You should have your electrician install the lighting before you install the light rail molding.

Let's look at the procedure for under-cabinet light rail:

1. Measure all lengths where you'll install molding.

2. Using a miter saw or fine-toothed hand saw, carefully cut lengths of molding to your dimensions.

3. If you will have strips of molding meeting at a corner, you'll need to make a miter cut. This is a 45-degree angle cut to allow the two pieces to join perpendicularly. Your miter saw can be set to do perfect miter cuts. If you're using a hand saw, you'll need a miter box to make the cuts. This guides the saw at the proper angle.

4. Attach lengths of molding temporarily with C-clamps to make sure they fit properly. If not, make adjustments and recut if necessary.

5. You can install under-cabinet light rail with adhesive caulking if you wish. Glue the lengths of molding in place, then attach the C-clamps again to hold them in place until the glue dries.

6. You can also install light rail with thin finishing nails or micro nails using a micro nail gun. Attach light rail in place with C-clamps, then using a thin drill bit, pre-drill holes for the finishing nails. Don't drill the whole way in—you should leave

something for the finishing nails to bite into. Gently tap finishing nails in place, or use a micro nail gun to nail in place.

7. Fill tiny nail holes with a bit of caulk, or with a wax stick that matches the cabinet finish. If you use caulk, carefully paint over the caulk with finishing paint that matches the cabinets.

> **CAUTION** **Don't Get Burned!**
>
> Moldings are expensive, so it's not uncommon for do-it-yourselfers to be a bit jittery about cutting it. Don't be concerned, though, because you should have ordered extra length to allow you some leeway when cutting. At installation time, if you're unsure of your measurements, it's a good idea to cut an extra 1/16" longer than you think you might need. You can always cut it back, but you can't make it any longer. At least, not without having to insert a tiny piece and making the whole length of molding look bad.
>
> Here's another tip: Before you cut the length of molding you need, always cut 1/4" off the end of the piece to ensure you have a clean cut to work with. Molding isn't always square when it comes out of the factory, and you could end up with a bad cut as a result.

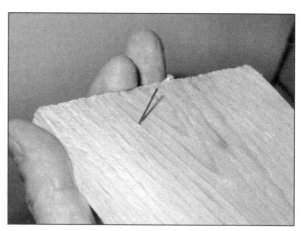

This is a micro nail. As you can see, it lives up to its name!

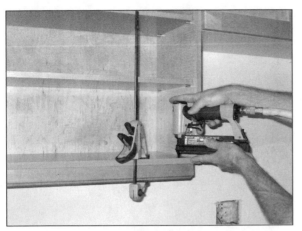

We attached the light rail with micro nails, using a nail gun.

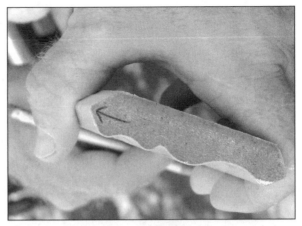

This is our crown molding. The arrow is pointing toward the bottom. You can see the biggest cove, or dip, is at the top.

Installing crown molding is a slightly different process. The light rail mounted straight against the bottom of the cabinet. But crown molding will be turned at a 45-degree angle and pushed against the ceiling and top of the cabinets, covering the line where the cabinets and ceiling meet. The beauty of this is that if there's a slight gap between the ceiling and cabinets, the crown molding will cover it. Because of the molding sitting at an angle, you must take extra care when cutting crown molding, and especially the miter cuts for corners. This is explained further in the procedure outline and photos.

Crown molding can be pretty elaborate, and it can be confusing trying to figure out which side is the top side. Here's how to tell: The biggest cove, or dip, is on top, and there are more grooves on the bottom.

Here's a quick note: If you have European full overlay cabinets, which don't have a frame, you would have to install starter strip between the cabinets and the ceiling so you can attach the crown molding to the starter strip. The nice thing about this is that you can cut the starter strip to the exact height you need to meet the ceiling.

1. Measure all areas where crown molding will be placed.

2. Turn crown molding upside down to cut it. Also, you must lay it at a 45-degree angle on the saw in order to get the proper angle at the corners. Looking at the profile of the molding, you'll see two flat sides—set them flush to the back and bottom of the saw.

3. Check your measurements on each piece before and after making the cuts. Put corners together to make sure they fit well.

4. To install crown molding, push the piece against the ceiling and cabinet front. You can open a cabinet door and use it to help support longer lengths.

5. Your mounting options are the same as for the light rail. Use micro nails, or finishing nails after pre-drilling holes.

Measure all areas for crown molding. Since it's likely to be a long run, you may want someone to help you hold the end of the measuring tape for greater accuracy.

Hold crown molding in place while pre-drilling holes or attaching with micro nails. We used finishing nails.

Lay crown molding at a 45-degree angle on the miter saw to cut it. Note the profile of the molding in this photo—two flat areas rest on the saw. Also, you can tell it's been placed upside down, because the largest cove, which is always on top, is shown here at the bottom.

Cutting Corners

No, I'm not talking about taking shortcuts. I'll explain how to properly cut inside corners and outside corners when cutting crown molding.

- Inside corners: Cut your 45-degree miter cut *toward* the measurement— that is, assume you've measured from the corner you are cutting *toward* the opposite end.

- Outside corners: Cut the 45-degree miter cut *away from* the measurement.

Practice, practice, practice! Before you cut your expensive molding, buy an eight-foot length of cheap trim and practice cutting inside and outside corners, so you don't end up wasting the limited amount of molding that comes with your cabinets.

This is an inside corner, with the angle pointing toward the inside of the corner.

This is an outside corner—the angle points outward from the corner.

A miter saw makes cutting exact angles easy. This is set up to cut an inside corner. To cut an outside corner, the saw would be rotated 90-degrees to the right, or counterclockwise.

Toekick Installation

Toekick is easy to install. Simply measure the length you need off the wall, cut, and install.

Before you do, remember the shims you probably had to install to level and square the cabinets? You need to cut off the excessive length of shims before installing toekick.

Here's the procedure:

1. Cut off shims flush with the cabinet. Use a razor knife to cut as close as possible so shims don't interfere with the toekick.

2. Measure your required toekick lengths. Be sure to measure a length that's flush with the face of the cabinet. Some cabinet faces extend farther than the side of the cabinet, so this is important to remember or the toekick will look bad.

3. Cut toekick to the required lengths.

4. Attach toekick using an adhesive such as Liquid Nails, finishing nails, or micro nails.

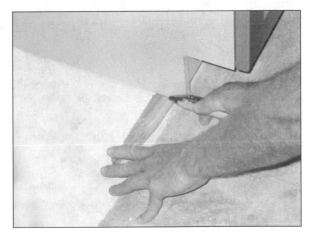

Cut all the shims that were left in place after leveling the cabinets.

Make sure toekick is flush with the sides of the cabinets.

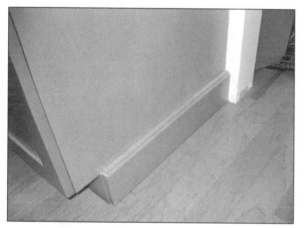

You may also need baseboard, which is like the toe-kick, but used on the sides of cabinets that are visible. The top of baseboard is finished.

After you've installed all moldings, perform touch-up work as follows:

1. Cover nail or micro nail holes with a bit of caulk, or with a wax stick that matches your cabinets.

2. Caulk the seam between crown molding and the ceiling, wiping excess caulk with a damp sponge or cloth.

3. Caulk any gaps that may be present at the corner joints of moldings, wiping excess. For this task, use caulk that matches the cabinets, or let white caulk set, then paint over it carefully with touch-up paint that matches the cabinets. If gaps are small, a wax stick may work well here, too, instead of caulk.

It's okay to use white caulk where crown molding meets the ceiling, if the ceiling is white or you plan to paint the ceiling, and thus the caulk. Otherwise, try to match the ceiling color, or the cabinet color.

Use a damp sponge to wipe excess caulk at the crown molding.

If you don't use colored caulk, you can paint it with touch-up paint to match the cabinets.

You've finished your cabinet installation! Congratulations! Now we'll move to the sink and take care of plumbing issues.

Sink and Plumbing

You're heading into the home stretch of your installation. It's time to install the sink, if you haven't had it done already by a countertop contractor.

Whether your sink is porcelain or stainless steel, single or double bowl, this procedure applies.

1. Install the faucet on your new sink before placing it in the cabinet. If your setup has a separate sprayer, you'll install that, too.
2. Connect the supply lines to the faucet, and the line for the sprayer if you have one.

3. Apply a line of kitchen or bath caulk around the top edge of the sink opening, where the sink will overlap the countertop.
4. With the help of an assistant, lift the sink and carefully place it into the opening in the countertop, making sure the faucet supply lines drop into the sink cabinet.
5. If your sink is stainless steel, it will need to be clamped to the countertop. Install the special sink clips. If it's porcelain, it doesn't require these clips.
6. Remove excess caulk around the sink with your finger, making sure it's spread evenly around the sink.
7. Run a line of caulk around the perimeter where the sink edge meets the countertop. Wipe excess with a damp sponge or cloth, and allow to set.

Our sink is an under-mount with a granite countertop, so the faucet is installed directly into the countertop. For something a little different, we installed the faucet at the corner of the single-bowl sink, which is a great look for this type of sink and countertop.

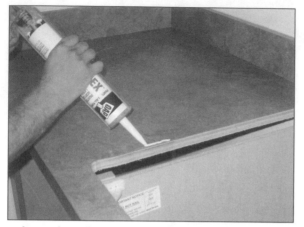

Place a line of caulk around the outside edge of the sink cutout.

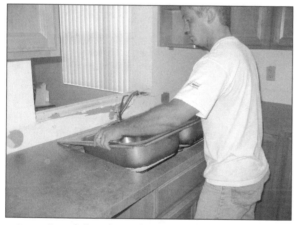

Drop (carefully!) the sink into place. If you have a cast iron sink, you'll probably need help lifting it into the cutout. For stainless sinks, attach the clips that hold the sink to the countertop on the inside of the sink base cabinet.

Now let's finish the plumbing work under the sink.

Sink Drain/Garbage Disposal Flange

You'll install either a sink drain or a garbage disposal flange in the drain hole. Here's the procedure for the sink drain:

1. The sink drain comes in two pieces that connect—one goes into the hole from the sink, the other meets it from the bottom of the sink. Apply plumber's putty around the inside edge of the drain, then press it firmly into the drain hole in the sink. Work around the circle to make sure it's evenly set. Wipe the excess putty away. If you have a garbage disposal, you'll install the flange that comes with it in the same manner just described. This flange is specially made to connect to the garbage disposal underneath.

2. Attach the bottom portion of the sink drain and tighten. Let it set for a bit, then tighten some more.

For the garbage disposal flange, there's a ring underneath that you'll snap into place. Tighten the screws, then let it set a bit and tighten the screws some more.

We'll get to the garbage disposal installation in a bit.

This is a garbage disposal flange. The part sitting on the counter goes under the sink, the parts being held are inserted from the top. A ring snaps the two sections together, and the screws are tightened to make a seal.

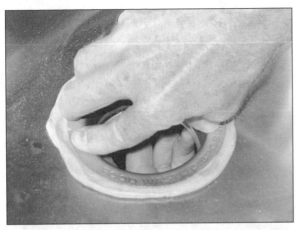

After lining the inside of the flange with plumber's putty, press it into the sink drain hole, snapping the bottom ring in place to attach the two sections.

Apply pressure around the flange to ensure a tight seal.

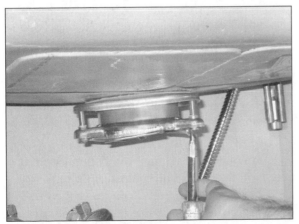

Tighten the screws under the sink, let it set a bit, then tighten some more.

Dishwasher Installation

This is a good time to begin your dishwasher installation, before you do all the other plumbing under the sink. Make sure you have the right length of supply line for the dishwasher if you purchased a new one—the supply lines, the electrical cord, and supply line connector don't come with the appliance. When you purchase your dishwasher, make sure you get these items.

1. Bring the dishwasher into the kitchen and place it near where you'll install it, turning the back toward the opening.

2. Connect the supply line to the dishwasher, located in the bottom front of the unit.

3. Before you slide the dishwasher into its place, feed the supply line, the drain line, and the power cord through the hole(s) you cut in the side of the sink base cabinet. At this time, you should also make sure an icemaker line is properly fed into the cabinet as well.

4. Carefully slide the dishwasher into place, making sure the lines don't kink as you do, and keeping the insulation flat against the unit as you push it into the opening.

5. Make sure the dishwasher is level. Adjust the legs or shim it if necessary.

6. Dishwashers are attached to the countertop with brackets that keep the unit from tipping forward when you're loading it. Screw these brackets into the underside of the countertop.

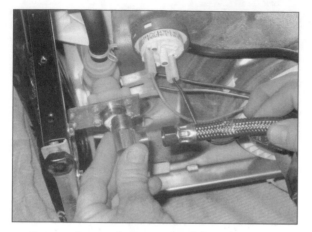

Connect the supply line to the dishwasher with a special fitting. It won't come with a new dishwasher—you have to order one when you buy the dishwasher.

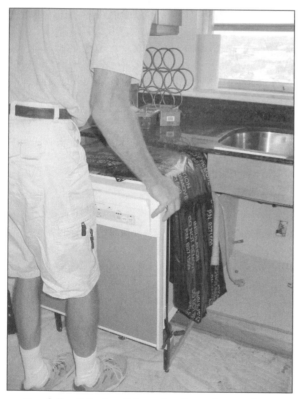

Carefully slide the dishwasher into place, taking care to not kink the lines or fold the insulation. Make sure the dishwasher is level when in place.

Now let's get to the rest of the plumbing.

Under-Sink Plumbing

All that plumbing that you disconnected when you took out your old kitchen now has to be reconnected. A good order in which to do the plumbing is to connect the faucet, supply lines and icemaker lines first—they're in the back and are easier to get to if you haven't done any other plumbing yet. Then connect the pipes, followed by the garbage disposal installation.

> **CAUTION Don't Get Burned!**
>
> If you have a new garbage disposal, and you have a dishwasher, don't forget to remove the "knockout" from the dishwasher drain hole in the garbage disposal. This is a plastic plug that's in place for consumers who don't have dishwashers. Simply insert a screwdriver and tap it until the plug pops out into the inside of the disposal, where you can retrieve it and toss it. This one comes from the files of "The Pros Make Mistakes, Too"—many people have installed a disposal, hooked up the dishwasher drain line, and ended up with a sink base cabinet full of water and/or a massive dishwasher backup because of forgetting to remove this plug.

1. Connect the faucet supply lines, the dishwasher supply line, and an icemaker supply line if you have one.

2. Reconnect the sink drain pipes. If you don't have a garbage disposal, you're done and can move on to the next section.

3. For a garbage disposal, follow the installation instructions that came with the disposal.

4. If you're reinstalling an existing disposal and don't have directions, simply work backward from how you uninstalled it. Hold the disposal up to the bottom of the flange and attach it by turning the flange by hand.

5. Attach the dishwasher drain line to the opening in the garbage disposal. Tighten the clamp that holds it in place.

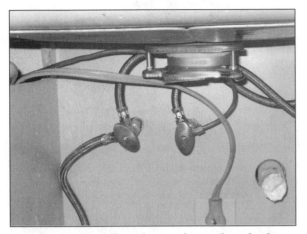

Connect faucet, dishwasher, and icemaker plumbing before reconnecting drain pipes for easier access.

Connect the disposal to the flange. Turn the flange by hand to make the seal.

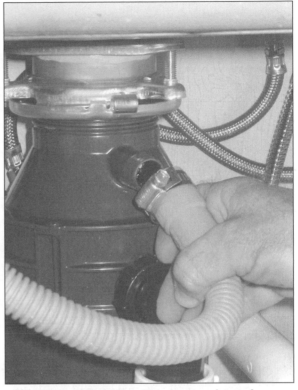

Attach the dishwasher drain hose to the garbage disposal, tightening the clamp. Don't forget to remove the knockout first!

Next, we'll install the over-the-range microwave. If you have a ventilation hood, read through this section, too.

Install Microwave/Hood

Installation procedure for a microwave or ventilation hood is pretty much the same. A new microwave will come with a mounting bracket that you'll have to install on the wall right under the cabinet. If you're reusing an existing microwave, you should use the mounting bracket that came with it. Vent hoods don't mount on a wall bracket—they're simply mounted to the bottom of the cabinet.

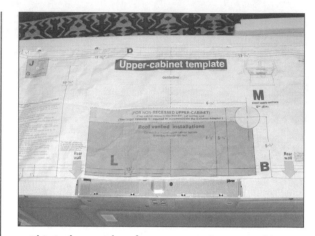

This is the template for our new microwave. Note the large rectangle in the foreground—this is the cutout for outside venting systems.

You'll need to drill holes in the bottom of the cabinet for the mounting screws, and to run the microwave's electrical plug or the vent hood's power wire through the bottom. (Hoods are hardwired and generally don't have plugs.) If you're venting to the outside for either microwave or hood, you'll also need to cut a hole for the duct opening.

Use the paper template supplied with a new microwave or hood to mark the location of mounting screws, power cord or wire, and duct opening if applicable, on the bottom of the cabinet. If you're reinstalling an existing microwave or hood, you can either carefully measure the locations of these items, or use paper to make a template yourself.

To make a template: Place a sufficiently large sheet of paper on top of the microwave or hood, marking "front" and "back" on the paper. Mark the mounting hole and power cord locations, and the duct opening if you need it. Then use the template in the installation steps that follow.

New microwaves and hoods will include installation instructions. Read them thoroughly and follow them, as they'll address any installation issues specific to the model of microwave or hood you've purchased. If you still have the manual for an existing microwave or hood, it will have installation instructions. However, we'll outline the basic installation steps here:

1. Attach the mounting bracket to the wall under the cabinet (microwave only). Insert screws into the studs, since the bracket will be holding a lot of weight.

2. Place the template against the bottom of the microwave cabinet, making sure the front of the template is along the front of the cabinet. With a pencil, mark the hole and duct locations through the template onto the bottom of the cabinet.

3. For a microwave, measure the width of the plug so you can cut a hole large enough to feed it through the bottom of the cabinet. For a vent, cut a hole large enough to feed the power wire or wires through.

4. Drill the holes through the bottom of the cabinet. Drill part of the way through from either the top or the bottom, and finish from the other side for a cleaner cut. If you're venting to the outside, cut the duct opening. For a hood, the holes you drill will be much smaller, for screws rather than bolts. Vent hoods are lighter and generally don't use large bolts with washers.

5. Place washers on the mounting bolts for a microwave. Have bolts and screws ready to use.

6. For microwave: Lift the microwave up toward the cabinet, and feed the power cord through the hole in the bottom of the cabinet. Tilt it forward, and hook the tabs on the back of the microwave onto the mounting bracket. When it's hooked, tilt the microwave back and lift up against the bottom of the cabinet.

7. Insert mounting bolts through the bottom of the cabinet and far enough to support the microwave so you can let go of it. Yes, the microwave's heavy, and you'll probably have to work quickly if you don't have a helper. Then fully set the bolts.

8. For a hood: Lift the hood up toward the cabinet, and feed the power wires through the opening into the cabinet. Lift the hood against the bottom of the cabinet.

9. Insert screws through the bottom of the cabinet into the hood and tighten.

Attach the mounting bracket to the wall, making sure it's flush against the bottom of the cabinet.

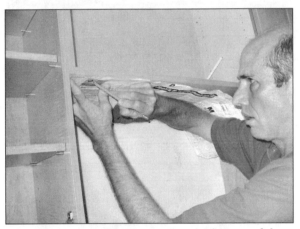

Hold the paper template against the bottom of the cabinet and mark where to drill mounting holes, and a hole for wires or electrical cord.

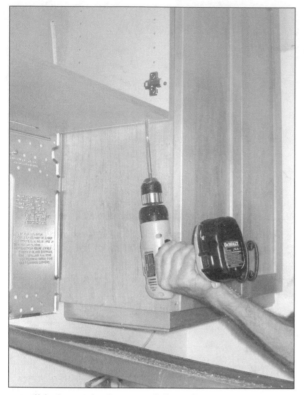

Drill holes in the bottom of the cabinet, starting on one side and finishing on the other for a cleaner cut.

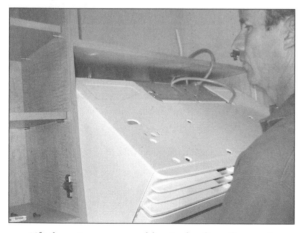

Lift the microwave and begin feeding the cord through the hole. Tilt the microwave forward and hook the back onto the mounting bracket.

Insert mounting bolts. You'll have to work quickly if you don't have an assistant helping you hold up the microwave.

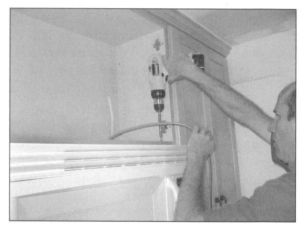

Drive bolts to attach the microwave to the cabinet completely.

Voila! The microwave is in place, and looks terrific!

This is a good time to have your electrician come in to finish up the electrical work, such as connecting the hood's power wires, and finish installing an electrical outlet for the microwave if you don't already have one there.

Install Remaining Appliances

You can now put your range and refrigerator in place. If you have a gas range, call your utility company to hook it up for you.

To install a cooktop, you'll need to cut an opening in your countertop in the same manner that you did the sink opening. Your solid-surface countertops would already have this opening cut. Follow the instructions that came with your cooktop for completing the installation. Basically, you drop it in and plug it in, or have your gas utility company connect a gas cooktop.

Plug in the range and slide it into place.

CAUTION **Don't Get Burned!**

Even if you disconnected a gas appliance, you should always have your utility company install gas appliances. They'll make sure it's working properly. Gas is too dangerous to mess with on your own—let the pros do it.

You only have the ceilings, walls, and floors to go. You're almost finished with your new kitchen!

Ceilings

If you planned to paint your ceiling, or apply ceiling tiles, you should do this now. Also, install any new lighting fixtures, or have your electrician do the work.

Our ceiling is going to be painted. But first, we installed a new track lighting fixture.

Now let's get to the floors.

Floor Installations

In this section, we'll outline the basic procedure for installing the three most popular types of flooring: Tile, vinyl, and wood. Again we'll note that you can install flooring before or after you install cabinets—the choice is up to you. Just remember that if you install flooring first, you must account for it in your cabinet heights.

Mike's Installer Notebook

Any condo residents out there? You may need to install a layer of cork under tile or wood flooring to help cut down on noise. Cork comes in rolls, like carpeting. Installation is pretty simple. Roll out the cork and cut it to fit the room. Roll it back, trowel on the adhesive recommended by your supplier, then roll the cork back over the adhesive and fit it to the walls. It's a good idea to run a roller over it to make it lie flat—the roller is being used on a wood floor in this photo). Then, install tile or wood on top of the cork.

After rolling out the cork and cutting it to fit the room, roll it back, then spread adhesive on the sub-floor with a trowel.

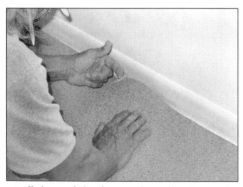

Roll the cork back over the adhesive and smooth, preferably with a roller.

Ceramic Tile Flooring

Laying tile flooring isn't really difficult, but it is labor-intensive. If you've chosen to lay your own tile, it's a good idea to plan your layout carefully to save time and frustration.

Here are some special tools and materials you'll need to lay tile floor:

◆ Tiles
◆ Adhesive—Use the type recommended by your tile supplier for the type of tile you're using.
◆ Grout—Typically a powder that you mix with water or other additive. Again, use what your tile supplier recommends for the type of tile you've chosen.
◆ Grout sealer—It's a good idea to seal the grout to keep it cleaner.
◆ Wet saw, tile cutter, and/or circular saw with masonry blade
◆ Straightedge
◆ Grout float—Used to apply grout
◆ Notched trowel—Used to apply adhesive
◆ Grout sponge—For wiping grout
◆ Chalk line
◆ Tile spacers

Inventory your tiles to make sure you have what you ordered, and that you have enough. Make sure tiles are free of dust before you begin to install them.

Depending on your house's construction, you may or may not choose to install a plywood sub-floor to lay tiles on top of. If your floor is a concrete slab, you can easily lay tiles directly on the concrete. For wood sub-floors, you may wish to lay plywood. Simply nail ¼" plywood sheets to the floor, cutting to size as needed. Then lay tiles on top of it.

Here's the procedure:

1. Find the center of the room. This is important—you want to lay tiles from the center to the edges to get a uniform look. Otherwise, you could end up with large tiles on one side and a sliver of tile on the opposite wall, which wouldn't look good. Mark the center of opposite walls and snap a chalk line between them. Mark the center of the remaining two opposite walls and snap a chalk line. Where these two lines intersect is the center of the room.

2. Do a trial run. Literally, a dry run before you mix any adhesive. Lay out some rows of tiles in each of the four sections of the room, taking the rows to the walls so you can see how it looks, and know how much cutting you may or may not have to do. Use the spacers to account for the grout lines. If something looks funny, or if you end up with tiles at one wall that would require too thin a cut to be practical, you can "fudge" your layout a bit, an inch or so either way, to remedy the problem and try to get the best visual result before actually putting tile into adhesive.

3. Start it straight. If you wish, you can lay a straight board in the center of the room along the line where you want to start laying the tiles, to help you lay the first tiles in a straight line. Or, you can follow the chalk line if you want.

4. Work in small areas. Mix enough adhesive to work in small areas at a time. If you don't, the adhesive might begin to harden before you finish. Spread the mortar over a small area using the notched trowel.

5. Set the first tile. Twist the tile into the mortar to set it firmly into the adhesive. Make sure it's straight, then place the spacers around it.

6. Set the rest of the tiles. Set the next tile, check that it's straight, then set another. Keep setting tiles, checking now and then to make sure your lines and rows are straight, and that tiles are level.

7. Cut tiles. When you come to a wall where you'll need to cut tiles, you may want to stop there and keep working elsewhere in the room until you reach a point where you've laid all the full tiles you can. Now you can turn your attention to cutting tiles and finishing off the job.

8. Remove the spacers. When the mortar begins to set, take out the spacers. Wipe excess adhesive that may have oozed onto tiles.

9. Let the adhesive set fully. Follow the instructions for the adhesive you've used and let it fully set for the amount of time specified. This generally means 24 hours at least.

10. Grout the spaces. Mix the grout according to directions. Using the grout float, scoop out enough to cover a small area, then, holding the float at a 45-degree angle, force the grout into the joints as far as possible, scraping off excess grout with the float as you go.

11. Sponge off excess. Let the grout cure a bit according to directions, generally about 20 minutes. Then use a damp sponge to wipe off excess grout and clean off the tiles, being careful not to take grout out of the joints.

12. Polish it off. After grout has fully cured according to directions, polish the tiles off with a clean, soft cloth.

A ½" notched trowel is a good idea, because when you come to a high spot in your floor, you can thin out the mortar more easily to make sure the floor is level.

Cutting Tile

Don't think you're a tile cutter? Follow these steps. You might buy some inexpensive tiles to practice on before getting down to the real job.

For a snap cutter:

1. Measure and mark your file. Draw your cutting line on the tile with a marker. Lay the tile on the tile cutter, making sure the centerline of the cutter lines up with the cutting line on the tile. Make sure the tile is square in the cutter so the cut line is straight.

2. Score the glaze. Draw the cutting wheel firmly across the tile once to cut through the glaze. Use protective eyewear and a dust mask when cutting.

3. Snap the tile. Snap cutters are all different and have different ways to snap the tile at the cut line. Basically they all work on the same principle: You apply pressure to the score line to cause the tile to snap at the cut.

For a tile saw:

1. Measure your tile and mark your cutting line.

2. Cut the tile in the same manner you would cut a wooden board on a table saw, cutting through it with firm, even pressure. Be sure to use protective eyewear and a dust mask when cutting!

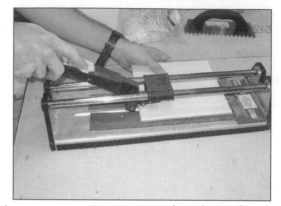

Snap cutters are inexpensive—about $20. When the blades are too dull to cut, simply toss it and buy another one. They're perfect for the do-it-yourselfer who might install tile once in many years.

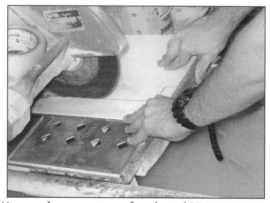

You can buy a wet saw for about $85, or rent one. Another option: mark tiles that require difficult cuts and take them to your local home improvement store to be cut.

Snap chalk lines for guides to laying tiles straight. Lay tiles out dry first to see how they'll run against the walls. Use tile spacers to account for grout lines.

Spread adhesive using a notched trowel. Spread in one direction only, and don't swirl the adhesive.

Allow adhesive to set for at least six hours, preferably overnight before grouting. Using a grout float held at a 45-degree angle, force grout into spaces between tiles. Level grout as closely as possible with the tile surface.

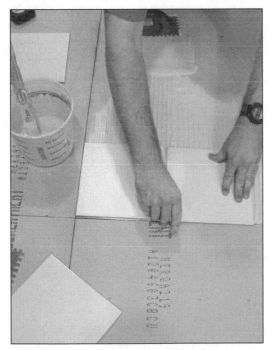

Lay tiles, pressing firmly into the adhesive. Use spacers to leave even grout lines.

After grout cures a bit (about 20 minutes), use a damp sponge or cloth to wipe off excess, being careful to not pull grout from spaces.

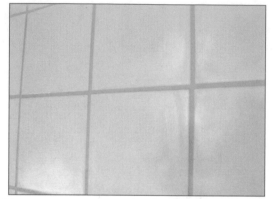

Allow grout to cure completely according to product directions. Wipe tiles with a damp sponge or cloth, then buff with a dry cloth.

Vinyl Tiles

Vinyl is available in sheets or tiles, though today, the popularity of vinyl tiles has increased greatly. They're much easier to install than sheet vinyl, and offer a greater flexibility for designing your own patterns using several colors or patterns. We'll describe how to install vinyl tiles.

Essentially, it's the same procedure just outlined for ceramic tile. But you don't need spacers, nor the mess of grout or even adhesive, since vinyl tiles are typically self-adhesive. Also, you don't need special equipment to cut vinyl tiles—a sharp razor knife and a good straight edge will do.

1. Make sure the surface you plan to adhere the vinyl tiles to is clean and free of dust and debris.

2. Follow steps 1–7 of the previous section, ceramic tile flooring, to set vinyl tiles. Make sure tiles are set right up against each other to prevent unsightly cracks between tiles that can also lead to loosening of tiles.

Wood Floor

Today's wood and wood laminate flooring is easier to install than ever. It used to be a long, tedious task, laying one plank after another and nailing them into the sub-floor. Now, wood is

almost as easy to lay as vinyl tile, as some brands are actually self-adhesive.

The most commonly used wood and wood laminate products are available in "tiles" that are at least three planks of wood wide, and fit together with a tongue-and-groove system. Those that aren't self-adhesive are installed like ceramic tile, applying adhesive to the floor with a trowel.

This wood "tile" uses a tongue-and-groove system for installation, along with adhesive spread with a trowel.

We installed wood floor in our kitchen. Here's how it's done:

1. Make sure the floor surface is clean of dust and debris. If you're using a cork underlay, install that first as described at the beginning of this section (we did this).

2. It's your choice whether to remove baseboards, install floor, then reinstall baseboards, or cut the wood flooring to fit up against the baseboards.

3. Lay some flooring as a dry run to see how it fits, and to determine your arrangement for visual appeal.

4. As with tile, you'll want to start somewhere near the middle of the room and work toward the wall. Smaller, individual planks are available for working a good fit to the wall.

5. Apply adhesive according to the directions for the particular product your floor supplier recommended.

6. Set the first pieces of flooring, making sure they're in a straight line. Insert the tongue from one wood tile into the groove of the next, then tap together firmly with your hand. Cut pieces as necessary to fit to the walls.

You can rent a roller like this from your home improvement store or other wood floor supplier. Stand on the bar and apply pressure as you slowly roll across the floor, pressing the wood firmly into the adhesive. Note the special tape holding the wood planks and tiles together.

Walls

The final step: Finishing your walls. Whether you're painting, hanging wallpaper, or applying some wood paneling such as beadboard, take special care to not damage your new cabinets and floor.

We won't tell you how to paint—that's pretty basic. But we will describe the basics of hanging wallpaper.

Hanging wallpaper can seem like a scary proposition, but it's easier than ever. Many wallpaper products are available that are pre-pasted, eliminating the mess that can come with using a separate paste. But even the ones that aren't don't pose as much of an installation nightmare as they used to. For kitchens, paper-backed wallpaper is recommended for its durability.

Use a large table in another room to cut wallpaper. It's a good idea to build one with plywood and sawhorses, or place a large sheet of plywood on top of a table. This way you don't have to be concerned about cutting on a good table.

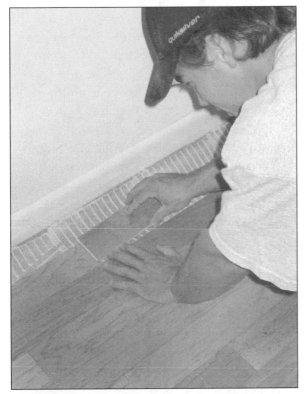

Wood floor today fits together easily with a tongue-and-groove system. In this photo, we're placing individual planks working up to the wall.

7. After you've laid a few wood tiles side by side, run special tape across them to hold the planks together. This tape is available from your wood floor supplier.

8. When you've completed a section, slowly walk a roller over the wood to press it firmly into the adhesive.

9. Let the adhesive cure according to directions before removing the special tape.

We'll cover the basics of wallpapering here. Before you start:

1. Make sure the walls are clean and free of nails, nail holes, and debris.

2. It's a good idea to use a primer paint before hanging the wallpaper.

3. Smooth any rough spots with sand paper, as they'll be visible through wallpaper.

4. Spread a drop cloth on the floor, over countertops, and anything else you need to protect from adhesive.

5. Remove light switch and outlet plates.

Here are some special materials you'll need:

◆ Sharp utility knife with extra blades

◆ Wallpaper tray

◆ Wallpaper brush

◆ Seam roller

◆ Broad knife (a smoothing tool)

1. Apply sizing to the walls. This is a product that makes walls easier for the paper to adhere to. Simply paint it on like paint.

2. If you have a patterned wallpaper, decide how you want the pattern to meet the ceiling.

3. Cut your first piece of wallpaper, about 6" longer than the wall. You'll want to overlap the ceiling and baseboard area a bit. (Note that you can remove baseboards if you wish and run the paper behind them, then reinstall the baseboards.)

4. For pre-pasted wallpapers, roll the sheet with the pasted side out. Soak it in a wallpaper water tray for the length of time specified for the product, usually about 15 to 20 seconds.

5. Take the roll out of the tray after you're sure the water has covered it all. Lay it paste-side up on the table, then fold both ends toward the middle. This is called booking, and it makes it easier to carry the sheet. To reduce mess, place the sheet in a plastic bag and take it into the kitchen.

6. Starting in a corner, if you have one to wallpaper, mark the wall at a width ¼" less than the paper width. Draw a level line down the wall from this point.

7. Open the sheet of paper and, starting at the top, press the paper to the edge of the ceiling, flush with your straight line. Make sure your pattern is where you want it to be. Try not to move the paper too much so you don't stretch it or cause wrinkles.

8. Use a wallpaper brush or a broad knife to smooth the paper, working from the ceiling down, using vertical sweeps.

9. Trim wallpaper at the ceiling and at the floorboards. Use a straightedge to cut against, cutting along the bottom of it.

10. Hang the next piece of wallpaper, again starting at the ceiling, lining up seams as closely as possible and matching any patterns.

11. After paper has been up for at least 20 minutes, press the seams with a seam roller, being careful not to push so hard that adhesive oozes from the seams. Roll upward with the roller, then wipe off any adhesive with a damp sponge or cloth.

12. At corners, paper should overlap by about ¼". Hang the next piece to overlap this one and fit it into the corner. Do this for both inside and outside corners.

13. Around doors and windows, cabinets, and backsplashes, fit paper as close to the casing, cabinet, or backsplash as possible, overlapping a bit, then trim to fit. Take extra care when cutting around cabinets and laminate backsplash!

14. At outlets and light switches, hang paper right over them, marking them to be cut later. Cut an X over the switch or outlet (turn the power off first!), then pull back the edges and trim, leaving enough paper

on the wall so the switch and outlet plates cover the edges.

Designer's Notebook

If you're so inclined, you can put wallpaper on light switch and electrical outlet plates. But if you do so, try to match the pattern where the switch is located. By doing this, the switch or outlet practically disappears into the wall, an interesting look.

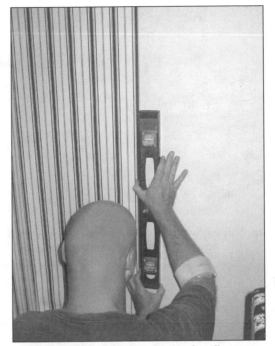

Use a level when placing sheets of wallpaper to make sure they're straight.

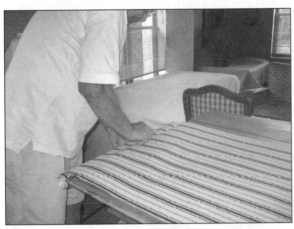

Use a large table to roll out wallpaper and cut it to size. A piece of plywood on two sawhorses will do.

This wallpaper required paste, which is rolled on with a paint roller. For pre-pasted, dip the roll in water for 15 seconds, then unroll and "book" according to directions.

Smooth wallpaper to get wrinkles and air bubbles out. Wallpaper should overlap crown molding and baseboard so you can cut it exactly to fit.

Carefully cut wallpaper at baseboards and crown moldings, cutting against a straight edge.

Can you see this covered outlet? Barely. It blends into the wallpaper pattern perfectly.

Ready to see the finished kitchen? It's an amazing transformation!

New Kitchen at Last!

It's time to unveil the new kitchen. Let's see how it progressed from a 1960s ugly duckling to the sleek, new kitchen we just showed you how to create.

Smooth seams with a seam roller. With a damp sponge or cloth, wipe away any paste that may seep through the seams.

Drab, monotone, lacking function ...

... to bold, colorful, and functional.

A better layout, with well-defined work centers.

A design "no-no" here and there, like the stove against a wall.

This shot was taken in front of two walls that weren't being used at all.

The same view, through the new cutout and over a bar, making use of the previously wasted space.

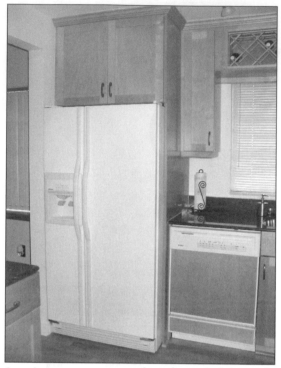

Imagine—easy access to those formerly little-used cabinets above the fridge!

The once-dead upper corner is now fully functional with this easy-reach cabinet.

This base cabinet has roll-out shelves and acts as a short pantry. It's located in a corner of the kitchen that previously had nothing in it and was completely wasted space.

A little high-style comes from glass doors.

This kitchen can be considered fairly typical. Even with the limited space, you can see that careful planning, good design and layout, educated kitchen element choices, and a do-it-yourself spirit can give a fantastic makeover to even the most outdated kitchens, and turn them into beautiful, functional, dream kitchens.

The kitchen you've always wanted is not beyond your reach. You now have the tools and knowledge you need to make sensible design decisions and intelligent purchases, as well as the step-by-step procedures to install all elements of a kitchen. Just add elbow grease, and you're good to go. Happy kitchen remodeling, and good luck!

The Least You Need to Know

- Don't begin installing your new kitchen elements until you have all the tools and safety equipment you'll need to do the job.

- Base cabinets must be level so the countertops are level. If the floor isn't level, you'll need to adjust the cabinets by placing shims under them. If the floor is off by $\frac{1}{16}$" or less across a six-foot span, you generally won't need to shim the cabinets.

- Inventory your cabinets as soon as they are delivered to make sure you've received what you ordered. Take immediate steps to correct any mistakes, as wrong items can delay your remodeling project.

- Re-check your measurements before starting. Minor adjustments can still be made in some instances, particularly floor to ceiling dimensions because you can adjust backsplash height if necessary.

- Order countertops as soon as you finish installing the base cabinets, since it takes at least a week to ten days for delivery.

- Install upper cabinets, making sure that any cabinets with "right" sides and "left" sides are placed properly before permanently mounting them.

- Install countertops, being careful not to scratch the surfaces. Use caulk that matches the countertop, the wall, or the cabinets.

- Add moldings and fillers. Take care when cutting fillers and moldings, since you have a limited amount of these items that match your cabinets.

- Perform plumbing tasks and install sink, dishwasher, and garbage disposal. Don't forget to remove the "knockout" from the dishwasher drain hole in the disposal *if* you have a dishwasher.

- Install appliances. If you have a gas range or cooktop, call your gas utility company to hook it up for you.

- Install lighting fixtures, or have your electrician install them for you if you're uncertain about working with electricity.

- Finish it up with floors, ceiling, and walls. Don't be tempted to walk on a tile floor too soon—you could shift the tiles and ruin the entire layout.

Glossary

adaptive design   Refers to design features adapted for handicapped people with special needs.

aesthetics   The artistic or visual aspects of a design.

appliance garage   An area under an upper cabinet enclosed with a tambour or lift-up door to house small appliances or other countertop items.

backsplash   The vertical wall space between the upper cabinets and the countertop.

built-in appliances   Appliances that are built into the cabinets.

bulkhead   Framework extending from the wall under the ceiling, an enclosure often carrying ductwork.

casing   Molding applied around the opening of a door or window.

convection oven   Method of cooking utilizing a fan to circulate air around the food, cooking it more quickly and evenly than conventional radiant cooking.

cooktop   Cooking surface set into a countertop without an oven below.

crown molding   Decorative material, usually matching the cabinets, that is installed along the top of cabinets, or at ceiling where cabinets meet it.

elevation   The drawing of a wall in two dimensions (height and width) as you would see it by standing in front of it.

ergonomic   The science of designing and arranging objects for the safest, easiest, and most efficient use for the human body.

Euro-style cabinets   Also called frameless, the cabinets are open-faced with no frames. There's only a thin line around doors and drawers when closed.

face frame cabinets   Cabinets that have a frame on the face, like a picture frame, which can be seen around the closed door or drawer.

faux painting   A method of painting that simulates other surfaces, such as stone, plaster, old or distressed surfaces, and so on.

filler   Vertical strip of material that matches the cabinets, used to fill in gaps and allow clearances between walls and cabinets or between two cabinets.

floating material   Used to level a floor if tile adhesive can't be removed from the sub-floor.

free-standing range   Range that's not integrated into the cabinets. Has finished sides and can stand alone, or fit in a space between two separate base cabinets.

half lazy Susan   A cabinet accessory, it's a half turntable used inside blind corner cabinets for easier access to cabinet contents.

halogen   Type of light bulb that uses thermal radiation from a white-hot tungsten filament to produce light.

Hoosier hutch   Freestanding piece of furniture that works well in kitchens.

induction cooking   Cooking technology in which cookware is heated using magnetic energy, requiring a ceramic cooktop with induction energy coils directly beneath the surface, and cookware made of a magnetic-based material. The cookware gets hot, but not the cooktop. When the pan is removed from the cooking element, it immediately begins to cool. Most steel and cast-iron cookware works with induction cooking, but aluminum, copper, and some stainless steel doesn't because they're not magnetic.

island   Freestanding cabinet or group of cabinets in the center of the kitchen. It can also include a seating area, a sink, or a cooktop.

laminate   Layers of wood, plastic or other material bonded together by heat and pressure. Used on cabinets and countertops.

lazy Susan   A round turntable used in corner cabinets for easy access to cabinet contents.

MDF   Medium-density fiber material used to make cabinets.

mullions   Large vertical members between a double-width window. However, in the kitchen design business, this term is commonly used to describe what is really a muntin.

muntins   Small members that divide the panes of glass in a window.

nomenclature   Codes that designate and describe cabinets. For example, W3030-12 means a Wall cabinet, 30" wide by 30" high by 12" deep.

peninsula   A section of cabinets exposed on three sides and attached to the main kitchen cabinets on one side only. Called a peninsula referring to geographical peninsulas, like the state of Florida. Peninsulas frequently include an extended countertop eating or serving area.

peninsula bar   A seating area at a peninsula, which can be bar height (42 inches) or counter height (36 inches).

perspective   In kitchen layout drawing, the point of view of the drawing.

plan view   A drawing or sketch of the kitchen or any room as if looking down upon the room.

pull-out trash cabinet   Cabinet that holds a trash container on pull-out drawer slides.

radiant cooking   Traditional thermal cooking.

range   Single appliance housing a cooking surface with oven below. (*See* freestanding range and slide-in range.)

reveal   An exposed area between the edge of trim and a cabinet, the edge of a cabinet door to the end of the cabinet, or between a cabinet and a window or door opening.

roll-out   Drawer in a cabinet that rolls out for easy access to contents.

scale   Sizing of design drawings to correspond to real life. Kitchen professionals' standard scale is ½" = 1 foot.

shims   Small strips of material, often wood, used for leveling cabinets with floors and walls.

slide-in range   Range that is placed between two cabinets and is integrated with the countertop. The sides are unfinished, and controls are located on the front panel of the unit so that the countertop can extend along the back of the appliance. There's no gap between the unit and the cabinets.

soffit   The underside of an architectural projection from a wall, such as a bulkhead.

starter strip   Strip of material installed between the ceiling and a cabinet that's to be mounted flush against the ceiling.

stile   A vertical framing member used in the front frame of a cabinet.

stock cabinets   Kitchen cabinets that aren't custom-made, but are regularly mass-produced.

toekick   The kick rail at the bottom of a base cabinet, recessed behind the front frame generally by about three inches.

trim kit   Kit used to mount appliances in a cabinet or on the wall, such as a microwave; or, a kit to mount cabinet panels to the front of appliances.

under-cabinet light rail   Molding that mounts under cabinets to finish them; named so because it also conceals under-cabinet lighting fixtures.

work centers   Areas of the kitchen where elements of a particular kitchen task are grouped for efficiency, such as cleanup center, cooking center, food preparation center, and so on.

work triangle   The path among the three major work areas of a kitchen: the cooking center, the cleanup center, and the food prep center.

Kitchen Design and Installation Resources

Professional Organizations

National Kitchen & Bath Association
687 Willow Grove Street
Hackettstown, NJ 07840
1-800-843-6522
Fax: 908-852-1695
www.nkba.org

General information for the consumer regarding standards for kitchen design, products, and installation.

Magazines Online

Kitchen and Home Design and Decorating

Better Homes and Gardens (www.bhg.com)
Country Sampler (www.sampler.com)

Country Sampler Decorating Ideas (www.sampler.com/decideas)

Home and Design (www.homeanddesign.com)

Kitchen and Bath Design News (www.kbdn.net)

Living Home Online (www.livinghome.com)

Old House Journal Online (www.oldhousejournal.com)

Urban Designer Kitchens (www.urbandesignerkitchens.com)

Home Improvement

The Family Handyman (www.familyhandyman.com)

Remodeling Online (www.remodeling.hw.net)

Design and How-To Websites

DIY: The Do It Yourself Network (www.diynet.com)

DIYOnline.com (www.diyonline.com)

DoItYourself.com (www.doityourself.com)

FlooringGuide.com (www.flooringguide.com)

HandymanUSA.com (www.handymanusa.com)

Home & Garden Television (HGTV) (www.hgtv.com)

HomeDepot.com (www.homedepot.com)

Homestore.com (www.homestore.com/ homegarden/homeimprovement)

Improvenet.com (www.improvenet.com)

Kitchens.com (www.kitchens.com)

Superkitchens.com (www.superkitchens.com)

This Old House Online (www.thisoldhouse.com)

Product Resources

Appliances

Amana Appliances
2800 220th Trail
Amana, IA 52204
1-800-843-0304
fax: 319-622-8345
www.amana.com

Frigidaire Home Products
250 Bobby Jones Expressway
Martinez, GA 30907
706-651-7122
fax: 706-651-7091
www.frigidaire.com

GE Appliances
Appliance Park
Louisville, KY 40225
502-452-4311, 1-800-626-2000
www.geappliances.com

Kenmore Appliances
Sears
3333 Beverly Road
Hoffman Estates, IL 60179
1-800-549-4505
www.Kenmore.com

KitchenAid
2000 M-63 N., MD 4302
Benton Harbor, MI 49022
616-923-2712
fax: 616-923-3214
www.kitchenaid.com/

In-Sink-Erator
A Division of Emerson
4700 21st Street
Racine, WI 53406-5093
1-800-558-5700
www.insinkerator.com

Maytag Appliances
403 W. 4th St. N.
Newton, IA 50208
641-787-7000
www.maytag.com

Sharp Electronics Corp.
Sharp Plaza
Mahwah, NJ 07430
201-529-8200, 1-800-be-sharp
fax: 201-529-8919
www.sharp-usa.com

Vent-A-Hood Co.
P.O. Box 830426
Richardson, TX 75083-0426
972-235-5201
fax: 972-235-5238
www.ventahood.com

Whirlpool Corp.
2000 M-63 North
Benton Harbor, MI 49022
616-923-5000, 1-800-253-3977
fax: 616-923-3872
www.whirlpool.com

Cabinet Manufacturers

Bremtown Kitchens
1456 State Rd. 331 N
Bremen, IN 46506
574-546-2781
fax: 574-546-2453
www.bremtown.com

Canac Kitchens
360 John Street
Thornhill, ON L3T 3M9
905-881-2153, 1-800-226-2248
fax: 905-881-9725
www.canackitchens.com

Holiday Kitchens
A Division of Mastercraft Industries, Inc.
120 West Allen Street
Rice Lake, WI 54868
www.holidaykitchens.com

KraftMaid Cabinetry
15535 S. State Ave.
Middlefield, OH 44062
610-589-5333
www.kraftmaid.com

CE Cabinets
A Divison of Maax, Inc.
5555 Des Rossignols Blvd.
Laval, Quebec H7L 5S7
Canada
450-625-4244
www.cecabinets.com

Merillat Industries
P.O. Box 1946
5353 W. US 223
Adrian, MI 49221
517-263-0771
www.merillat.com

Mill's Pride
250 S. Australian Ave. 13th Floor
West Palm Beach, FL 33401
561-655-3955
www.millspride.com

Plato Woodwork, Inc.
200 Third St. SW
Plato, MN 55370
320-238-2193, 1-800-328-5924
fax: 320-238-2131
www.platowoodwork.com

Schrock Handcrafted Cabinetry,
A Masterbrand Company
One Masterbrand Cabinets Drive
Jasper, IN 47546
812-482-2527
www.masterbrandcabinets.com

Wellborn Cabinet, Inc.
P.O. Box 1210
38669 Highway 77
Ashland, AL 36251
256-354-7151, 1-800-762-4475
fax: 256-354-1874
www.wellborn.com

Wood-Mode Cabinetry
One Second St.
Kreamer, PA 17833
570-374-2711, 1-800-635-7500
fax: 570-372-1422
www.wood-mode.com

Cabinet Refacing

Home Depot
www.homedepot.com

Mastercraft Cabinet Refacing
www.mastercraftindustries.com/refacing/

Sears Cabinet Refacing
www.sears.com

Countertops

Granite

Granitewerks Inc.
2218 N. Elston
Chicago, IL 60614
773-292-1202, 1-800-747-2648
fax: 773-292-0630
www.granitewerks.com

Keys Granite
8788 NW 27th St.
Miami, FL 33172
1-800-8-granite
www.keysgranite.com/

Tri-State Stone, Inc.
120 Southbridge Road
North Oxford, MA 01537
508-987-9311, 1-888-817-2188
fax: 508-987-9306

Laminate

Formica Corporation
10155 Reading Rd.
Cincinnati, OH 45241
1-800-FORMICA
fax: 513-786-3024
www.formica.com

Wilsonart International
2400 Wilson Place
Temple, TX 76503-6110
254-207-7000, 1-800-433-3222
fax: 254-207-2384
www.wilsonart.com

Solid Surface

Corian Dupont
Dupont Surfaces
P.O. Box 80016
Barley Mill Plaza 16-1174
Wilmington, DE 19880
302-892-7072
www.corian.com

Silestone
Consentino USA, Inc.
10707 Corporate Drive, Suite 136
Stafford, TX 77477
281-494-7277
fax: 281-494-7299
www.silestoneusa.com

Stainless Steel

Brooks Custom
A Division of Brooks Woodworking, Inc.
15 Kenisco Dr.
Mt. Kisco NY 10549
Phone/fax: 1-800-244-5432
www.brookswood.com

Frigo Design, Inc.
5860 McKinley Road
Brewerton, NY 13029
1-800-836-8746
www.frigodesign.com

John Boos & Co.
315 S. 1st St.
Effingham, IL 62401
217-347-7701
fax: 217-347-7705
www.johnboos.com

Wood/Butcher Block

Craft-Art
1876 Defoor Avenue, Bldg. C
Atlanta, GA 30318
404-352-5625
www.craft-art.com

John Boos & Co.
315 S. 1st Street
Effingham, IL 62401
217-347-7705
www.johnboos.com

Flooring

Tile

Dal Tile
7834 C.F. Hawn Frwy.
Dallas, TX 75217
214-398-1411, 1-800-933-TILE
fax: 214-309-4584
www.daltile.com

US Ceramic Tile Company
10233 Sandyville Road S.E.
East Sparta, OH 44626-9333
330-8665531, 1-800-321-0684
fax: 330-866-5370
www.usceramictileco.com

Wood

Bruce Hardwood Floors
18803 Dallas Parkway
Addison, TX 75248
972-931-3100, 1-800-256-0308
fax: 972-887-2234
www.brucehardwoodfloors.com

Pergo
P.O. Box 1775
Horsham, PA 19044-6775
1-800-33-PERGO
www.pergo.com

Vinyl

Amtico International Inc.
6480 Roswell Road
Atlanta, GA 30328
404-267-1900, 1-800-370-7324
fax: 404-267-1901
www.amtico.com

Armstrong World Industries
2500 Columbia Ave., Building 5
Lancaster, PA 17603
717-396-6425
fax: 717-396-6428
www.armstrong.com

Congoleum Corp.
P.O. Box 3127
Mercerville, NJ
609-584-3000
fax: 609-584-3518
www.congoleum.com

Lighting

Mepla-Alfit
130 Lexington Pkwy.
P.O. Box 1666
Lexington, NC 27295-8524
336-956-4600, 1-800-456-3752
fax: 336-956-4750
www.mepla-alfit.com

Hardware

Amerock Corp.
4000 Auburn St.,
P.O. Box 7018
Rockford, IL 61125-7018
815-969-6138
www.amerock.com

Cliffside Industries Ltd.
60 Wright Ave.
Lititz, PA 17543
1-800-873-9258
fax: 1-800-926-3435
www.cliffsideind.com

Hafele America Co,
3901 Cheyenne Dr.
Archdale, NC 27263
336-889-2322, 1-800-423-3531
fax: 336-431-3831
www.hafeleonline.com

Top Knobs (U.S.A.), Inc.
P.O. Box 779
Belle Mead, NJ 08502-4107
1-800-499-9095
fax: 1-888-486-7566
www.topknobsusa.com

Sinks and Faucets

American Standard
P.O. Box 6820
Piscataway, NJ 08855
732-980-3000, 1-800-442-1902
fax: 732-980-3335
www.americanstandard-us.com

Delta Faucet Co.
55 E. 111th St.
Indianapolis, IN 56280-1071
317-848-1812
fax: 317-573-3486
www.deltafaucet.com

Elkay Manufacturing Co.
2222 Camden Ct.
Oak Brook, IL 60523
630-574-8484
www.elkay.com

Franke
3050 Campus Dr., Ste. 500
Hatfield, PA 19440
215-822-6590, 1-800-626-5771
fax: 215-822-5873
www.franke.com/ksd

Kohler Company
444 Highland Drive
Kohler, WI 53044
920-457-4441, 1-800-4KOHLER
fax: 920-459-1505
www.kohlerco.com

Moen Inc.
25300 Al Moen Dr.
P.O. Box 8022
North Olmsted, OH 44070
216-962-2000, 1-800-321-8809
fax: 1-800-962-2770
www.moen.com

Price Pfister, Inc.
19701 Da Vinci
Lake Forest, CA 92610
1-800-732-8238
fax: 1-800-713-7080
www.pricepfister.com/

Useful Websites

Granite

Stoneinfo.com
www.stoneinfo.com/articles/
granite_countertops.html
This site offers a helpful comparison between granite and solid surface countertop materials.

Lighting

GELighting.com
http://www.gelighting.com/
Find tips for planning your kitchen lighting.

Tile

Ceramic-tile.com
www.ceramic-tile.com/

Infotile.com
www.infotile.com

FloorsTransformed.com
www.floorstransformed.com

The above three sites provide useful information, including product knowledge, and care and installation of tile for flooring or backsplash.

Appendix C

Graph Paper

Use the blank graph paper on the following pages to design your new kitchen.

Index

E